The Cinema of Disorientation

This book is dedicated to the memory of Sean Bonney (1969–2019),
a master of revelatory disorientation and incisive confusion.

The Cinema of Disorientation
Inviting Confusions

Dominic Lash

EDINBURGH
University Press

Edinburgh University Press is one of the leading university presses in the UK. We publish academic books and journals in our selected subject areas across the humanities and social sciences, combining cutting-edge scholarship with high editorial and production values to produce academic works of lasting importance. For more information visit our website: edinburghuniversitypress.com

© Dominic Lash, 2020, 2022

Edinburgh University Press Ltd
The Tun – Holyrood Road, 12(2f) Jackson's Entry, Edinburgh EH8 8PJ

First published in hardback by Edinburgh University Press 2020

Typeset in Garamond MT Pro by
Servis Filmsetting Ltd, Stockport, Cheshire,
and printed and bound by CPI Group (UK) Ltd,
Croydon, CR0 4YY

A CIP record for this book is available from the British Library

ISBN 978 1 4744 62778 (hardback)
ISBN 978 1 4744 6278 5 (paperback)
ISBN 978 1 4744 6279 2 (webready PDF)
ISBN 978 1 4744 6280 8 (epub)

The right of Dominic Lash to be identified as the author of this work has been asserted in accordance with the Copyright, Designs and Patents Act 1988, and the Copyright and Related Rights Regulations 2003 (SI No. 2498).

Contents

List of Illustrations	vii
Acknowledgements	ix
Introduction	1
Prospectus	13

Part 1: Confusion as Fusion: Metalepsis, Completeness and Coherence

Chapter 1: Metalepsis in Film and Its Implications	27
Chapter 2: Genres within Genres within Genres: Nested Narrative and Metalepsis	39
Chapter 3: 'Disappeared where it's real hard to disappear': Three Ways of Getting Lost in *INLAND EMPIRE*	51
Chapter 4: Achieving Coherence: Diegesis and Death in *Holy Motors*	69

Part 2: Disorientating Figures and Figures of Disorientation

Chapter 5: Figuring (Out) Films: Figuration in Narrative Cinema	91
Chapter 6: Distinguishing the Indistinguishable: Figures of Imperceptibility and Impossibility in *Lost Highway* and *Caché*	105
Chapter 7: Homes for Displaced Figures: Pedro Costa's *Colossal Youth*	117
Chapter 8: Sink or Swim: Immersing Ourselves in Jean-Luc Godard's *Adieu au langage*	133

Conclusion: Method-Free Orientation	153
Appendix: *Colossal Youth* Scene Breakdown	159
Notes	165
Bibliography	181
Filmography	191
Index	195

List of Illustrations

FIGURES

I.1	A reflection enters the frame . . . but turns out not to be that of Alan Gray, as we are likely to have assumed.	3
I.2	We assume the camera movement tracks Gray's attention, but his mind – and body – are elsewhere.	4
I.3	A tear – or not?	10
P.1	Visually similar images can represent either *looking out* or *looking in*.	22
2.1	The structure of David Mitchell's novel *Cloud Atlas*.	42
2.2	The structure of the entire film *Cloud Atlas*.	43
2.3	The structure of a twenty-minute segment from *Cloud Atlas*.	44
2.4	The structure of *The Forbidden Room*.	47
3.1	Sandy, Lula and Nikki: Laura Dern speaks while barely moving her lips, variously conveying concern and curiosity (*Blue Velvet* (1986)), fear and desire (*Wild at Heart* (1990)) or sorrow and guilt (*INLAND EMPIRE*).	61
4.1	The fraudulent porthole.	76
6.1	Fujiwara's shots (2), (3), (4) and (5) from the corridor sequence in *The Night of the Demon*.	107
6.2	From the opening of *Caché*.	108
6.3	Mirror images hiding in plain sight in *Lost Highway*.	113
6.4	Hiding in plain sight at the end of *Caché*.	114
6.5	Instances of violence in *Caché* and *Lost Highway*.	115
C.1	Confusion rectified?	157
C.2	Ethan is shut out but the viewer is not shut in.	158

TABLE

8.1	*Adieu au langage*	145

Acknowledgements

This book has emerged – whether fully formed or not I leave it for others to judge – from the chrysalis of a PhD thesis at the University of Bristol. I'm enormously grateful to Alex Clayton for his initial encouragement of my inchoate ideas and his sterling and patient work as a supervisor, as well as to Kristian Moen for crucial and well-timed interventions. I couldn't have undertaken this research without the support of a University of Bristol scholarship. Many thanks also for invaluable midwifery by my examiners, Catherine Wheatley and Sarah Street, the two anonymous reviewers of the initial book proposal (one of whom subsequently outed himself as Andrew Klevan), and the anonymous reader of the initial manuscript. My fellow PhD students at Bristol formed, and continue to form, the nucleus of a terrific community, always ready with a dissenting opinion. Love and thanks in particular to Eve Benhamou, Gareth Evans, Miguel Gaggiotti, Sarah Kelley, Lara Perski, Polly Rose and Steven Roberts. And extra doses of gratitude to Hoi Lun Law, who has probably read more of my work and given more thoughtful feedback on it than is permitted by the Geneva Conventions. I presented material related to the contents of this book at the *Screen* conference in 2018, the *BAFTSS* conferences in 2017 and 2018, and the 'Methodologies in Film-Philosophy' symposium at King's College London in 2017, and am very grateful to all the organisers, my fellow panellists and everyone that asked a question or offered feedback. Many thanks also to all the students – at Bristol, Reading and King's College London – that I have taught while working on this book, as well as to my teaching colleagues, with whom I may not have explicitly discussed the material herein but who have certainly helped shape my thinking and expression. Thanks in particular to Pete Falconer, Elena Gorfinkel, Jacqueline Maingard, Adam O'Brien and Lisa Purse. Gillian Leslie and her colleagues at Edinburgh University Press have been a delight to work with. I'm grateful to my parents for more than I could possibly sum up here. My greatest thanks go to Kate for sticking with me on our ongoing programme of mutual confusion and delightful disorientation.

'Cinema is the art of surprise and disorientation, the art that creates constant confusion.'

Adrian Martin, *Mysteries of Cinema*

'Confusion – yeah!'

Prince, 'It's Gonna Be A Beautiful Night'

Introduction

> You kind of get lost. And getting lost is *beautiful*. (David Lynch, in Barney 2009: 225)

John Boorman's 1972 film *Deliverance* is preoccupied with being lost. Before he and his three companions embark on their fateful trip down the Cahulawassee River, Lewis (Burt Reynolds) announces with bravado, 'I never been lost in my life'. When he eventually manages to find said river, however, Lewis gives the lie to his earlier comment by admitting that 'sometimes you have to lose yourself before you can find anything'. Between these two remarks Drew (Ronny Cox) bows out of a guitar and banjo duel with a local youth, happily declaring 'I'm lost!' He has lost his place in the music, which is a spatial metaphor for a non-spatial phenomenon. The boy has shown greater mastery than Drew, who is forced to admit to having become disorientated, but entering this state proves to be a joyful and exuberant experience, one that, as David Lynch says, can even be beautiful. Not that this is always the case; as the film continues, being lost comes to take on increasingly nightmarish dimensions. In fact, although we certainly could say that *Deliverance* is about four men getting lost on a river, it might be more accurately described as being about disorientation and confusion. Ami Harbin has suggested that '[t]o become disoriented is, roughly, to lose one's bearings in relation to others, environments, and life projects' (Harbin 2016: xi). All three of these features can be seen in Boorman's film. Its final section, for example, follows its protagonists as they lose their bearings in relation to their 'life projects' in attempting to cover up what happened on the river. Their relation to others becomes, at times, fatally confused: Ed (Jon Voigt) kills a man because he mistakes him for somebody else. And the film ironically explores the relationship between environment and disorientation by indicating a way in which the men could be said *not* to get lost. Their confidence in their spatial location is undermined by two local mountain men who tell them, before brutally assaulting them, that 'this river don't go to Aintry'. In fact, as it turns out, it *does*. The protagonists, in a sense, knew where they were the whole time, but this realisation only goes to show quite how profoundly disorientated they have become.

We might have assumed that as long as we have *some* idea of where we are, we can't – strictly speaking – be lost: 'I'm not *lost*, I just don't know exactly where I am.' It is, however, perfectly natural, on finding yourself, say, in a city you don't know very well, to say to yourself, or to someone that you stop to ask for directions, 'I do have *some* idea of where I am, but I'm a little bit lost.' That this is the case must have something to do with the fact that having a rough idea of where one is can sometimes be very helpful (if, say, I need to get north of the river and all I know is that I'm currently south of it) but is in other situations of almost no help at all. If I don't know where the street I'm on lies in relation to the street I need to get to, then knowing that both streets are on the same side of the river does nothing except to reassure me that at least things could be worse – I could be *even more* lost! From the fact that there can be degrees of being lost it does not, therefore, follow that the closer one is to being on track, the less lost one is, as the example of *Deliverance* indicates. The questions of where one is and of what one knows about where one is, although intimately related, are distinct.

Deliverance is not a film that this book will be returning to, but it serves neatly to indicate a number of the central concerns of *The Cinema of Disorientation: Inviting Confusions*. Focusing on critical accounts of some profoundly disorientating films, but also including theoretical and methodological reflections, *The Cinema of Disorientation* aims at exploring something of the variety of ways both characters in films and we, a film's viewers, can become confused and disorientated. It discusses both cognitive and affective aspects of disorientation (what we 'know' about where we are and how it feels when we know less about it than we might like), but its focus is consistently critical and hermeneutic. How might a focus on disorientation and confusion help us to understand better – to do critical justice to – films and the experience of watching films? *The Cinema of Disorientation* hopes, in attempting to answer this question, to demonstrate the interest and attraction of cinematic disorientation and confusion. While by no means arguing that they are always valuable or interesting in and of themselves, the book does claim that our understanding of film is enriched by coming to terms with those occasions in which, as Lewis says, 'you have to lose yourself before you can find anything'.[1]

It is certainly true that films can disorient or confuse as the result of carelessness – poor editing that leaves an audience pointlessly muddled about spatial relationships, for example – but this book focuses on situations in which the experience is productively occasioned, giving rise to aesthetic and phenomenological richness.[2] Let me illustrate this with two tiny examples from Carl Th. Dreyer's *Vampyr* (1932). Early in the film, the Lord of the Manor (Maurice Schutz) appears to Allan Gray (Nicolas de Gunzburg). Gray is in bed (the previous intertitle refers to 'his restless sleep' ['seinen unruhigen

 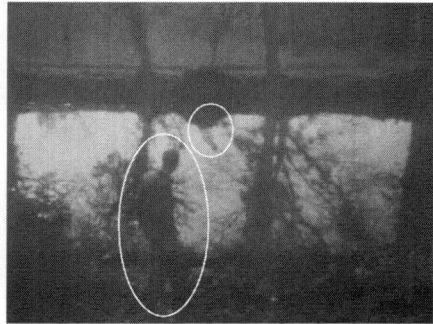

Figure I.1 *A reflection enters the frame . . . but turns out not to be that of Alan Gray, as we are likely to have assumed.*

Schlaf']), and the Lord enters his room by unlocking – from the outside – a door that has been locked from the inside. The Lord leaves Gray a package, then departs. The whole scene unfolds like a dream. Later, however, we see that Gray *really does* possess the package that the Lord left him. How can this be possible? The film's opening titles tell us that Gray's 'preoccupation with the mad ideas of bygone centuries' has turned him into 'a dreamer and visionary for whom the boundary between reality and the supernatural has been lost' (my translation). The film makes the viewer, also, lose their clear sense not only of this boundary but of others including (but not limited to) the boundaries between sleep and waking; past and present; fantasy and reality; and even the living and the dead. Gilberto Perez describes how, in *Vampyr*, 'everything appears eerily blurred in a no man's land between life and death' (Perez 1998: 124).

The film does not, however, confuse viewers only through its fantastical narrative; more localised devices also create subtly disorientating effects. In the scene immediately after the Lord of the Manor's arrival, we see Gray set off purposefully from the inn where he is staying. Dreyer cuts to a weathervane (a silhouette of an angel) and then to a shot of a river running horizontally across the centre of the frame, bounded above and below by its tree-lined banks. A reflection in the water picks its way from left to right on the far bank: Gray, we surely assume. But we only just have time to realise, with a jolt, that there is *no body* giving rise to the reflection before Gray appears at the bottom of the image, entering the frame also from the left, but on the near bank (see Figure I.1; the next scene shows that the impossible reflection is one of a number of shadows that are supernaturally able to act independently of the bodies that give rise to them). A comparable disruption of time, space and identity occurs later when Gray emerges from a trapdoor, looking intently to his left (screen right – see Figure I.2). The camera tracks

 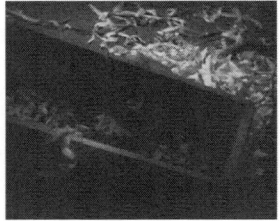 

Figure I.2 *We assume the camera movement tracks Gray's attention, but his mind – and body – are elsewhere.*

right to reveal a coffin. In so doing it is, we assume, directing our attention to match Gray's. But then the camera suddenly pans left and catches Gray in the middle distance already departing, walking *away* from the coffin through a doorway. These examples are not in accordance with 'classical' practice as it is usually understood, which is constructed in such a way that it 'passes relatively unnoticed' (Bordwell 1985: 164), but neither are the techniques deployed here designed to be clearly visible.

In fact, until we re-watch and analyse such sequences, we are likely to notice 'something wrong' but unlikely to be very clear as to why we feel this way. Whether the disorientation has been produced by disrupting the connection between what a character appears to be attending to and what the film attends to (as in the second example, with the coffin), or by fantastically disrupting the laws of physics (as with the riverbank example), in both cases we notice that our expectations – or, perhaps better, our *assumptions* – have been subverted, but doing so takes precedence over noticing *how*, or even noticing *what*, those expectations or assumptions were.[3] Stanley Cavell observes that 'facts of a frame, so far as these are to confirm critical understanding, are not determinable apart from that understanding itself' (Cavell 1979a: 224). That is to say that it is not possible to determine which aspects of a film ('facts of a frame') are pertinent to our understanding of it *before* we understand it. We almost always understand, or think we understand, *something*, however partial, provisional or ultimately mistaken this understanding may turn out to be; disorientation is rarely, if ever, total. These two moments in *Vampyr* (and many more like them) disorientate us by playing with – even, we might say, by taking advantage of – the assumptions we use to make sense of films. My interpretation of these moments is therefore at variance with Mark Nash's attempt to read the film exclusively in terms of Tzvetan Todorov's notion that hesitation between possible explanations is what characterises the fantastic (Nash 1976).[4] Although some disorientating effects elsewhere in the film *do* rely on hesitation (or on something even stronger, a kind of undecidability), it is not hesitation that is decisive here but the realisation that one has *already* formed an interpretation but has done so erroneously: our disorientation is caused by the fact that we *do not* hesitate. Our understanding of a film is not merely the prosaic basis on which we build interpretations (V. F. Perkins powerfully argues this in Perkins 1990), nor is it essentially retrospective, a way of accounting for our experiences after the fact. Understanding is always operative and always under negotiation, continually shifting and developing; examining disorientating films can help bring this process clearly into view.

OTHER TAKES ON DISORIENTATION

Insofar as this book is about film criticism as well as about films its proposals for the practice of film criticism are conducted for the most part implicitly, by exemplification. The hermeneutic traditions that most interest me are united by their shared interest in, and respect for, the film as text, as unfashionable as such an approach may be in some quarters.[5] They attempt a responsible engagement with cinema which does not deny the contribution of personal response, but which attempts to ground such responses in the details of the film, arguing for a position in such a way that others can return to the film and decide whether or not they are persuaded by an argument. After this Introduction I offer a more detailed Prospectus of *The Cinema of Disorientation: Inviting Confusions*, detailing the book's main subjects (confusion and disorientation), the body of work on which it concentrates (which I refer to as the contemporary cinema of disorientation) and the means by which I will conduct my examinations (which centre upon a critical focus on figuration). Before this, however, I will close this introduction by briefly distinguishing my approach from three related, but distinct, strands in contemporary film studies: certain forms of cognitivism, phenomenology and neo-formalism.

Cognitive studies of film have taught us a great deal about the different ways we understand and engage with disorientating films, clarifying what viewer disorientation can tell us about the cognitive processes involved in film viewing. David Bordwell, for example, has explored the role of schemata in our comprehension of films, drawing on sources such as Constructivist psychology and the art historian E. H. Gombrich to make the important point that we do not watch films as if we were empty vessels waiting passively to be filled with data but organise our perception and comprehension according to structured expectations: 'organized clusters of knowledge guide our hypothesis making' (Bordwell 1985: 31). This is certainly an important insight; my accounts of two moments from *Vampyr* above could be described in terms of the film's subversion of schemata. My divergence from some cognitivist film studies that have followed in the wake of work by Bordwell and other scholars such as Noël Carroll and Gregory Currie is to some extent a matter of emphasis and focus. In some of these accounts disorientation and confusion appear mainly as obstacles to viewer engagement, whereas I do not make any such assumption. In this I depart somewhat from the work of psychologist Paul J. Silvia, who argues that in a 'functional sense, interest and confusion are opposites. Interest motivates learning, exploring, seeking information, and engaging with new things . . . confusion presumably motivates withdrawing, avoiding, and shifting to something different' (Silvia 2010: 79). Although Silvia by no means argues that confusion is without value, he sees this value as residing chiefly in confusion's potential for signalling to us that something needs fixing; confusion 'informs people that they do not comprehend what is happening and that some shift in action is thus needed' (Silvia 2009: 49). In a pedagogical context, for example, '[i]f people learn that confusion is a signal that something is awry cognitively, then they can use it as information about the effectiveness of their learning strategies' (Silvia 2010: 79). The fact that Silvia construes interest and confusion as 'opposites', even if only in a 'functional sense', does not readily allow for the possibility of becoming intrigued by something precisely *because* it is confusing. He allows for confusion to *lead to* interest, but not for it to *be interesting* (except, of course, to a psychologist). I concur instead with Niall Martin and Mireille Rosello's desire 'to separate the idea of an affective reaction [to disorientation] from the assumption that the affect will always be negative' and endorse their claim that such a reaction 'could vary from curiosity, wonder or enchantment to aggressive rejection' (Martin and Rosello 2016: 2).

There has in recent years been an upsurge of cognitivist interest in what are referred to as 'puzzle films', including some of those films on the margins of the Hollywood mainstream that overlap with my objects of study in this book, such as *INLAND EMPIRE*. Miklós Kiss and Steven Willemsen's book *Impossible Puzzle Films* is a prime example. While I am in full agreement with their claim 'most contemporary complex narratives are in some ways dependent on principles and conventions of classical film narration' (Kiss and Willemsen 2017: 22), I situate myself at some distance from their intention to employ 'naturalistic, evidence-based inquiries [which] also need to be evaluated and interpreted in light of traditional film-scholarly concepts and expertise' as part of a 'cognitive-based approach to film [which] can thus be summarised as a science-based mode of observing, describing and interpreting how the relation between artworks and viewers "works"' (*ibid.*: 29). To begin with, such studies are potentially problematic when, as is the case with Kiss and Willemsen's book, they do not deal with a sufficiently large body of data from which to draw robust 'science-based' conclusions.[6] I also do not believe that there is such a thing as the 'value-free' approach at which the authors aim (see *ibid.*: 3). All studies of film involve presumptions of value (such as hierarchies of significance) just as much as the viewing of films does (see Perkins 1993: 191 for an excellent expression of this point); we might even refer to such presumptions as evaluative schemata. The phenomenological aspect of *The Cinema of Disorientation* aims to explore our experience of disorientating films with a view to gaining a better grasp of our values and presumptions rather than attempting to do without them.[7]

My chief reservation about these kinds of cognitivist study, however, concerns the richness of the critical accounts they generate. The intention to account for 'how the relation between artworks and viewers "works"' risks rendering individual films merely as instantiations of cognitive processes rather than as critical objects in their own right. Gregory Currie, for example, explicitly declares that his book *Image and Mind* 'aims at conclusions of maximum generality rather than a concentration on particular works, schools or genres' (Currie 1995: xi). Such conclusions are without doubt valuable and necessary, but it is also true that any claim that some observation, feature or property x pertains to all films can be – strictly speaking – falsified simply by finding one film to which x does not pertain. I am tempted to claim that this book aims to supplement studies aimed at 'conclusions of maximum generality' by focusing on 'confusions of maximum specificity'.

The laudable goal of theoretical clarity can sometimes lead to critical distortion. Kiss and Willemsen, for example, chastise a piece by William Brown (see Brown 2014) because it 'confuses the cognitive effort of narrative comprehension (that is, the construction of referential and explicit narrative meaning) with the variety and richness of simple or complex perceptual and interpretive responses to these films (also involving more implicit and symptomatic meanings)' (Kiss and Willemsen 2017: 45). The possibility that films themselves might productively 'confuse' these different dimensions is not even entertained, because a rigid distinction between 'narrative comprehension' and 'perceptual and interpretive responses' is assumed to hold a priori.

The very generality that is one of the cognitivist approach's chief virtues sets up pitfalls whenever such enquiries intersect with the detailed interpretive study of individual films. This is demonstrated by the article 'Towards an Embodied Poetics of Cinema' by Maarten Coëgnarts and Peter Kravanja, which shares much of Kiss and Willemsen's cognitivist framework. The authors read a leftwards panning movement in Antonioni's *The Passenger* (1975) that passes from Jack Nicholson's character, David Locke, alone in his hotel room, to a conversation that took place at a diegetically earlier point between Locke and the now-dead David Robertson (Charles Mulvehill) as an instance of the metaphor 'passage in time is motion in space' (Coëgnarts and Kravanja 2012: 5ff.). The viewer does not, however, know that the movement is back in time until, through an open door, we see Locke and Robertson in conversation. (The fact that we can hear the conversation has until this point been explained by the fact that Locke is replaying a tape he made of the two men talking.) There is therefore a disorientating surprise for the viewer not at the point when we first hear the men's voices, but only when we also see them, something the idea of a direct mapping between space and time has difficulty in accommodating.[8] Fully exploring both the nature and the consequences of this disorientation would require, as in the examples from *Vampyr* above, an exploration of the disruption of the viewer's initial interpretation (or hypothesis, to use Bordwell's language), in which there is movement in space but *no* movement in time.

The Cinema of Disorientation aims at greater critical specificity because this will deepen our understanding of the particular films in question with no serious damage to generality (every demonstrated achievement of a film is, necessarily, a possible achievement within the medium of film). In addition, such an approach will facilitate an attention to context and its consequences, which is absolutely crucial in studying disorientation and confusion because they are phenomena fundamentally bound up with relationships of different kinds. As Andrew Klevan writes in his *Aesthetic Evaluation and Film*:

> The meaning or effect of a word or thing shifts depending on the context – the particular sentence, speaker, and situation – in which it appears. The same principle applies to an image, a gesture, a cut, or a camera movement within a film. They are not equivalent to images, gestures, cuts, and camera movements in other films. This is why the critic needs to be phenomenologically responsive to the particular case. (Klevan 2018: 77)

But what kind of phenomenological responsiveness, exactly, is required? By introducing a version of Merleau-Ponty's phenomenology into film studies with her book *The Address of the Eye*, Vivian Sobchack both initiated a valuable debate and drew the attention of scholars to unfairly neglected aspects of the experience of film viewing. Unfortunately, however, her version of phenomenology tends to be as insensitive to the details of individual cases as the kinds of cognitive approach just discussed. When Sobchack writes, for example, that '[t]hrough the address of our own vision, we speak back to the cinematic expression before us, using a visual language that is also tactile, that takes hold of and actively grasps the perceptual expression, the seeing, the direct experience of that anonymously present, sensing and sentient "other"' (Sobchack 1992: 9), her approach does not readily open up further avenues for critical exploration because it simply posits the film as 'that anonymously present, sensing and sentient "other"'. Sobchack's phenomenology does not appear very open to questions such as: 'What distinguishes films that *do* seem to express the experience of some kind of 'other' from those that don't?'; or,

'In what circumstances does our vision seem more or less "tactile"?' If her account applies to all films equally, then any film is as amenable to phenomenological study as any other. In a certain sense this is of course true, but there also is also both the room and the need for a more phenomenologically evaluative criticism. Daniel Yacavone points out that such was in fact Merleau-Ponty's own practice:

> Sobchack's overriding focus on what are presented as fundamental visual, spatial, and affective features of all live-action films, as tied to perceptual conditions of the film *medium* and its *technology*, stands in sharp contrast to Merleau-Ponty's emphasis on variable *artistic form*, *style*, and *expression* in cinema, together with temporality and rhythm. (Yacavone 2016: 160)

Writing recently about films that could certainly be seen as fitting into the cinema of disorientation – Terrence Malick's *To the Wonder* (2012) and Shane Carruth's *Upstream Color* (2013) – Sobchack makes the excellent observation that the films 'compelled our attention to their every frame and gesture, and yet, even after multiple viewings . . . also continued to refuse us', leading her to ask: 'How does one resolve the paradox of an experience that was both immersive and alienating?' (Sobchack 2014: 50). This question resonates very closely with the issues I want to explore in this book, addressing as it does not only the vast range of affective possibilities that disorientation can generate (as we saw earlier in the way that being lost in *Deliverance* produces joy at one point and murder at another) but also the way that such contradictory outcomes can become 'confused' with one another: '*both* immersive *and* alienating'. However, after referring to conventions of narrative film such as the 'cognitive and cumulative enchaining of events through cause and effect' (*ibid.*), Sobchack goes on to say that both Malick's and Carruth's films

> . . . refuse all these established conventions, however – as well as our usual ways of experiencing and making sense of them. Instead of cognitive, reflective, and after-the-fact sense-making, they make sense – if we let them – in the phenomenological 'now' of seeing, hearing, and touching (if always also at a distance). (*ibid.*: 51)

A consequence, or perhaps a corollary, of Sobchack's brand of phenomenology seems to be an understanding of meaning in which bodily, non-discursive meaning becomes something more precious, more genuine, than cognitive or linguistic meaning. *The Cinema of Disorientation* aims at resisting this dichotomy between the 'cognitive' and the 'phenomenological'. I think it is at best misleading to say that these films, and others like them, 'refuse' all 'established conventions'. Perhaps they 'resist' them, 'obstruct' them, 'obscure' them, or even (ugly word) 'problematise' them – but to say any of these things is

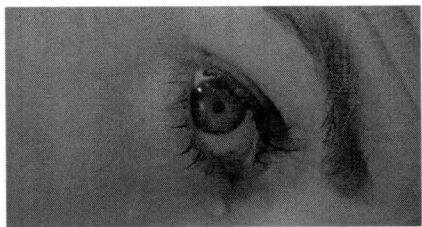 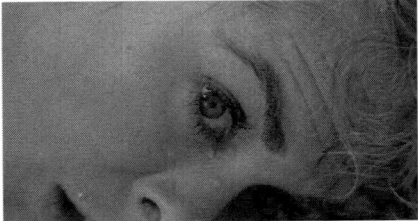

Figure I.3 *A tear – or not?*

not to say that such conventions are simply irrelevant in cases like these. As my earlier examples from *Vampyr* aimed at demonstrating, we make use of what Sobchack calls the 'cognitive ... enchaining of events through cause and effect' (*ibid.*: 50) not only afterwards but also *during* viewing – otherwise the effect could not be 'cumulative'. (To reiterate, one of the chief strengths of cognitivist film studies is what it has taught us about how this process works.) Surely these cognitive processes must also be part of any phenomenology worth its salt; otherwise phenomenology – in its (laudable) interest in 'seeing, hearing, and touching' – is in danger of becoming a kind of anti-intellectualism.[9]

Eugenie Brinkema has very bracingly reacted against this kind of cognitive/affective dichotomy, arguing in *The Forms of the Affects* that attending to affect requires *more* – not less – close reading, because affect is 'a problematic of structure, form, and aesthetics' (Brinkema 2014: xvi). I am fully in sympathy with this argument, but once again I find that the significance of close detail sometimes gets distorted, this time by Brinkema's dedication to the conceptual rhetoric of her arguments. For example, Brinkema makes much of the confusing encounter with something just below the eye of Marion's (Janet Leigh) corpse in Hitchcock's *Psycho* (1960) that *might* be a tear.

This uncertainty – is it a tear, or just a drop of water? – is transformed by Brinkema into something fundamentally undecidable: 'Such a tear that does not drop but folds points to a subjectless affect, bound up in an exteriority, uncoupled from emotion, interiority, expressivity, mimesis, humanism, spectatorship, and bodies' (*ibid.*: 45). If, however, we look closely at the perhaps-tear, its track indicates that it has descended *beneath* Marion's eye – which is to say, to the left of the image as we look at it (because she is lying on the floor, on her left side, facing us). It is thicker towards the bottom than the top; I cannot see any thinning or distortion towards its right side (as we look at it) which would indicate that it has travelled diagonally down, to the left, from the tear duct in the corner of her eye. Were the drop of water a tear, it would have to have emerged from that corner and then travelled down her nose, but it is a little difficult to imagine that in that case – even if she had shed the tear while upright, before falling – gravity and the contours of her face would have caused it to end up where it does in fact lie, with the shape it does in fact have. A reading strategy that ignores bodies – their biology and physics as much as their history and psychology – could not investigate these issues. To do so is not to conclusively demonstrate that it is not a tear, but it is to say that close reading provides reasons to think that it is not. To argue this is not to close the door to an even closer reading that finds contrary evidence, nor is it to preclude investigating the ways in which the drop is tear-like, or questioning what it is that prompts us either to believe, for a time, that it is a tear or to treat it as one. As with Coëgnarts's and Kravanja's treatment of the panning movement in *The Passenger*, Brinkema's account has difficulty in examining in detail the progress in time of the viewer's reaction; a more phenomenological account holds out the possibility of greater richness, as long as such an account does not, like Sobchack, think that phenomenology should have nothing to do with 'reflective . . . sense-making'.

Such an account could, instead, emphasise the process of sense-*making*, which does not entail ignoring the role of the senses; it is, after all, *sense*-making we are interested in. There is pathos in the very fact of being caused to wonder about the distinction between a tear and a mere drop of water since, after death, a tear on a face is – in a stronger sense than applies when someone is alive – nothing but a drop of water. If we think we are seeing a tear, only to conclude that we are not, the sense of water-as-tear itself undergoes a kind of dying, or at least a coming-into-question. To examine the traces of the track of the 'tear' in Hitchcock's image, as well as the temporality and sequentiality of its presentation to the viewer, and the confusion that this prompts, is to engage in a closer reading of the drop's materiality and textuality – what Brinkema calls its 'ineluctably specific complexity' (*ibid*.: 21) – than her text in fact does. Brinkema's eagerness to get beyond the true/false distinction seems to cause her to break her reading off early. Since reading is 'interminable' (*ibid*.: xiv), it must always be the case that we do so, but that only makes it all the more incumbent upon us not to do so *too* early.

By pointing to what I find to be limitations in some of the most important other ways in which film studies has investigated confusion and disorientation I by no means wish to argue for an atheoretical critical practice. On the contrary, I am interested in criticism as a praxis that can explore its theoretical assumptions in the very process of criticising; attention to detail and to the implications of detail can be both a critical and a theoretical discipline. I hope, then, that as well as offering readings of important, challenging, but still under-discussed recent films, the value of *The Cinema of Disorientation:*

Inviting Confusions will also lie in the ways it defends certain theoretical propositions about film and makes methodological recommendations concerning film criticism. Confusion can be valuable, both while watching a film and in writing about it, and I hope to show how.

Prospectus

In this Prospectus I aim to offer a concise account of *The Cinema of Disorientation: Inviting Confusions*, under three main headings. First, I shall detail the book's main subject (confusion and disorientation) and something of its philosophical underpinnings; second, I will explain the body of work on which it concentrates (the cinema of disorientation); and finally I shall set out the means by which I will conduct my examinations (a critical focus on figuration). Finally, I will give an outline of the structure of the book as a whole.

I should say something briefly here about my use of the terms *confusion* and *disorientation*. I have not found it necessary or useful systematically to distinguish them, so in some contexts they are more or less interchangeable. Elsewhere, however, *disorientation* refers more to the subjective state of the viewer[1] (I have not tended to refer to films themselves as disorientated) and *confusion* to qualities of films themselves, in the ways discussed immediately below. This should be clear from the context.

TOPIC: INVITING CONFUSIONS

This book is about inviting confusions in two senses: first, in the sense that I propose that the aesthetics of film will profit from welcoming – rather than resisting and attempting to diminish – confusion; and, second, in the sense that the book aims to demonstrate exactly what it is about many of the confusions to be found in film that might be considered inviting. But it is important to be clear that in saying this I am referring to two related but distinct senses of confusion, the first familiar, the second a little peculiar to contemporary ears.[2] First, there is confusion as the name of something experienced by the audience. This is the familiar affective sense, whose meaning is very close to that of disorientation ('I'm confused!'); it is a possible *effect* of confusion in the second sense.[3] This second sense refers to the confusion which we find in the films themselves. In saying this I am not using the word pejoratively (indeed part of my purpose is to counter critics who find the films I discuss confused in just such a sense), but rather in a sense related to that which Alexander Baumgarten, the eighteenth-century founder of aesthetics, thought was particular to aesthetic cognition. Terry Eagleton explains that ' "[c]onfusion" here means not "muddle" but "fusion": in their organic interpenetration, the elements of aesthetic representation resist that discrimination into discrete units which is characteristic of conceptual thought' (Eagleton 1990: 15). This sense of confusion can pertain not only to aesthetic cognition but also to perception itself. Baumgarten's usage derives from Leibniz, for whom 'clear' ideas were contrasted not with 'confused' ideas but rather with 'obscure' ones. 'Distinct' and 'confused' are the two subcategories of clear ideas, as Simon William Grote – drawing on Leibniz's 1684 'Meditations on Knowledge, Truth and Ideas' – explains:

> An idea is clear, in that it allows one to recognize what thing is being represented, because it contains representations of those characteristics of the thing that allow one to distinguish it from other things. An idea is confused, as opposed to distinct, in that those distinguishing characteristics are not made explicit, so that the thing represented cannot immediately be classified according to a definition. (Grote 2010: 113)[4]

None of this means that conceptual thought can have nothing to do with aesthetic objects – as Eagleton puts it, such objects 'resist' thought, they do not 'escape' it – but that discourse about them must *take account* of this resistance (and perhaps also *account for* it). The particular narrative and ontological 'confusions' found in these films are a subcategory of, and perhaps even an allegory for, a phenomenon of resistance to analysis (in the sense of a neat carving up into separate parts) that is present in aesthetic cognition generally speaking.[5] The resistance of aesthetic objects to discrimination does not require us to avoid deploying distinctions – such as, for example, those between emotion and logic, form and content, or diegesis and affect – so long as we continually remind ourselves that all applications of such distinctions to 'confused' phenomena must remain, at least to some extent, local and provisional. It is not the function (or, at least, it is not the *only* function) of distinctions to divide things into two neat categories. A distinction may be of value and interest even if cases exist that call the distinction itself into question because this can help us come to understand exactly what is at stake in it. Precisely because they 'cannot immediately be classified according to a definition' confused objects of thought invite – perhaps even demand – interpretation.

Following this line of thought, I do not offer in this book a theory of disorientation that adjudicates as to whether confusion is primarily a subjective state or an objective property. It is true that *Inviting Confusions* concentrates on demonstrable qualities of the films discussed; it is not a psychological study. And yet I have only been directed to the features I concentrate on because of psychological confusions I have experienced, and my discussion of them is always related to these experiences. (This lies behind my definition of the cinema of disorientation – see below.) This book operates according to the principles that (1) confusion or disorientation must be shown to be textually warranted and must sustain critical interest, and (2) that it is only by critical interpretation that this can be demonstrated – it cannot be 'proved'. In my everyday experience of films it may often be the case that I'm confused because I didn't watch carefully enough, or because I had already confused two things that the film could reasonably expect me to be able to distinguish (Newcastle upon Tyne and Newcastle under Lyme, for example, which Wikipedia tells me are 'not to be confused'). Confusions such as this are surely a fascinating topic for the psychology or sociology of film viewing, but they are not the subject of this book.

The concept of orientation can itself be seen to involve a confusion (in Baumgarten's sense) between the subjective and the objective. In this it, of course, shares something fundamental with the notion of the aesthetic. In a 1786 paper entitled 'What is Orientation in Thinking', Baumgarten's famous admirer Immanuel Kant explored this confusion by means of the word's etymology:

> To *orientate* oneself, in the proper sense of the word, means to use a given direction . . . in order to find the others, and in particular that of the *sunrise* . . . For this purpose, however, I must necessarily be able to feel a difference in my own *subject*, namely, that between my right and left hands . . . Thus, in spite of all the objective data of the sky, I orient myself *geographically* purely by means of a *subjective* distinction . . . (Kant 1991: 238–9)

For Kant, even the literal meaning of 'orient' combines or 'confuses' space and time, the objective and the subjective, the (objective) moment of the dawn – when the sun is in the east, the orient – and my (subjective) sense of the difference between my two hands.[6] The lesson Kant draws from this etymology is that the proper meaning of orientation in thinking is 'to be guided, in one's conviction of truth, by a subjective principle of reason where objective principles of reason are inadequate' (*ibid.*: 240). Without wishing to misrepresent the problems with which Kant is chiefly concerned in this essay – which have to do with the relationship between faith, ethics and reason – his account is pertinent to the aesthetic issues that are my focus in this book. 'Objective principles of reason' are never sufficient for criticism, but accounting for the role of the subjective does not have to mean explaining away personal response as an accident of biography ('Apichatpong Weerasethakul is one of our greatest directors – I love anything that reminds me of that wonderful holiday in Thailand'). Rather, it involves attending to the relationship between the particular paths that the critic follows and the ways that the film in question gives itself up to exploration. No critic can explore a film from every possible avenue and there will inevitably be a subjective dimension in the choice of approach, but there is no way to excise this subjectivity in order to be left with the purely objective. As Simon Jarvis has written in arguing for a 'material phenomenology':

> Until affective impressionality is recognized as the substance that most certainly exists, it will continue to be ruled out of court as merely idiotic, as singular, as personal, as subjective, and it will continue to be the case that the first move in any account of aesthetic experience will be to cross out, to fail accurately to listen to, the experience the inquirer has actually had, in favor of an experience she thinks she ought to have had, because she thinks other people are likely to have had it. (Jarvis 2002: 12)

Writing critically on the films covered in this book raises this issue with urgency because it is frequently unclear which critical path is the most likely to reduce disorientation. But given that a path must be chosen, one's interpretational choices as a critic are emphasised all the more prominently. *The Cinema of Disorientation* sees this emphasis not as a way of jettisoning objectivity in order more directly to access my own subjective experience as a film viewer, but precisely as a means of gaining insight into the peculiar confusions between the subjective and the objective that characterise both film viewing and film criticism. As Theodor Adorno puts it (showing his Kantian roots and using, rather appropriately for our purposes, at least two spatial metaphors):

> The more the observer adds to the process, the greater the energy with which he penetrates the artwork, the more he then becomes aware of objectivity from within. He takes part in objectivity when his energy, even that of his misguided 'projection', extinguishes itself in the artwork. The subjective detour may totally miss the mark, but without the detour no objectivity becomes evident. (Adorno 2004: 229)

We cannot arrive at objectivity simply by deleting the subjective because artworks only exist as such when encountered subjectively. Thus, as Adorno and Jarvis both argue, we have to *pass through* the subjective to reach any kind of aesthetic objectivity.

The critical judgements offered in this book aim, then, to ground themselves in textual evidence but they are also based in my own individual experience of the films discussed. If in places I use the first-person plural this does not represent an attempt to force the reader into agreement but is an invitation to the reader to see whether or not they perceive things that way. The thinking behind this exactly parallels Stanley Cavell's account of so-called ordinary language philosophy:

> The philosopher appealing to everyday language turns to the reader not to convince him without proof but to get him to prove something, test something, against himself. He is saying: Look and find out whether you can see what I see, wish to say what I wish to say. Of course he seems to answer or beg his own question by posing it in plural form [. . .] But this plural is still first person [. . .] All the philosopher, this kind of philosopher, can do is to express, as fully as he can, his world, and attract our undivided attention to our own. (Cavell 2015: 89)

The Cinema of Disorientation does not, then, aim to produce a standard set of reliable criteria by means of which we might categorise disorientating films and master our disorientation. The aesthetic criteria it proposes have, instead, more in common with Cavell's view of Wittgensteinian linguistic criteria. This is a complicated and thorny subject, but for my purposes it will suffice to refer to Steven J. Affeldt's explanation that, for Cavell's Wittgenstein, 'the search for criteria . . . occurs in response to a crisis – either confusion in the face of some empirical phenomenon or philosophical disorientation' (Affeldt 1998: 12). Or, as Cavell himself puts it in *The Claim of Reason*: 'Official criteria are appealed to when judgements of assessment must be declared; Wittgensteinian criteria are appealed to when we "don't know our way about"' (Cavell 1979b: 34). *The Cinema of Disorientation* does not propose that disorientation is a virtue that should never be lessened; it is more interested in how films provoke disorientation and the different ways in which we produce criteria in order to re-orientate ourselves in response to the specific challenges of individual films than in generating a toolkit for reducing disorientation. (Affeldt remarks that for Cavell, 'the sense of our criteria and of our talk of our criteria arises only in response to, and reaches only so far as is called for by, the specific confusions or disorientations that we actually encounter' (Affeldt 1998: 13).) As Cavell puts it himself, 'in using ordinary or official criteria we *start out* with a known kind of object whereas in using Wittgensteinian criteria we *end up* knowing a kind of object' (Cavell 1979b: 16). This book hopes to end up knowing the films it discusses better.

BODY OF WORK: THE CINEMA OF DISORIENTATION

To this end, the book focuses on examples taken from what I have decided to name the cinema of disorientation. (The term itself is modelled after the notion of a 'cinema of distraction', itself based on Siegfried Kracauer's discussion of what he saw as a 'cult of distraction' in the cinemas of Weimar Berlin, but beyond that I intend no reference to Kracauer's ideas; see Kracauer 1987 [1926].)[7] The cinema of disorientation refers to a tendency in film rather than a genre, and it can only be identified critically. This tendency cuts across different genres and subgenres. Thus, to take the films this book concentrates on as examples, David Lynch's *INLAND EMPIRE* (2006) might be seen as a kind of puzzle film, Leos Carax's *Holy Motors* (2012) as an instance of art cinema, Pedro Costa's *Colossal Youth* (2006) as part of the slow cinema movement and Jean-Luc Godard's *Adieu au langage* (2014) as having a relationship to the essay film. Whatever their provenance, however, this book argues that in each case disorientation is, deliberately, made into a central component of the viewing experience; appropriately coming to terms with this disorientation is therefore crucial to adequately interpreting and evaluating such films.

The group of films about which the latter claim is true – which is to say, those films concerning which no interpretation can be adequate that fails to address their disorientating aspects – comprise the cinema of disorientation. The relation between film and viewer is primary to my sense of this tendency, but it is also crucial to pay attention to the way these films *represent* disorientation. As well as disorienting their viewers, they very frequently concentrate on disorientated characters; indeed, the latter (how they represent disorientation) is frequently central to the former (how they generate disorientation). Having said this, the analyses in this book are distinct from a recent strand of interesting work in film studies that focuses on disorientation primarily in terms of politics and identity. Murat Aydemir, for example, has explored queer orientation in Gus Van Sant's *Elephant* (Aydemir 2016), while Olivia Landry has analysed the relation between disorientation and personal and political trauma in Christian Petzold's *Phoenix* (Landry 2017). I have no wish to evade or play down political themes (they make an appearance, for example, in my discussions of trafficking and migration in relation to *INLAND EMPIRE* and *Colossal Youth*), but my priorities are different from these studies. While I by no means deny that disorientation can be fundamentally political, I do not think that it is always and inherently so (except insofar as anything is potentially politically relevant). My focus is aesthetic, which does not at all mean that I aim to be apolitical but that in this book politics are a necessary part of the process of reading films as art, rather than – as is the case in Aydemir's and Landry's articles – aesthetics being a component of an essentially political investigation that takes place by means of the study of film.[8]

I claim, then, that the cinema of disorientation is a tendency or category that runs through the history of cinema, as is indicated by the following list of twenty films – mostly otherwise unmentioned in this book – that I consider part of the cinema of disorientation. (I have restricted myself to one film per director.) The list is fairly arbitrary, but it does attempt to cover something of a range of periods, genres and countries of origin; I'm sure most readers will instantly think of other possible candidates that could have been included here.

Some examples of the cinema of disorientation:

A Page of Madness (Teinosuke Kinugasa, 1926; Japan)
The Testament of Dr. Mabuse (Fritz Lang, 1933; Germany)
Laura (Otto Preminger, 1944; USA)
The Seventh Victim (Mark Robson, 1945; USA)
Invasion of the Body Snatchers (Don Siegel, 1956; USA)
Last Year at Marienbad (Alain Resnais, 1961; France)
Seconds (John Frankenheimer, 1966; USA)
Céline et Julie vont en bateau (Jacques Rivette, 1974; France)
Mirror (Andrei Tarkovsky, 1975; USSR)
Three Women (Robert Altman, 1977; USA)
The Suspended Vocation (Raúl Ruiz, 1978; France)
Bad Timing (Nicholas Roeg, 1980; United Kingdom)
Days of Eclipse (Alexander Sokurov, 1988; USSR)
New Rose Hotel (Abel Ferrara, 1998; USA)
Khrustalyov, My Car! (Aleksei German, 1998; Russia)
Oldboy (Park Chan-wook, 2003; South Korea)
Syndromes and a Century (Apichatpong Weerasethakul, 2006; Thailand)
Timecrimes (Nacho Vigalondo, 2007; Spain)
The Master (Paul Thomas Anderson, 2012; USA)
mother! (Darren Aronofsky, 2017; USA)

The Cinema of Disorientation is not a work of film history, and I do not have a particular historical argument to make about the development of the cinema of disorientation; its emergence seems to be a perennially renewable possibility, so any thumbnail outline would inevitably be selective to the point of distortion. Other scholars have engaged in very fruitful work in exploring the ways that different forms of disorientation have become prominent at different times, such as the emergence of film noir in the aftermath of the Second World War, or the various pressures and influences that gave rise to modernism more generally; see, for example, Naremore (1998) and Kovács (2007). (An excellent study focusing on a single disorientating film – Kinugasa's *A Page of Madness* – that carefully unpacks the cultural specificity of its disorientating aspects is Lewinsky (1997).) I want simply to say that the cinema of disorientation is alive and well at the present time and so the category is, at the very least, *current*. Thus, even in the absence of historical arguments as such, it is my hope that by focusing this book's attention on some recent films that disorientate and confuse in ways that seem to me to be both critically interesting and diverse I will be able contribute something to our understanding of the current state of film. The films I have chosen to discuss, however, by no means represent a full spectrum of the contemporary possibilities of the cinema of disorientation. Instead, this book focuses on recent instances of *extremely* – but *differently* – disorientating films. I hope to demonstrate the continuity of these films with more mainstream practice. This is not because I want to undermine their radicality, but because I want to show how much more there is to say even about films as bewildering as these beyond remarks such as 'of course you were confused – that was the point!' (Another approach would have been to explore the extent to which disorientation and confusion are part of our experience of films that might seem straightforward, but that is a project for another book.)

Approach: Attending to Figuration

Two specific concepts are central to my attempt to produce accounts of instances of the cinema of disorientation that will do them justice: *metalepsis* and *figuration*. Through the work of Gérard Genette and others, metalepsis has come to be used to designate instances of narrative wherein levels that 'ought not' to be able to come into contact with one another nevertheless do. In *Daffy Duck & Egghead* (Tex Avery, 1937), when Egghead implores an audience member to sit down, and eventually shoots him when he refuses, that is an example of metalepsis. So, too (it seems), is the first scene I mentioned from Dreyer's *Vampyr*, in which a dream visitation is nonetheless able to give Gray a physical book. Metalepsis can be a very helpful concept, whether one is investigating particular types of narrative confusion (in the non-pejorative sense) or the audience confusion (in the regular sense) which such narrative 'confusions' may result in. Studying metalepsis, then, involves both of the senses of confusion with which this book is concerned, and is a device that readily gives rise to feelings of disorientation; it thus offers a convenient starting point for my investigations.

Traditionally, metalepsis is considered as a rhetorical figure. Figuration is, then, a much more general concept than metalepsis. Indeed, words such as 'figure', 'figurative' and 'figural' have a huge range of senses. But the senses that particularly interest me relate to the way that two particular meanings of the word *figurative* intersect with one another in film. In studies of rhetoric or literature, the figurative exists in opposition to the literal: figurative language is language that is not – or not merely, or not entirely – literal. In visual art, however, the notion of the figurative exists in opposition not to the literal but to the *abstract*; abstract art is non-figurative. These two senses could be seen to pull in opposite directions: in visual art figuration is a move *towards* 'replication', while in literature it pulls *away* from it – away from direct, literal, factual statements. Film is particularly interestingly placed because – in its multi-layered deployment of image, sound and language – it makes use of phenomena that can be described using either sense of the word.

The disorientations produced by my examples from *Vampyr* (see Figures I.1 and I.2) make use of both senses of the figurative. The disorientations are produced via the visual means by which people and objects are represented (one sense of 'figuration'), but they would not be as disturbing as they are without the symbolic, metaphorical or metonymic import of these representations (their 'figuration' in a more literary sense). The sight of a shadow without a source is disturbing because of the disruption of causal order it signifies; the image of a man ignoring a coffin makes us suspect that the coffin serves as a metonym for his own death. This 'confusion' of procedures of figuration is extremely widespread in narrative cinema, so let me attempt to make what I mean a little clearer with a canonical instance of classical cinema, albeit 'a film with a classical narrative structure that nevertheless resists classical narration' (Lehman 2004: 240): John Ford's *The Searchers* (1956).

Ford's film famously includes a number of shots that look out from an enclosed space through an opening. The first shot of the film – what Robert Pippin calls 'our orienting shot' (Pippin 2010: 110) – does so, as does the movie's final shot; one other very important shot does the same; and there are also shots looking out from inside a teepee and from within a cave. Peter Lehman notes that '[t]he doorway motif with its elaborate use of both outer and inner doorways as well as teepee openings and mouths of caves is elaborately complex' (Lehman 2004: 250), but argues shortly afterwards that 'the shot viewing the action through the mouth of the cave . . . is entirely motivated by the visual rhyme of the composition' (*ibid.*: 251). I would, however, follow Nicole Brenez when she argues (vis-à-vis another film from 1956, George Cukor's *A Star is Born*) that it 'is not merely a matter of rhymes aiming to establish a thematic coherence but of constructing a film through the form of a passage between altered images' (Brenez 2007: 21).[9] These shots in *The Searchers* are figuratively connected *both* in the sense of their metaphorical import (which relates to the many crucial boundaries that the film tests via its themes of miscegenation and incest, not to mention the possibility of discerning what is going on inside a person from what they show on the outside) *and* in the visual sense: the images literally resemble one another.

The ways that these phenomena interpenetrate make particular *narrational* phenomena possible. Many commentators have noted the relationship between the way the camera moves outwards in the opening shot, only to retreat within in the film's final image. I have not, however, seen much discussion of the relationship between outward and inward movement in the first two 'doorway' shots.[10] The opening of the film clearly represents a look from the *inside out*, from the – at least apparently – safe homestead to the exterior

Figure P.1 *Visually similar images can represent either* looking out *or* looking in.

and the unexpected (and in a number of ways disturbing) arrival of Ethan Edwards (John Wayne). But the second use of such a shot occurs after the whole family, including Ethan's (illicitly) beloved Martha (Dorothy Jordan), has been killed and its female members raped. This time, the use of a very similar image represents a look from the *outside in*, and hence indicates that the deaths of Martha and the other family members are so horrific that they can only be represented by not being shown: we see only Martha's torn and bloodstained dress, and what we understand to be Ethan's gaze at her corpse. This point is made all the more powerfully because of what Brenez calls the 'passage' from the opening – outwardly directed – shot to the shot of Ethan looking in. Both the similarities and differences between the two images are crucial: the visual similarity calls attention to the narrative and symbolic differences.[11]

This phenomenon is related to what George M. Wilson calls 'rhetorical figures of narrational instruction' (Wilson 1986: 49), but instead of Wilson's exploration of the way rhetoric can organise our view of, or relation to, a narrative, I mean here to emphasise something simpler but more fundamental: 'rhetorical figures of narration', perhaps. We cannot wholly separate the narrational from the symbolic: the film's narration *itself* proceeds, in part, through particular means whose figuration is connected in both the literary and the visual senses of the word. My claim in this book is that the potential confusions (in both senses) that figurations may give rise to in any narrative film are exacerbated in the films discussed precisely because of their disorientating, frequently metaleptical, narratives.

THE STRUCTURE OF THIS BOOK

It may perhaps be said that *The Cinema of Disorientation* lacks a unifying theoretical argument. In that the book does not construct a unified theory of disorientation, this may be true (although its structure is logically conceived) but – if so – this is because I have strived to avoid the kind of theoretical clarification that considers its business to be the policing of firm distinctions, thereby obscuring the fact that much of what is of theoretical interest blurs distinctions. My claim – and it is a theoretical claim – is that confusion and disorientation are of this nature. Besides, there are many theoretical arguments contained in this book and I hope that their connections will become apparent over its course. (For example, it makes theoretical claims about the relationship between orientation and coherence, and defends a specific definition of figuration.) I also hope that it is more than a writerly conceit that I do not begin by setting forth all these arguments in outline. To do so would risk misrepresenting the kind of critical/theoretical attitude that this book aims to exemplify and to recommend. (Skip to the conclusion if you are eager to see more discussion of this point.)[12] Nevertheless, a rough sketch of the territory may well be of use, and so I now provide one.

The book is divided into two sections, each further divided into four chapters. Part 1 is entitled 'Confusion as Fusion: Metalepsis, Completeness and Coherence'. Its first chapter will articulate the nature and significance of metalepsis in film, as well as some of its ontological and rhetorical implications. This first theoretical chapter, then, is concerned particularly with issues of diegesis and narration. It is followed by a chapter on *Cloud Atlas* (2012) and *The Forbidden Room* (2015). Each of these films contains an unusually large number of nested narratives that are distinguished by genre, and that sometimes involve, or at least border on, metalepsis. Genre is usually seen as an aid to orientation: identifying a film's genre situates it in a landscape of other films. This chapter, however, explores the ways that combining multiple genres in a single film can either aid orientation or produce disorientation, and to what end. *INLAND EMPIRE* and *Holy Motors* also combine different genres with nested narratives, but in even more complex and bewildering ways. Chapter 3 focuses on the way that *INLAND EMPIRE* demonstrates how critical consistency can exist in tension with completeness. Can consistency – reduction or elimination of disorientation – only be achieved at the price of certain exclusions? What happens if we are forced to leave different things out in different readings? With regard to Carax's film, I will argue that cohesion and consistency can be as disorientating as their absence. *Holy Motors* cues us to set aside certain expectations, only to wrong-foot us later on by unexpectedly reintroducing them; it shows that connections are not always conducive to orientation, but can in fact be disorientating. But having shown that coherence can be disorientating, I will argue that the film ultimately achieves coherence not *despite* its disorientating elements, but *by means of* them.

Part 2 of *The Cinema of Disorientation* is entitled 'Disorientating Figures and Figures of Disorientation'. Its four chapters parallel the structure of Part 1: an initial theoretical chapter is followed by a chapter developing some of the theoretical ideas developed therein via an analysis of a small group of films, after which two more chapters each treat a single film in detail. The first chapter of Part 2 deals with issues of signification and discourse, extending the discussion of metalepsis in the book's first chapter to an exploration of the wider phenomenon of which it is a part, namely figuration. The next chapter compares some specific figures in David Lynch's *Lost Highway* (1997) and Michael Haneke's *Caché* (2005) and explores how, in what I refer to as a kind of 'figurality by indiscernibility', these films exploit difficulties in distinguishing images so as to disorientate the viewer and thereby figure that which cannot be directly represented. Detailed analyses of Pedro Costa's *Colossal Youth* (2006) and Jean-Luc Godard's *Adieu au langage* (2014) make up the book's final two chapters. Both films disorientate, but through opposite strategies: *Colossal Youth* by often seeming not to give us enough to go on, *Adieu au langage* by giving us far too much to keep a handle on. Despite this contrast, in both cases the films' figurative procedures can be shown to reveal a great deal more narrative content and consistency than is initially apparent. I shall explore a range of senses of figure that help articulate the ways *Colossal Youth* simultaneously orientates and disorientates its audience, and use the notion of immersion to explore the ways we can become 'lost' in *Adieu au langage* both in the orientational sense that is primary throughout this book, and in the other sense of becoming absorbed in it, somehow in the midst of it.

Part 1

*Confusion as Fusion:
Metalepsis, Completeness and Coherence*

CHAPTER 1

Metalepsis in Film and Its Implications

WHAT IS CALLED METALEPSIS?

Stories within stories are anything but rare in the cinema. An arbitrary and highly selective list of films where they feature strongly would include *Mabel's Dramatic Career* (1913), *Sherlock Jr.* (1924), *Hiroshima mon amour* (1959), *The Saragossa Manuscript* (1965), *La Nuit américaine* (1973), *Céline et Julie vont en bateau* (1974), *The French Lieutenant's Woman* (1980), *Videodrome* (1983), *eXistenZ* (1999), *Adaptation* (2002), *Hable con ella* (2002), *Synecdoche, New York* (2008), *Inception* (2010), *Cloud Atlas* (2012) and *The Forbidden Room* (2015). When we encounter a narrative within another narrative we are dealing, in a certain sense, with an ontological hierarchy. In the most general sense (from the perspective of our 'real' world) everything in a narrative is on the same ontological level – is, precisely, narrative. When, however, a narrative contains another narrative, then from the perspective of the containing narrative (according to which the 'container' is not narrative but reality), the contained narrative *is*, nevertheless, still narrative. The two narratives are thus ontologically distinct and, generally, there cannot be direct exchange between the two: such exchange is as impossible as it would be for J. K. Rowling to meet Harry Potter. But, nevertheless, nested narratives not infrequently *do* feature such supposedly 'impossible' crossovers. Entanglements between nested stories within a single work are increasingly being studied under the rubric of metalepsis (see, for example, Kiss 2012 and Buckland 2013). Gérard Genette, whose *Figures III* (1972) formulated the basics of the modern understanding of metalepsis, subsequently devoted a whole book to the subject (Genette 2004).

The origins of the term and the history of its usage are complicated and at times contradictory. Genette has sorted through these various meanings and come to the conclusion that the clearest and most useful application of the term is to call metalepsis any procedure 'which unites, in one sense or another, the author and their work, or more generally the producer of a representation with that representation itself' (*ibid*: 14; my translation). This definition comes, in the course of Genette's book, to broaden out slightly to refer to any situation where *ontologically distinct levels* (whether properly so, or merely fictionally so, from within the diegesis) encounter one another. If a character from a film escapes from the film and begins to exist in the world that produced the film, as Tom Baxter (Jeff Daniels) does in Woody Allen's *The Purple Rose of Cairo* (1985), then this is metaleptical – and not only when Baxter meets the actor who 'produced' him, Gil Shepherd (also Jeff Daniels, of course).

In this chapter I will sketch out the nature and role of metalepsis in cinema, including its relation to questions of ontology and rhetoric, and indicate the relevance of the concept to the questions of confusion and disorientation with which I am concerned. I will, however, address those questions less directly than in the critical chapters that follow; my purpose in this first chapter is to prepare the ground and develop some tools that will prove useful later on. I shall do so first by clarifying the relationship between metalepsis and the fantastic. This will lead to a discussion of the ontology of fiction that is guided by attention to metalepsis, after which the chapter will conclude by claiming that metalepsis is best seen not merely as a question of the logic of fictional worlds but as, fundamentally, a matter of rhetoric. Metalepsis, I will argue, can guide us to an understanding of the way a work of fiction solicits the attentions and emotions of its audience. It can do this by prompting us to attend to the intersection – or confusion, in Baumgarten's sense – of a number of different logical or rhetorical dimensions (narrational, affective, etc.) and by encouraging us, instead of attempting to separate them tidily at all costs, to remain sensitive to the ways they impinge on one another.

Metalepsis and the Fantastic – Misconceptions and Possibilities

It is easy to overstate the disruptive potential of metalepsis. Since I do believe that it is of the nature of metalepsis easily to give rise to the fantastic or the paradoxical, it is particularly important to be clear that this is not its only function, nor always a consequence of its presence. Thomas Morsch rightly points out that '[m]etalepses are neither a specifically postmodern stylistic device, whose reach would be restricted to the corresponding genres, nor do they necessarily have anti-illusionistic effects. Depending on context and on how they are deployed, metalepses may instead serve to enhance and stabilize fiction' (Morsch 2012: 114). Earlier in the same article, however, he himself makes the very mistake that he warns against when he remarks that '[m]etalepsis not only places part and whole, lower-order and higher-order levels, in a mirroring relationship, like the device of *mise en abyme*, but it also lets each pass over into the other in a paradoxical manner not amenable to the logic of "realism"' (*ibid.*: 111). This is going too far since, as Genette shows, even the nineteenth-century realist novel is full of examples of metalepsis not aimed at disrupting the logic of the fictional world. One well-known example is when Balzac ('or, if you prefer, the narrator of *Illusion perdues*') writes that '*while* the venerable churchman climbs the ramps of Angloulême, it won't be useless to explain, etc.' (Genette 2004: 22; Genette's emphasis, my translation). The metalepsis here emphasises that it takes time to climb a ramp by declaring that this gives the narrator time to convey some other information while the climbing is taking place. Adopting the conceit of doing something else *while* an event is happening in the fictional world is to mimic the way the real world works, in which certain actions require a certain amount of time, and to downplay the ability of fiction to dispose of time and space in any manner it sees fit.

We might, however, wonder whether metalepsis *in cinema* tends more universally towards the fantastic and paradoxical than it does in literature, because effects such as Genette's example from Balzac rely on the identity between the narrator's enunciation and the substance of the narrative, an identity which comes naturally to literature but that cinema can only, at best, imitate. In 1910, Berthold Viertel published an essay entitled 'Im Kinematographentheater', or 'In the Cinematic Theatre', where he described the experience of sitting in a Viennese movie theatre watching the German and Austrian kaisers watch a film that had been recorded that very morning and depicted none other than themselves:

> [The two rulers] saw a true likeness of themselves, one that appeared to speak, salute, and laugh. And the audience in the picture applauded. And the audience in the theater also applauded. And the monarchs in the picture showed their appreciation. And the real monarchs showed their appreciation in reality. But then, all of a sudden, one of the films ripped, and the theater went dark. At that very moment, shivers went down my spine. What? Did that tear also go through the real people? Horrified, I asked myself, who here is the real one? (Viertel, in Kaes et al. 2016: 78)

Viertel has a disturbing and disorientating metaleptical experience in the absence of any intention to generate one on the part of the filmmaker or projectionist. The experience of cinematic duplication is exhilarating (even the kaisers applaud) but also horrific and corrosive of our trust in the correspondence of our senses to reality. What kind of existence do cinematic images possess, and how does 'real' reality relate to the indexical representation of reality? Which of the two is the more real? Cinema confronts us with what Viertel refers to as 'this terrifying doubleness [Doppelgängertum] of representation' (*ibid.*). Doublings and doppelgängers are prominent in a number of films made in the decade after Viertel's article, exploring the horror of the idea that our uniqueness can be undermined, but also implicitly exploring the very nature of cinematic representation itself.[1] Viertel's account is also suggestively reminiscent of specific moments in much later films. There is, for example, the ripping of the film which is also the ripping of a face at the beginning of a famous sequence in Ingmar Bergman's *Persona* (1966). Towards the end of *INLAND EMPIRE*, the character played by Laura Dern watches herself on the big screen, 'in a dark theatre, before they bring the lights up', just as the kaisers did in 1910. The photograph's very realism (which the movement of cinema amplifies) is also the source of its most fantastic quality, that of *duplication*. It is this profound link between (realist) representation and (fantastical) duplication that enables these troubling metaleptical effects. By becoming lost (absorbed) in a film we cannot, it seems, help but open ourselves up to the possibility of disorientation.

ON THE ONTOLOGY OF FICTION: ÉTIENNE SOURIAU

> and after I had seen
> That spectacle, for many days, my brain
> Worked with a dim and undetermined sense
> Of unknown modes of being
>
> (Wordsworth, *The Prelude* (1805), I, 417–20)

It is a distinctive fact about the cinematic apparatus that it involves multiple channels of signification. In this it is unlike, for example, the novel. Christian Metz writes that '[a] novel is made only of words, so we can say that in this sense it has only one "channel" . . . In cinema the signifying material is more diverse (images, sounds, dialogue, and so on), so there are many channels' (Metz 2016: 170). This is certainly true, although a novel can *feel* as if it has multiple channels, hence the great interest of tone and irony to the analyst (the very possibility of free indirect discourse relies on a separation between the words of the narration and what it actually *says*). The exploration of the impossible seems characteristic of art, as in paintings that evoke movement, or music that evokes stillness. Alain Badiou sees it as particularly characteristic of cinema: 'No painting will ever become music, no dance will ever turn into poem. All direct attempts of this sort are in vain. Nevertheless, cinema is effectively the organization of these impossible movements' (Badiou 2005: 82). I suggest that novels have one channel but explore the ways they can seem to have many, whereas cinema with its multiple and manifold channels explores the ways they can be entwined with one another.[2]

One reason that cinema lends itself so readily to metaleptical narrative may then be to do with its pluricodal nature and the resultant fact that it can be seen as composed of different *levels*. Making connections between different levels is part of cinema's bread and butter. One well-known, and still useful, taxonomy of cinematic levels is that put forward by Étienne Souriau in his article 'La Structure de l'univers filmique et le vocabulaire de la filmologie', published in the *Revue international de filmologie* (Souriau 1951). Thus, although I would not claim that cinema is intrinsically metaleptical, the way metalepsis highlights the intersection of different narrative levels can sensitise us to the way that an interaction between levels, in a more general sense, is characteristic of cinema.

Souriau's taxonomy involves seven levels, as follows: the *afilmic* (the real and ordinary world independent of the film), the *profilmic* (the space photographed by the film camera), the *filmographic* (the film as a physical, material, chemical object; the celluloid strip – or today the digital file), the *screenic* or *filmophanic* (the film as projected on the screen), the *diegetic* (the imaginary world created by the film),[3] the *spectatorial* (all the subjective phenomena brought into play by the perceptual, mental and psychological activities of film viewers) and finally the *creatorial* (the implied activity of the creator(s) of the film). The list is suggestive and useful, but even such a synoptic view is not exhaustive because multiple layers can be in operation simultaneously *within* and *across* Souriau's categories: think, for example, of the possible operations of geometric, chromatic, gestural, sonic, musical, verbal and written information in a single film sequence.[4] The interpretation of a gesture, say, might require reference, at the very least, to the afilmic, profilmic, diegetic and spectatorial levels. In Howard Hawks's *The Big Sleep* (1946), when Vivian Rutledge (Lauren Bacall) finally, at the encouragement of Philip Marlowe (Humphrey Bogart), gives in and scratches her leg, we can only interpret her scratch by referring to contemporary social customs about the display of female legs in the presence of a male, and feminine decorum more generally (afilmic); to the actual scratch that Lauren Bacall, sat on a desk before a camera in 1945, gave herself (profilmic); to the significance of the encouragement to scratch, and the acquiescence to it, in the context of the developing relationship between Rutledge and Marlowe (diegetic); and to our positioning as spectators (presumed to be male?) who are, via the camera, shown a certain amount of Mrs Rutledge's leg (spectatorial). That which is theoretically separate (although simultaneous) also proves able to intersect. Even in a straightforward scene such as this, different levels can become, we might say, *entangled* with one another. (Should that, for example, be Lauren Bacall's leg rather than Mrs Rutledge's?)

In situations whose explanation requires simultaneous reference to multiple levels we might even speak of 'metaleptical explanation'. This might seem a rather baggy concept, as it could reasonably apply to any situation in which the production of a film affected its final state ('the lead actor was drunk the whole time, that's why he has so few lines'). So it would be preferable to restrict its use to cases in which an explanation seems impossible without reference to multiple levels (my previous example could always be diegetically explained away by, say, the character's taciturn disposition). As an example of an instance where a metaleptical explanation would be illuminating, I offer George M. Wilson's remark that, at the end of Michael Haneke's *Caché* (2005), 'it is implicitly suggested that we don't know that all of the image-track has not been fictionally derived from mysterious security cameras that somehow seem to be effectively present everywhere' (Wilson 2011: 101). Given the extent to which Haneke's film trades on the friction between our desire for a diegetically consistent explanation of its mysteries and the film's refusal to provide one, offering an explanation so resolutely diegetic – if nonetheless bordering on the fantastic, and therefore in tension with the general tenor of the diegesis – seems to me more of a distortion than a clarification. Better, I suggest, to admit that the question cannot be solved from one side alone and to offer a metaleptical explanation that combines a diegetic aspect with reference to the spectatorial and creatorial levels and the way the film manipulates and deliberately frustrates spectator desire.[5]

The ontological distinctions between the levels of Souriau's taxonomy are various and complex. The profilmic, for example, could be considered a subset of the afilmic, ontologically similar but distinguished by the fact that it is the target of a particular form of representation (that provided by the film camera). The diegetic level is distinct because its contents are fictional. But how does the ontology of fiction relate to that of the extrafictional, 'real' world? Is the fictional simply the non-existent, of the same order as subjective fantasy? Besides his work explicitly on cinema, Souriau was a philosopher involved in issues of aesthetics and ontology much more generally; indeed, he 'was a philosopher before he was an aesthetician' (Lowry 1985: 76). For Souriau, '[a]rt differs . . . from most human activities, which are oriented towards events. Art is directed towards the production of beings, and thus toward ontology' (*ibid.*: 77). Hence the importance of a key term for Souriau, that of *instauration*, or, as paraphrased by Luce de Vitry-Maubrey, 'the ensemble of processes which result in establishing a being whose presence, solidity, and autonomy of existence are incontestable' (Vitry-Maubrey, *La pensée cosmologique d'Etienne Souriau* (Paris: Klincksieck, 1974), p. 219; quoted in Lowry 1985: 75). But what kind of being is this? In 1943, a decade before the lecture outlining his taxonomy of cinematic levels, Souriau published *The Different Modes of Existence* (Souriau 2015), a difficult and curious but also very stimulating attempt to allow for the possibility that when we say 'to exist' we do not always mean the same thing or, to put it another way, that there are different ways of existing.

Such abstract speculations may seem a little remote from metalepsis and cinema but if diegesis is something that operates according to our sense of reality, and if we want to understand how and why a diegesis can be confusing or disorientating, it is important to know as much as possible about that sense of reality. Souriau's comments about fictional existence are particularly relevant and interesting. As explicated by Isabelle Stengers and Bruno Latour in their introduction to the recent republication of Souriau's book, the philosopher is asking whether

> we finally have the right to grant existence to beings hitherto dismissed as belonging to the 'purely subjective,' for example, to the beings of fiction? To those phantoms, chimeras and imaginaries that are sometimes so inconsistent that we have great difficulty recalling or reconstructing the experience, and yet which sometimes seem endowed with such an insistence that they seem more 'real' than the M. Durands, Duponds or Dufours with whom we are summoned to coexist? (Stengers and Latour, in Souriau 2015: 57–8)

Particularly interesting here is the pairing of the *inconsistent* with the *insistent*: perhaps it is exactly this combination which characterises fictional beings? Souriau argues that '[t]hese *mock-existences* or pseudo-realities are real; but also counterfeit in that they formally imitate the *réique*[6] status, without having its consistency or, if we want to speak in this way, its matter' (Souriau 2015: 154). Both consistency and inconsistency are crucial to the fictional. It is not just that a degree of consistency is required for credibility; it is also impossible for fictional beings to be *without* inconsistency – there is no way they can possess the consistency of non-fictional beings. So fictional beings are merely imaginary, then? Not so fast, Souriau warns. As Stengers and Latour put it, 'the reader supports the work, but for all that he is not at liberty' (Stengers and Latour, in Souriau 2015: 60):

> There is a consistency specific to the beings of fiction, a specific type of objectivity that Souriau describes by the pretty word *syndoxic*. In a certain way, we all share Don Juan, Lucien de Rubempré, Papageno, the Venus de Milo, Madonna or *Friends*. Certainly this is about *doxa*, but a *doxa* that is sufficiently held in common that we can recognize these beings as having a specific form of monumentality. Our tastes can vary, but they focus on elements that are sufficiently apportioned to enable a shared analysis. (*ibid.*: 58)

Rachel from *Friends* does not exist in the same way that you or I exist, but her existence or non-existence is not simply a private matter. Hence one can, for example, say false things about her (such as that she marries Chandler Bing). What marks out fictional beings is not merely that their existence is purely phenomenological, but that they 'formally imitate the *réique* status, without having its consistency' (Souriau 2015: 154); they are distinguished from passing feelings or perceptions precisely in that they appear to have a more stable, consistent existence – akin to that of non-fictional beings – that they in fact lack. Fictional beings lack both the consistency of the non-fictional and the freedom of the purely imaginary. Their existence is constrained. Ultimately, fictional beings exist by means of our *solicitude*, the care or attention we give them. Souriau's work indicates that if metalepsis foregrounds questions of fictional ontology, then it is necessary for us to consider our relation to the fictional beings in question, to examine the ways they solicit our attention, emotions or desires. One common name for this kind of solicitation is rhetoric, to which, in the final section of this chapter, I now turn my attention.

METALEPSIS AND RHETORIC

Given that diegesis and ontology are crucial for the presence of metaleptical effects, one might think that these categories could be used to provide classificatory criteria, distinguishing films with multiple narratives but no metalepsis from those that do exhibit it. We could even construct something of a sliding scale. For example, Paul Thomas Anderson's *Magnolia* (1999) features nine narrative strands, but all of them take place in the same world at the same time: no metalepsis here. In *Cloud Atlas*, on the other hand, although all its narratives take place in the same world, they do so at different times spanning hundreds of years. Even without the intimations of reincarnation that dot the narrative, the presence in one narrative strand of written or filmed narratives (and an LP) that derive from another strand move us into a more metaleptical situation, though perhaps still only on the threshold of metalepsis proper. (I shall clarify this in the following chapter.) It is only when characters from fictions that are diegetically fictional, or that originate in diegetic dreams or fantasies, interact that we have metalepsis proper: no metalepsis without at least a hint of the fantastic, it appears. Certainly, when narrative strands that have previously remained separate finally intersect, this is not enough to qualify as metalepsis, lest the term's extension proliferate uncontrollably. And yet this particular account will not quite do, because metalepsis is not simply a question of *fabula* (narrative events considered in the order they happen within the fictional world), but also of *syuzhet* (the order in which the events are presented in the film). It is not merely a phenomenon that pertains to the logic of fictional worlds, permitting us to ignore the specific images, words and sounds which give rise to those worlds; metalepsis is also a matter of narration and figuration.

Take, for example, the famous 'Wise Up' sequence in *Magnolia*, in which Aimee Mann's song 'Wise Up' links the film's nine protagonists, who all sing it at the same time, though they remain separate from one another and have no knowledge that the other characters are also singing the same song. Ascribing a (diegetic) mystical connection to explain the sequence would be crass. Clearly, compared with the film up to this point, the sequence is unrealistic, but something unrealistic does not automatically become fantastic. It is tempting to deploy the distinction between rhetorical and ontological metalepsis that some scholars have seen as implicit in Genette's work and argue that we are dealing here merely with a rhetorical metalepsis – one based only in the film's means of expression – rather than a more disorientating and destabilising ontological metalepsis grounded in the logic of the diegesis itself (see, for example, Ryan 2006: chapter 9, and Pier 2016, in particular section 3.2.1). But it seems to me that this distinction is another example of an often-helpful notion that becomes unhelpful if we think it divides the field neatly in two. Are all the characters in the 'Wise Up' sequence 'really' singing? That is, if we could transport ourselves into the diegetic world, would we see them singing – or is the song 'merely' a rhetorical device employed by the film, or by Paul Thomas Anderson? Kendall Walton would say that the question is whether they are 'fictionally singing', and might also say that it is an example of what he calls a 'silly question' (see Walton 1990: 174–83), a view with which I am sympathetic (as I indicate in the final paragraph of this chapter). And yet it would be hard to argue that film doesn't solicit the question *at all*, which I think is one reason why the sequence somehow 'feels' metaleptical.[7] The film is our only means of transport into its world – and the way it achieves this is entirely by means of its rhetoric. The issue would not be solved by claiming that they are clearly not all 'really singing' because this would only raise the further question of what they *are* 'really' doing instead. Had the film wanted to clearly signal that they are not 'really' singing – that, for example, the characters are themselves imagining each other singing – it could have done, and it does not. But even had it done so, it would have done so by rhetorical means. Relative to a fictional world, the distinction between rhetorical and ontological metalepsis is itself established and maintained only by rhetorical means.[8]

I think that the sequence is better approached in terms of dramatic mode and aesthetic risk, via what I suggested above one might call a metaleptical explanation – an explanation that combines diegetic logic with rhetorical and affective impact. George Toles argues something very similar:

> Anderson takes a mammoth risk by inserting a musical sequence so late in his narrative, without any preliminary warning or formal preparation for

> an eruption into song that is as serious as it is surreal . . . The entire fragile edifice of the film might well collapse if the 'Wise Up' sequence registers as nothing more than bathos and authorial hubris. Anderson jettisons one well-established framework of representation (messy, snarled-up realism) and replaces it with a framework that is overtly choreographed, stylized, and highly compressed. He paradoxically makes his gentle, formally and emotionally contained musical montage *dangerous* by so brashly disregarding the rules of proper film storytelling and constructing his climax on a foundation of coincidence . . . And the number recklessly flirts with absurdity, apparent in such decisions as . . . having two singers . . . performing in states of unconsciousness. (Toles 2016: 15)

Were the sequence to exist on its own as a music video there would be nothing dangerous, confusing or metaleptical about it: the *song* would seem the primary diegetic level, one that is 'illustrated', we might say, by its application to a range of different narratives. Diegetic questions are certainly not irrelevant to the sequence (it is clear enough that coincidence is somehow the sequence's diegetic foundation, not magic or telepathy) but they are not primary: what is primary is the set piece's aesthetic tightrope walk, which we could characterise as a highly self-aware instance of what Alex Clayton, following V. F. Perkins, calls aesthetic suspense. Clayton's account of aesthetic suspense meshes tightly with Toles's discussion of the 'Wise Up' sequence: it involves 'moments [which] punctuate without quite puncturing the film's drama and invitation to emotional investment', perhaps a play with 'arriv[ing] at, but not . . . pass[ing], the edge of absurdity' (Perkins's words, quoted by Clayton), or a director's deliberate toying with their 'pact of tolerance' with the spectator (Clayton 2016: 209 and 201). Tolerance is not the same as credibility, but straining either involves similar stakes. Are the risks that are taken with regard to the audience's credulity and patience, or with their sense that their emotional and aesthetic involvement in the film thus far has been solicited fairly, adequately compensated by the particular affective and aesthetic qualities of the musical sequence?

The crucial lesson I take from this example, and with which I will close this chapter, is that diegetic questions cannot always be neatly sliced off from other questions – such as questions of form, tone and mood – which we might broadly claim to be aspects of a film's rhetoric. Or, to put it another way, the distinction between rhetorical and ontological metalepsis is not absolute. This means that we should be wary of assuming that it is always desirable to avoid, as Kiss and Willemsen put it, confusing 'the cognitive effort of narrative comprehension . . . with the variety and richness of simple or complex perceptual and interpretive responses', at least if we take confusion in Baumgarten's sense (Kiss and Willemsen 2017: 45). Without gauging the rhetorical stance of a film or a sequence in a film we are unlikely to be able to say anything useful about any metaleptical qualities it may possess; examining those metaleptical qualities can, in turn, be of importance in forming a view about the kind of rhetoric that is in play.

I agree with Toles about coincidence in the 'Wise Up' sequence, but I am not so sure about absurdity – or rather, he is right to say that absurdity is *flirted* with. We are likely to feel a touch of absurdity when an unconscious character sings, but this will only persist if we insist that the diegetic status of every incident in a film can always be pinned down (once again: are they *really* singing or not?). Not all questions about diegetic status have an answer that is revealing: sometimes they may be best left unasked. Some forms of disorientation can, then, be the result of persisting in pursuing unsolicited, unnecessary and inappropriate questions. The questions we struggle with most should, surely, be those that are solicited by the work under consideration: as I will demonstrate in Chapter 3, *INLAND EMPIRE* solicits questions about its diegesis to a degree that the 'Wise Up' sequence in *Magnolia* does not. To claim that problems concerning diegetic status must always have a solution is to refuse to recognise that diegetic status is a production, not a fact.[9]

CHAPTER 2

Genres within Genres within Genres: Nested Narrative and Metalepsis

Genre is usually seen as an aid to orientation: identifying a film's genre situates it in a landscape of other films and assists the viewer in forming appropriate expectations. This very orientational function, however, might render us all the more vulnerable to disorientation. If, in a murder mystery set in the 1920s, suspicion were suddenly to fall on a character we considered already in the clear, we might be surprised but we would not be half as disorientated as we would be if a spaceship suddenly made an appearance. Genre could be said to increase orientation at the price of narrowing the range of what a film can present without provoking disorientation. These issues are, however, complicated by the two films that this chapter will explore because each film contains an unusually large number of nested (or quasi-nested) narratives that are distinguished by genre. There are six in *Cloud Atlas* (Tom Tykwer, Lana Wachowski and Lilly Wachowski, 2012) and seventeen in *The Forbidden Room* (Guy Maddin and Evan Johnson, 2015), which are nested within each other to various degrees; at its most extreme Maddin and Johnson's film goes nine stories deep.[1]

How might combining multiple genres in a single film either aid orientation or produce disorientation, and to what end? Both *Cloud Atlas* and *The Forbidden Room* have generated intense experiences of disorientation and confusion in viewers. Roger Ebert waxed lyrical about the kind of narrative surrender he believed appropriate to watching *Cloud Atlas*:

> Now that I've seen it the second time, I know I'd like to see it a third time – but I no longer believe repeated viewings will solve anything . . . On my second viewing, I gave up any attempt to work out the logical connections between the segments, stories and characters . . . But, oh, what a film this is! . . . And what a leap by the directors, who free themselves from the chains of narrative continuity. (Ebert 2012)

Eric Hynes describes his experience of watching *The Forbidden Room* at the Sundance film festival as follows: 'You lose the thread. You lose any sense of time . . . Looking around the room after the conclusion of *The Forbidden Room*, I saw looks of bewilderment, joy, and post-hypnosis disorientation, often on the same faces' (Hynes 2015). Hynes also notes the way that, in Maddin and Johnson's film, narrative confusion is matched by – bleeds into – its visual style: 'One story leads to, blends with, morphs into, and invades another, seemingly without rhyme or mercy. Meanwhile the surface of the picture blends and morphs as well, changing color and quality like a deep-fried dream. Or nightmare. Or phantasmagoric fish tank. Or Lava Lamp' (*ibid.*).

Does the complexity with which different genres are combined in these two films mean, as Adam Lowenstein writes in an excellent article about the films of Ben Wheatley and Amy Jump, that *Cloud Atlas* and *The Forbidden Room* cause us to lose 'our genre bearings' (Lowenstein 2016: 7)? In what follows I will argue that they in fact achieve different ends. The forms of disorientation that Lowenstein discovers in Wheatley's films are 'skilfully achieved by layering viewer relations to cinematic space atop viewer relations to cinematic genre'; the films lurch from one genre to another, thus progressively undercutting the viewer's confidence in the very kind of film that they are watching. Wheatley and Jump's films, according to Lowenstein, take advantage of the vulnerability to disorientation that genre entails – as I discussed above – in order increasingly to disorientate us as they proceed, only ultimately to abandon the viewer: '[W]e often wish we could find our way back to the familiar cinematic spaces and genre codes to which we are accustomed, but Wheatley has gleefully erased the map and set the house on fire. There is no going back' (*ibid.*: 5). The experiences generated by *Cloud Atlas* and *The Forbidden Room* are rather different. Their generic multiplicity is not a surprise that is sprung on the viewer but a feature that becomes apparent almost immediately. My emphasis here is therefore different from Lowenstein's because I will argue that these films offer an opportunity to examine the ways that a 'confusion' of genres within one film can serve both orientational and disorientational functions.

This chapter focuses, then, on a comparison between *Cloud Atlas* and *The Forbidden Room* in order to explore the relationship between multiple or nested narratives, genre and disorientation. It also follows on from the investigation of metalepsis in the previous chapter. The more distinct narrative levels a film contains, the more possibilities for metalepsis it affords. In studying precisely how the dense narrative layering works in these two films we will find once again (as in the 'Wise Up' sequence in *Magnolia*, for example) that a film's rhetoric can create an experience that feels metaleptical – involving some kind of blurring or confusion between distinct narrative levels – without metalepsis 'proper' (or ontological metalepsis) necessarily being present. The sheer quantity of narratives contained in these two films also provides an opportunity to investigate the relationship between quantitative complexity and disorientation. Particularly in cognitive film studies, disorientating films are frequently referred to within a rubric of complexity; Kiss and Willemsen's *Impossible Puzzle Films*, for example, is subtitled *A Cognitive Approach to Contemporary Complex Cinema*. I will, however, argue that complexity and disorientation are concepts that need to be kept distinct. For all the similarities that I have indicated, *Cloud Atlas* and *The Forbidden Room* are profoundly different films, and one way of accounting for this difference is to distinguish carefully between complexity and disorientation. The chapter will discuss the structure of each film and the nature of the disorientation it provokes (beginning with *Cloud Atlas* and following with *The Forbidden Room*) before discussing the role of metalepsis in each film and its relation to confusion (in its various senses).

CLOUD ATLAS

Cloud Atlas is adapted, in many ways very faithfully, from David Mitchell's 2004 novel of the same name. The novel features six different narrative threads which the film faithfully replicates. Each thread takes place in the same fictional world, but at increasingly later points in history. The six narratives are as follows, in (fictional) historical order. First, the 1849 story of Adam Ewing (Jim Sturgess), the son-in-law of a slave trader who is duped and poisoned by one Dr Henry Goose (Tom Hanks) before eventually being rescued by a freed slave called Autua (David Gyasi) and dedicating his life to abolitionism. Second, the 1936 story of Robert Frobisher (Ben Whishaw), a young composer who becomes amanuensis to the aging Vyvyan Ayrs (Jim Broadbent), an experience that culminates in Frobisher's suicide, but not before he completes his 'Cloud Atlas Sextet'. Third, the exposure of a conspiracy involving nuclear power by a young journalist called Luisa Rey (Halle Berry) in the San Francisco of 1973. Fourth, the story of the imprisonment in a nursing home, in 2012, of Timothy Cavendish (Jim Broadbent), a charming but somewhat disreputable publisher, by his disgruntled brother, and Cavendish's subsequent escape. Fifth, a futuristic tale set in Neo-Seoul in 2144 about the rebellion against a dystopian authoritarian regime called Unanimity by a 'fabricant' called Sonmi-451 (Doona Bae). Sixth, and finally, a post-apocalyptic story set in 2321 involving a tribesman, Zachry Bailey (Tom Hanks), and his developing relationship with one of the so-called Prescients (who retain the use of advanced technology) called Meronym (Hale Berry).

Mitchell derived the structure of his novel from Italo Calvino's famous work of 1979, *If on a winter's night a traveller*, but while the great achievement of that book is to make continuity out of discontinuity – constantly interrupting its narratives with new narratives (and never returning to a story once it

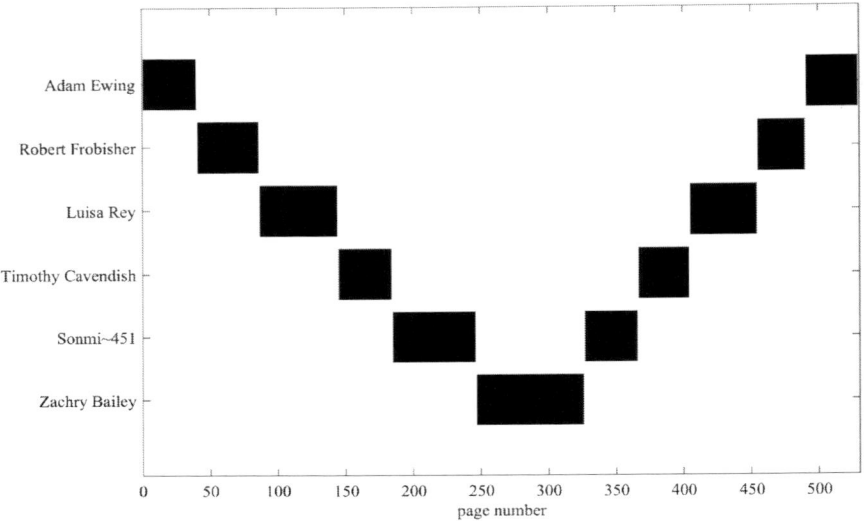

Figure 2.1 *The structure of David Mitchell's novel* Cloud Atlas.

has been dropped) and yet still retaining the rhythms of a satisfying novel – Mitchell makes sure he returns, eventually, to each story that he begins and neatly finishes it off. The resulting structure is virtuosic but simple. We encounter the stories in historical order; each of them is interrupted at some point, until the sixth narrative, which is uninterrupted, and after the conclusion of which we complete each of the other stories in reverse historical order. Figure 2.1 demonstrates this graphically.

If we look at a diagram of the structure of the *film*, on the other hand (Figure 2.2), even though it uses exactly the same six narrative threads with very little alteration (there is a seventh level because there is a framing narration, but this features the same characters as the sixth level) we see that the structure looks rather frightful.

It appears significantly more complicated than the book – as, of course, in a sense it is. This visual representation is, however, potentially rather misleading. After a brief introduction of about three and a half minutes which cuts rapidly between the different strands, presenting each of them twice (which is certainly likely to prove confusing on a first viewing), the next half hour of the film introduces each thread, in historical order, as happens in the novel; this can be seen clearly in Figure 2.2. If the challenge for the viewer in the introduction is the rapidity of cutting between entirely different narratives, set at different times and occupying different genres, and that we are encountering for the first time, then the challenge in the next section is to retain a grasp on each narrative, given that we stay with each one for minutes at a time and

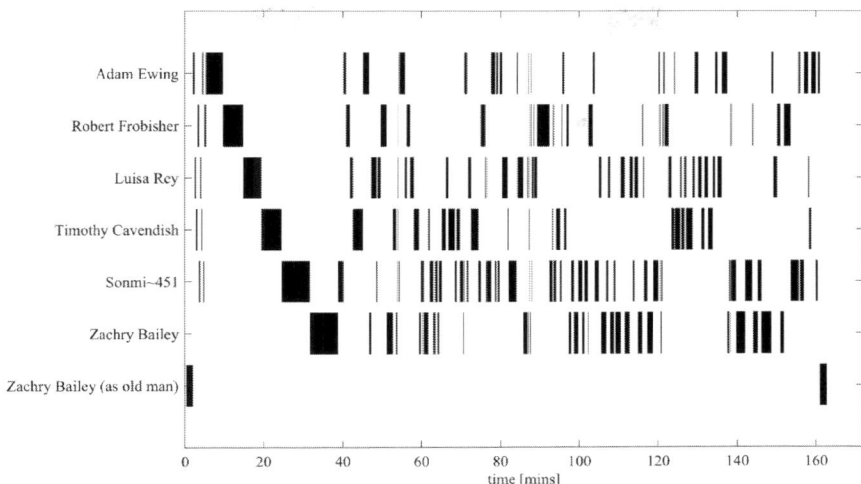

Figure 2.2 *The structure of the entire film* Cloud Atlas.

are given no reminders of the other narratives. That there are six parallel narratives enables the film to achieve a delicate balance; six is just enough narratives that on first encounter the sheer quantity of narrative information might well seem overwhelming and disorientating, but it is also few enough that with increasing familiarity, orienting oneself within each strand becomes increasingly easy. Omer M. Mozaffar writes that he 'suspect[s] that this film will successfully alienate or confuse most of its viewers' but that '[i]f you have the patience, it might take forty minutes to begin to understand it, and to subsequently immerse yourself into it' (Mozaffar 2012). Indeed, from about the forty-minute mark the film's editing, including between its different narrative strands, is consistently rapid, in familiar post-classical Hollywood style. Via its very adroit construction this fluidity assists rather than obscures viewer orientation, as will become clearer if we look in more detail at a twenty-minute segment of the film, from one hour twenty to one hour forty (Figure 2.3).

For the most part only some of the strands are kept in play at any one time; thus the viewer is not kept away from any one strand for long enough to forget it entirely, but is also, usually, not required to keep all six threads equally present in their minds. When we do move to a new strand narrative or verbal connections underline the logic of the transition. So, for example, shortly after the ninety-three-minute mark, Robert Frobisher announces his plan to make his escape from Vyvyan Ayres, after which the next few minutes alternate the stories of the escapes of Sonmi-451 from Unanimity and of Timothy Cavendish from his nursing home. A return to Frobisher allows him to refer to the book he is reading – Ewing's journal – in order to clarify for the

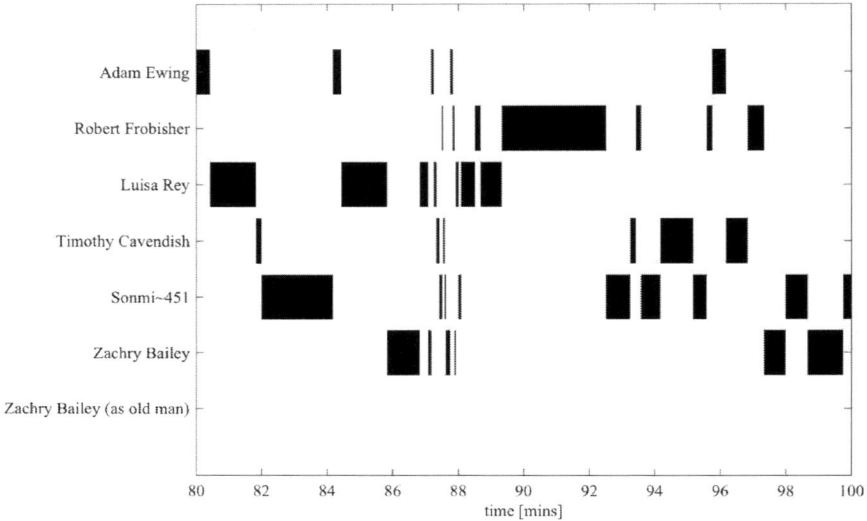

Figure 2.3 *The structure of a twenty-minute segment from* Cloud Atlas.

viewer, for the first time, that Goose is poisoning his 'friend'. Frobisher then announces that 'from this point on there was no going back', which enables the film to pivot to the Zachry Bailey narrative, which now alternates with Sonmi-451's story. In both of these strands there is indeed 'no going back': Sonmi-451 has now violently escaped from Unanimity, thus committing herself to the rebellion, while Zachry and Meronym have scaled a particularly precipitous rock face.

There is, in this section, one exception to the film's tendency to restrict the number of strands in play at any moment. Around the eighty-seven minute mark a voice-over in which the character Isaac Sachs (Tom Hanks) from the 1973 strand ruminates about the mutability of life and the forces of destiny ('yesterday my life was headed in one direction; today, it is headed in another . . . these forces that often remake time and space, that can shape and alter who we imagine ourself [*sic*] to be, begin long before we are born and continue after we perish') plays over images from all the strands. Rather than disorientating the viewer, however, this gesture serves an obviously unifying and clarifying function. Finally, each strand, of course, represents a different genre; our recognition of this helps prevent us confusing them one with another. I must admit that I find Ebert's claim that he 'no longer believe[s] repeated viewings will solve anything' to be itself confusing, or at least puzzling, since my experience is how easily one masters the art of keeping one's bearings among the six narratives even during one's first viewing. Rather than a confusion of genres what we find in *Cloud Atlas* is more like a compendium of genres, any of which could have served on its own as the basis for a Hollywood film. The film does not cause us to lose 'our genre bearings' so much as use genre to help us get and keep our bearings.

THE FORBIDDEN ROOM

Although there are occasional indications in *Cloud Atlas* that its earlier narratives exist within its later narratives, *as narratives* (Robert Frobisher, for example, becomes engrossed in reading Adam Ewing's account of his travels), *The Forbidden Room* is based much more extensively – indeed obsessively – on embedded narratives. Constantly, a character or entity of some kind in one strand tells a story, during which at some point another character or entity starts telling another story, and so forth. (Something of the film's exuberantly absurdist flavour may be gleaned from the fact that one of these storytelling entities is a dreaming volcano, and another the hairs of a dead man's moustache.) The film originated in a project called *Séances* that involved filming, mostly before a live audience, new films with the titles of films that are either lost or were never made, such as Murnau's *Der Januskopf* (1920), a version of the Jekyll and Hyde story, and Naruse's *The Strength of a Moustache* (Hige no Chikara, 1931). Although it is not a silent film, *The Forbidden Room* involves much affectionate pastiche of the silent cinema, replicating its impression rather than slavishly copying its grammar (close-ups and hand-held cameras, for example, are deployed in ways they rarely, if ever, were in the silent era), but also displaying a sound grasp of its principles and rhetoric (particularly in the use of intertitles).

Tony Rayns suggests that writing a synopsis of the film is 'a fool's game' because 'the film's relentless profusion is its whole point' (Rayns 2015). Certainly giving an account of its seventeen narratives even in the brief manner in which I outlined the narrative strands of *Cloud Atlas* would try the patience of the reader. But it would be as well to give something of its flavour, which I shall do by very briefly describing its first few segments. It would appear that the entire film takes place in a bathtub, as Rayns explains: 'The framing material, in which Maddin regular Louis Negin performs a monologue written by the poet John Ashbery on bath-time etiquette, was suggested by a lost 1937 short by Dwain Esper, *How to Take a Bath*' (ibid.).[2] From this monologue we move to a submarine (initially a bath toy) called the SS *Plunger*, whose crew are panicking because the explosive substance they are transporting is melting and will explode if they ever surface, while their captain has locked himself in his room. A forester somehow makes his way onto the vessel and proceeds to tell the story of his attempt to rescue his beloved Margot from the fearsome Red Wolves. During the rescue attempt Margot has a dream in which she is an amnesiac and hears a nightclub singer sing a song (actually performed by the group Sparks) entitled 'The Final Derriere' about a man's attempt to cure his obsession with bottoms. And so on.

It might appear from this account that orientation was the last thing on the filmmakers' minds, and yet Maddin has indicated that they did intend genre to serve an orientational function, just as it does in *Cloud Atlas*. Given the film's density the variety of genres it includes presents 'a chance to help the viewers remember where the heck they were in any of these complicated nestings we were always planning to give them . . . We knew we wanted to help people. So they would be able to say, we're in the virgin sacrifice volcano movie. We're in the submarine picture' (Rapold 2015). The film matches its aquatic – bathtime – framing by making the experience of plunging into deeper narrative layers and later resurfacing a central part of the viewer's experience. Once the film has delved a few narrative levels down there is next to no chance of remembering precisely how we got there. Maddin has indicated that this experience was central to what he wanted to construct with the film:

> I like the feeling when you're coming out of nested narratives of being reminded where you are . . . About ten years ago I watched John Brahm's *The Locket* (1946), which is about a woman who is a pathological liar, and we see her only through the flashbacks of three different men – Brian Aherne, Gene Raymond, and Robert Mitchum – as they tell their stories to each other . . . And I just loved watching it because you really get so caught up in each story that then when you come out of it again you remember, oh yeah, I was two or three narratives deep. It's kind of fun to get your bearings again, and then get lost again and then remember. (Peranson 2015)

Crucial to the texture of *The Forbidden Room* is the difference between going 'down' (which is often surprisingly straightforward, no matter how ridiculous the link between framing story and framed story) and coming back 'up', which exploits our distant memory of the journey down to replicate something of the feeling of a half-remembered dream. There is certainly disorientation, but very importantly it is *not* total; rather, the film foregrounds the process both of disorientation and reorientation; as Maddin says, '[i]t's kind of fun to get your bearings again, and then get lost again'.

The film flirts with a deliberately misleading sense of lack of discipline, when in fact its structure could not be more meticulously planned. (As Johnson puts it, '[t]he movie looks messy but it has a firm spine' (Hynes 2015).) Every descent to a new narrative level is (eventually) dutifully followed by the reverse move back up the chain of nested narratives. Beyond this, the film is structured along three large gestures of narrative descent and resurfacing, each one more complex (involving more stories) than the last.

Whereas *Cloud Atlas* aims to keep its viewers orientated, once they have been 'trained' by the opening forty minutes, *The Forbidden Room* achieves an increasingly intense rhythm via the proliferating density and absurdity of the nested stories. A disorientating and exhausting sense of excess was precisely what Maddin and Johnson were aiming at; the relentlessness of its bewildering narrative nestings deliberately risks pushing what, as we saw in the last chapter, Alex Clayton refers to as the film's 'pact of tolerance' with its audience as far as it will go, and perhaps beyond (Clayton 2016: 201). As Maddin told Mark Peranson: 'If we had two instead of three acts, with this Russian-doll concentricity of nested narratives, it would have come in an hour shorter. But then it wouldn't have been too much, it wouldn't have been exhausting . . .' (Peranson 2015).

The notion that *The Forbidden Room* might have anything as neat as a three-act structure might seem absurd to somebody who has just watched the film for the first time, but it can be clearly seen if we set out its structure in a diagram – see Figure 2.4. (Here the levels do not, as in *Cloud Atlas*, refer to specific stories but only to how far down the chain of embedded narratives we have travelled. At some points segments on the same level do make up part of the same story because some narratives recur, but at other points they are entirely separate.) This diagram appears a great deal clearer than that of *Cloud Atlas*, but in fact the reverse case obtains. In the earlier film a

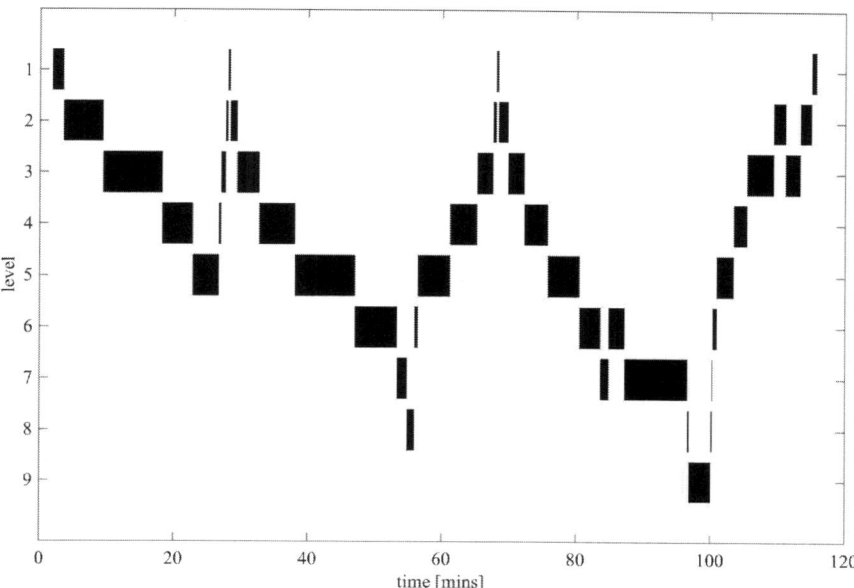

Figure 2.4   *The structure of* The Forbidden Room.

complicated-looking diagram belied the relative clarity of the viewing experience, whereas here the film's exceptionally meticulous structure clashes with the experience of actually watching it; as each act goes deeper and deeper into further and further embedded narratives our chance of keeping our bearings diminishes. But each ascent up the chain also holds out the possibility that if we concentrate just that bit harder we might get the hang of it. We might congratulate ourselves – particularly early in act three – for having started to get the hang of things (after two previous chances to practise), only for the film's complexity to outstrip our capacity once again. As Maddin puts it: 'You want people to feel washed up, panting, on some far shore, after barely surviving a drowning in narrative' (Romney 2015).

METALEPSIS?

Do we, then, find metalepsis taking place between the vast number of narrative strands and diegetic levels contained in *Cloud Atlas* and *The Forbidden Room*? Despite the manifold opportunities for it that such density affords, if metalepsis proper (i.e. ontological metalepsis) refers to an intersection of worlds that ought to be impossible – such as when a cartoon character shoots a member of the audience – then the surprise in both these films might be how little of this kind of metalepsis either film contains, despite the fact that both of them consistently provoke what we might call the feeling of metalepsis or the metaleptical, the feeling that stories that appear to have nothing to do with each other nevertheless come into some kind of contact. We could designate the metalepsis in these films as largely rhetorical, but what is interesting – with respect to the particular disorientations provoked by these two films – is the extent to which this rhetorical metalepsis is experienced by the viewer as somehow ontological. It is this feeling, for example, that appears to have confused some viewers of *Cloud Atlas*. Roger Ebert's reference to his failure 'to work out the logical connections between the segments, stories and characters' (Ebert 2012) seems prompted by a feeling that what is unusual about the film is that it does not fully spell out the *diegetic* connections between its strands. In fact, however, there are far more diegetic connections in the film than Ebert allows for, particularly when we allow for the film's hints at reincarnation, as indicated by a comet-shaped birthmark that is shared by a number of the protagonists. So, for example, Luisa Rey feels she has heard the 'Cloud Atlas Sextet' before, even though she is told that the LP containing it is vanishingly rare, because she is the reincarnation of Robert Frobisher, its composer. Reincarnation is certainly a fantastic connection between the narratives, but it is not – narratively speaking – illogical or impossible if we are dealing with a diegetic world in which reincarnation is a reality. Ontological metalepsis may require impossible or fantastic connections between diegetic levels, but not every such fantastic connection is metaleptical.

This being the case, although Luisa's memory of the Sextet is not a case of ontological metalepsis, strictly speaking, it clearly comes close to it, given that for most of us reincarnation and the possibility of remembering aspects of one's past lives are not realities, and given that – as I argued in the previous chapter – metalepsis (of whatever type) relies on the fact that the diegetic status of a narrative is not an objectively existing reality but the result of a film's rhetoric. *Cloud Atlas*'s rhetorical metalepses are generated largely through the ontological dimensions of its diegesis. The film deploys a rather deft sleight of hand, creating an impression of ontological metalepsis that it then disavows by making a kind of 'metalepsis' a reality within its diegesis. *The Forbidden Room*, on the other hand, creates feelings of metalepsis mostly through quantity and by surprise. The sheer absurdity of the transitions from one narrative to another make them feel metaleptical, by giving them a sense of worlds colliding impossibly. (To give one, not at all untypical, example: a pair of bananas that have been turned into aswangs (Filipino vampires) tell an amnesiac young woman the story of a man who attempts to cover up his failure to buy his wife a birthday present by passing off his possessions as a collection of duplicate items he bought for her, only to be faced with the problem of explaining what has happened to his own possessions.) If, however, my account of these films thus far has given the impression that the rhetoric of *Cloud Atlas* aims at an initial disorientation that subsides, as opposed to *The Forbidden Room*, which continually renews and reinvokes its powers of disorientation, this is only partially correct. Some of the connections between *Cloud Atlas*'s narrative threads are by no means as clarificatory as those already discussed, and thus my account needs complicating; I shall conclude this chapter by doing so.

As readers may have noticed in my plot summary of *Cloud Atlas*, many of the film's actors play more than one part. However, insofar as there are characters that correspond to one another in each strand, the casting does not follow this logic. Indeed, it seems that the casting is at times used deliberately to misdirect – to confuse – the viewer. The first character we see in the film is Zachry Bailey, played by Tom Hanks, in the narrative strand set furthest into the future. After this we move back to 1849 and meet Adam Ewing, played by Jim Sturgess. As Ewing strides across a pebbled beach we hear his voice-over announce, 'and thus it was that I made the acquaintance of Dr. Henry Goose, the man I hoped might cure me of my affliction'. Ewing approaches a man dressed in a waistcoat and straw hat, his back to us, digging in the beach. He turns to face the camera and we realise that he, too, is played by Hanks. The fact that an actor might play more than one character in this film is established right at the outset, not even two-and-a-half minutes into a nearly three-hour film; given the historical range covered by the film, we might well guess early on that these characters are reincarnations of one another in some sense. What we are certain not to guess is that it is *Ewing*, not Goose, who is reincarnated as Zachry, as the comet-shaped birthmark eventually indicates. Goose is in fact the first of the film's various devil figures, what Zachry calls in his opening monologue 'that fangy devil, Old Georgie hisself'.

Some have found the film's use of recasting to be a defect. Mozaffar declares that 'the plot(s) would be far more coherent if the same (mostly big name) actors and actresses (primarily Tom Hanks, Halle Berry, Susan Sarandon, Jim Broadbent, Hugh Grant, Keith David, and [Hugo] Weaving) were not re-used for almost every thread' and admits that 'this makes for a very distracting process' but claims that it ultimately contributes to the film's representation of the desire for 'complete liberation from all constraints' (Mozaffar 2012). I certainly agree that searching for the actor beneath the often very extensive makeup and prosthetics can be distracting. But I would account for its effect rather differently. We could say that there is a productive, quasi-metaleptical confusion between some of the film's themes (concerning the human connections between people apparently at a great remove from one another, whether chronologically, geographically, racially, sexually or otherwise) and the filmic devices (specifically the casting) that it deploys. The film, for example, deliberately recasts across racial and gender lines. Jim Sturgess and James D'Arcy play Korean characters in one segment, which might have given rise to substantial controversy except that this casting decision is clearly designed to take its place within a film in which Halle Berry and Doona Bae play white women, Hugo Weaving and Ben Whishaw play women and Susan Sarandon (very briefly) plays a man.[3] The fact that this recasting does not match up with the diegetic connections between the threads (such as recasting the same actor as the reincarnations of the same character) does not, *pace* Mozaffar, suggest that utopia would be a world without distinction, but instead disturbs the film's tendency towards a rather excessive neatness.[4] What risks at times coming across as a rather woolly paean to the continuity of the human spirit and the relationship between contingency and destiny is enriched by the confusion the casting engenders; it satisfyingly thickens the plot and ensures that there is some intriguing movement back and forth between orientation and disorientation, rather than the traffic running in only one direction. It is in this play with different levels and kinds of disorientation that *Cloud Atlas* and *The Forbidden Room*, for all their vast differences, indicate a shared awareness of some of the rewards cinematic confusion can offer.

CHAPTER 3

'Disappeared where it's real hard to disappear': Three Ways of Getting Lost in INLAND EMPIRE

Early on in David Lynch's *INLAND EMPIRE* (2006), Nikki Grace (Laura Dern) and Devon Berk (Justin Theroux) are beginning their first rehearsal on the set of their new film, *On High in Blue Tomorrows*. Also present are director Kingsley Stewart (Jeremy Irons) and his assistant Freddie (Harry Dean Stanton). Freddie hears a noise from the soundstage, which is supposed to have been cleared of other people. Devon goes to investigate, makes chase, but eventually loses whoever it is behind a row of theatrical flats representing the house belonging to Sue Blue, Nikki's character in the film. On his return to the others, Nikki asks Devon who it was. He replies that whoever they were, they 'disappeared where it's real hard to disappear'. It eventually transpires that what has taken place is an entanglement of reality and fiction, a metalepsis: the intruder was Sue Blue herself (or perhaps Nikki-playing-Sue, at a different point in time). Later in the film we see the intrusion from the intruder's point of view: following an arrow written shakily on a metal door below the words 'Axxon N.', Dern's character emerges onto the soundstage, looking – impossibly – at herself. She runs, is pursued by Devon, then opens a door in what should be merely a facade and takes refuge in a building that should not exist.

Where is it 'real hard to disappear'? And why? These scenes in *INLAND EMPIRE* activate ideas of location and confusion, logic and paradox. In this chapter I propose that attempting to produce a single, wholly consistent and coherent interpretation of Lynch's film may be misguided, but that this does not imply that we should just give ourselves up to disorientation.[1] I shall demonstrate a more fruitful approach by pursuing three different strategies for reading the film, each of which develops out of – and responds to – omissions in the previous reading. This chapter aims at interrogating the global coherence of *INLAND EMPIRE* and its relationship to our orientational strategies. I argue that Lynch's film only achieves coherence at the expense of completeness and can thus cohere in a number of different ways; significance will turn out to depend on our interpretive decisions. I shall try and show this by moving through three different strategies for reading the film, each of which takes its origin in what the previous strategy overlooked or omitted. This is by no means to say that we can make *INLAND EMPIRE* mean 'anything we want it to'; on the contrary, I will try to show how the film – as text – is responsive to our critical decisions. But we cannot securely rely on the film to indicate which of its elements are the most important and thus, more than with most films, what we decide to omit in any given reading (and all readings must omit *something*) is likely to turn out, in an alternative reading, to be of central importance.

More than any other of Lynch's works, in fact, *INLAND EMPIRE* brings coherence into conflict with completeness. No reading of the film that I have encountered finds a convincing place for everything in the film. But neither does the fact that each reading has lacunae mean that no reading is possible other than one based on purely subjective assertion. The film is constructed in such a way as to render possible a large number of mutually incompatible readings, which are each consistent as long as they pay the price of omitting one or more elements. The film's form recalls something Ezra Pound once said about the form of his *Cantos*: 'It had to be a form that wouldn't exclude something merely because it didn't fit' (quoted in McGann 1988: 8). Michel Chion observes that '[e]ven as he seeks to recreate a unity, Lynch seems to aim for the part as such to subsist, the part which is incommensurable with the whole' (Chion 1995: 181). As a young man, Lynch made 'kits' out of the parts of dissected animals, pointing out the difference between a complete collection of parts and a whole; hence Chion's decision to name his alphabetical discussion of important elements in Lynch's work as a 'Lynch-kit', and to describe it as 'an attempt to reconstitute an impossible whole' (*ibid.*: 161). It is not that we have no idea where we are with regard to the film, but that we cannot know *exactly* where we are. Something always remains unlocatable. As Brian Rourke puts it: 'While the viewer can pursue a dizzying array of options in imposing coherence on the film, none works without remainder' (Rourke 2016). I would merely question Rourke's use of the word 'imposing' here, which to me implies an excessively one-sided view, wherein the film outstrips all coherence and thus requires that – if we want to demand coherence of it – we can produce it only by distorting the film by using frameworks imported from elsewhere. I believe the situation to be more delicate than this. Clearly *INLAND EMPIRE* – like all films – is shaped by the process of its construction; as Dennis Lim explains, it 'was written a scene at a time and shot fitfully over a period of three years, without an ending in mind or (to begin with) a unifying structure' (Lim 2015: 167). But the film as we have it is a single work and, I argue, a unified work, even if it often puts our understanding of what it means to be such a work under serious strain. The film offers us plenty of interpretive invitations to which we can respond, but we must also be sensitive to the pitfalls they present and the gaps or limitations they exhibit.

I should, however, make it clear that I am not arguing that the film encourages precisely the progression between different reading strategies that my chapter follows, nor does everything I have to say fit neatly into one of the three approaches. My hope is rather that the structure I have used may demonstrate, or perhaps even dramatise, an oscillation between, on the one hand, a confidence that the film is responsive to our investigation of it and, on the other, a nagging feeling that one cannot fit it all together without contradiction or remainder. I do not propose the exact trajectory outlined here as the best, let alone the only, possible account of a critical response that does justice to the film. Rather, I hope to establish the possibility that searching for appropriate orientational criteria may lead us to have this *kind* of critical relationship with it.

Projections

Before embarking on the first reading strategy, some brief words on the film's central narrative and rhetorical figure are in order. In the very first moments of the film a beam of light illuminates or projects the outlines of the words INLAND EMPIRE in capital letters. At pivotal narrative moments in the film Lynch deploys a type of shot sequence that I shall call the projection sequence, wherein a character's literal and psychological points of view seem to intertwine in an 'impossible' – metaleptical – fashion. A character is shown looking towards something; a reverse shot indicates that what they are looking at is themselves, at another point in space and time; finally, another shot shows that one of the two versions of the character has disappeared. They have 'projected into' another version of themselves. A phenomenon of psychological derivation is made into a 'literal' – if fantastical – diegetic reality. Projection becomes, in *INLAND EMPIRE*, not merely a useful metaphor for grasping the film's thematic operations, but also a feature of the narrative.

Warren Buckland points out that this device 'is highly unusual, but not unique; Kubrick uses it towards the end of *2001* (1968), when Bowman is in the white room and sees an older version of himself. Once we see the older Bowman, the younger one disappears, and the film continues with the older man' (Buckland 2013: 243). Comparable sequences also appear in *Meshes of the Afternoon*, a short 1943 film made by Maya Deren with her husband Alexander Hammid, in which a dreamer (played by Deren) watches herself from a window. Each dream-self seems to generate yet another self, but unlike in *INLAND EMPIRE* these projections do not replace one another but multiply, until three different Derens sit around the kitchen table. The device also has a precursor in Lynch's previous film: there is an apparent shot/reverse shot of a single character at the beginning of the second part of *Mulholland Dr.* (2001). Diane Selwyn (Naomi Watts), who we have previously known as Betty Elms, is distraught at the break-up of her relationship with Camilla Rhodes (Laura Elena Harring). We see Diane from behind, standing at her kitchen sink. She turns to her left, at which point her dishevelled face, which has clearly been crying, breaks into a smile as she says 'Camilla! You've come back!' A reverse shot shows us Camilla at her most glamorous. Tears of emotion come to Diane's eyes, and she sighs in excitement, only for her tears and sighs of joy to become sobs of horror as her face contorts into a grimace. Another apparent reverse shot again shows us Diane, but washed-out and hard-faced, seeming to look towards her hysterical self with weary contempt. The editing here shows us the collapse of fantasy into reality: the longed-for return of the lover is only a figment of the imagination and hence there is nothing to see but oneself. In *INLAND EMPIRE*, however, the diegetic status of the projection shots is more ambiguous; we cannot be at all confident that it is possible to recuperate them in a non-fantastic fashion as the representations of a disturbed mind.

The first 'projection sequence' happens at the end of the visit Nikki Grace receives from Grace Zabriskie's 'Visitor #1'. Following her visitor's pointing finger, Nikki looks across the room and sees herself a day later, about to hear from her agent that she has got the part of Sue Blue; a reverse shot shows only an empty room, into which her butler comes with the telephone.[2] The second occurs when, as we have seen, Sue (played by Nikki) unexpectedly finds herself on the soundstage of *On High in Blue Tomorrows*, looking back through time at herself during the first read-through. The 'earlier' Nikki, rather than the intruder, disappears. The two projection sequences, then, differ in terms of which version of Laura Dern's character(s) it is that disappears. In the first sequence it is the watcher who disappears; in the second sequence, the watcher remains while the one being watched vanishes. We could, just about, explain the first projection sequence as a simple temporal ellipsis, a jump forward in time (perhaps Nikki did not 'really' see herself on the sofa), but the second time an event we have already seen is altered. When Sue emerges on to the soundstage her gaze causes her earlier self to disappear; the clarity of the distinctions between what is diegetically real and diegetically fictional, between what happened 'then' and what is happening 'now', begins to become seriously compromised. What are we to make of this?

Strategy 1: The Lost Girl

It seems sensible to commence an attempt to come to terms with the disorientation provoked by *INLAND EMPIRE* by trying to accommodate as much of the filmic text as possible. The film opens with a bewildering abundance of material which I will attempt to give a flavour of. Two black and white sequences follow the film's opening image of the projector beam and the title. The first consists mostly of close-ups of a turntable – its needle and the record spinning upon it – over which we hear a male voice scratchily announcing '*Axxon N.*, the longest running radio play in history! Tonight, continuing in the Baltic region, a grey winter day in an old hotel.' Then we see a hotel corridor and a man and woman. The latter says, in Polish, that she doesn't recognise the hallway. Their faces blurred, they enter the room and discuss 'what whores do'; blurred facial close-ups indicate that the man does indeed get the woman to have sex with him. She says, twice, that she is afraid. Then the low, threatening drones that have accompanied all the images thus far give way to the lighter, ethereal sounds of a female voice claiming that she 'sing[s] this poem to you, on the other side I see'. The image, still black and white, resolves into the woman sitting on the bed, alone, though her face is still blurred out, as if to protect her identity in the manner of surveillance footage shown on television. We cut to her point of view of the other side of the room; her abandoned shoes are still lying on the floor next to the sofa and there is a standard lamp in the corner.

Then there is an abrupt transition to colour. A close-up looking directly into a camera lens (though exactly what kind of lens is difficult to tell) is superimposed on a slightly wider version of the penultimate black and white shot. A dark-haired woman is sitting on a bed covered in a green bedspread, naked apart from a red dress that she holds against herself; she will only be named as the Lost Girl at the very end of the film, if we pay attention to the credits (she is played by Karolina Gruszka). She is not looking towards us but off to screen right towards, as the next shot reveals, a television showing only static. We briefly see the television over her shoulder and then, finally, are given a close-up of her face, tears streaming down her cheeks. Her television screen shows strange sped-up images of three humans with large rabbit heads in a room that resembles a sitcom set, followed by a woman walking to the front door of a palatial house. This, we will soon learn, is the material that is immediately to follow in *INLAND EMPIRE*. We zoom in on this Lost Girl's crying eyes as the voice sings 'It's far away, far away from me', before we dissolve to the rabbits' room and watch, now at normal speed, what the Lost Girl was watching.

Despite the sense of disorientation that this complex and bizarre opening is, I think, sure to generate in every first-time viewer, there is a great deal in it that prompts us both to consider the Lost Girl as the centre of the film and to identify to some extent with her, both emotionally and perspectivally. There is her evident pain and suffering, as well as the affective qualities of the music, and there is also the fact that what she watches on her television turns out to be the same – or at least very similar – to what we then watch on the cinema screen. Perhaps the disorientation that the film's complexity prompts in us as spectators is intended to mimic the Lost Girl's own confusion and desolation. A relatively coherent account of *INLAND EMPIRE* as the Lost Girl's story is, in fact, not too difficult to construct. Her next appearance makes it clear that her contact with Nikki/Sue is crucial: she provides Laura Dern's character(s) with the means 'to see' (by burning a hole in silk and looking through it while wearing a watch). We and Nikki/Sue are given views of the Lost Girl's past, in which she seems possibly to have been married to the man we know as the Phantom (Krzysztof Majchrzak) and to have committed at least one murder. She later contacts the man we know both as Nikki Grace's husband and, in another reality, as Sue Blue's husband (played by Peter J. Lucas) in some kind of seance, and laments that she doesn't know where she is. But the gun that Lucas's character is given after the seance enables Nikki, once she has fully acknowledged that the Lost Girl is watching her, to destroy the Phantom and to liberate the Lost Girl with a kiss. At this point Nikki disappears, having fulfilled her purpose, and the Lost Girl is tearfully reunited with her husband (Peter J. Lucas again) and their son (identified in the credits as 'Smithy's son'), who we see for the first and only time. The resolution of the problem that was established at the beginning is underlined by the only other appearance of the song we hear at the beginning of the film (written by Lynch, it is titled 'Polish Poem', and sung by Chrysta Bell). The song is only now allowed to run for its full length; at its end we learn that, finally, 'something is happening'.

A number of critics agree that *INLAND EMPIRE* is the Lost Girl's story. Todd McGowan is clear that the film's centre is the Lost Girl, who has a 'traumatising sexual encounter', after which 'she sits on a chair [*sic*] crying and watching the television, which unfolds a fantasmic drama that ultimately transforms her situation and reunites her with her husband and son' (McGowan 2010: 8). VanCleeve Taggart sees the film's nested narratives as consisting, precisely, of a hierarchy of nested projections (Taggart n.d.). Although, plausibly, Taggart locates the Lost Girl herself as a character within *Axxon N.*, she nonetheless views her as the 'projector' of everything she watches on her television, which is to say the vast majority of *INLAND EMPIRE*. But considering the Lost Girl as central in this way does not require us to buy into the narrative of her redemption. For Jonathan Goodwin the resolution of her narrative is savagely ironic:

The idol materializes, and the kiss signifies the completion of the Lost Girl's atonement fantasy. She is reunited with her husband and family. But the actual message here is that nothing has changed. The film's epilogue depicts the vehicle of transformation – the actress Nikki Grace – in an enlightened state being ritually praised by prostitutes, figurants, and other cinematic illusions. The Lost Girl has returned to her, by comparison, drab reality and is now satisfied with it; but the implicit comparison with the exultancy of Grace's ascent makes her atonement and reconciliation seem almost a cruel joke. (Goodwin 2014: 318)

Goodwin's reading is ingenious but I have difficulty seeing it as supported by the film. There is little in the film that specifically indicates that the emotional reunion of the nuclear family should be considered 'drab'. The Lost Girl is not returned, satisfied, to a reality she was previously dissatisfied with but is released from a prison – the hotel room – into the reality and the relationships she was desperate to reconnect with. (When we are first shown her modern husband's duplicate in the Polish past – Peter J. Lucas with a moustache – we cut three times to the familiar close-up of the Lost Girl, her lips parting in yearning and suppressed anticipation; we also cut to her, weeping more intensely than usual, when we see him murdered.) We have earlier seen Peter J. Lucas in the same set beating Dern's character – the Lost Girl's surrogate, we assume – because he says he can't father children but she is nevertheless pregnant. Now he comes in happily with a young boy, and so forgiveness (whether of his brutality, her infidelity or both) may not be far from our minds. And since we have seen another version of him lying dead on a Polish street, we might also think of resurrection. (Or, since she previously had to be contacted via a seance, perhaps it is the Lost Girl herself who is resurrected.) The film gives us few reasons I can see to suppose that forgiveness or returning to life are, at this point, to be considered as 'cruel jokes'.

Nevertheless, the double ending is certainly problematic, and Taggart's reading is therefore a little too neat in its construction of a fully coherent hierarchy of projections. As the film moves towards its ending, the connections that seemed previously to be parallel threads of narrative in different times, as some kind of curse doomed the same story to happen over and over again, now appear to be collapsing in on one another, leaving us with the Lost Girl, no longer lost but found, the curse having been lifted. And yet, if Nikki is merely the Lost Girl's fantasmic projection, or at least merely the instrument of her liberation or redemption, should she not leave the film after the kiss which makes her disappear? But, as Goodwin notes, she does not. Instead, we find her back again in what was once the rabbits' room, looking out at an empty auditorium from which we hear the sound of applause (she is, after all, an actor), after which we return to the meeting with her first visitor. The first time around she had a vision of the action which, it turned out, comprised the majority of the film. This time she has a vision of herself sitting serenely in a pale blue dress, and it is this same self who appears in the final, ecstatic coda. The two different versions of the soundstage scene occur within half an hour of each other, but the viewer has to wait almost two and a half hours to see a different version of this first projection sequence, giving it great structural and affective weight. If Nikki is merely the Lost Girl's fantasy or projection, should the coda not be the Lost Girl's vision? But there is no indication that the Lost Girl has any more visions after, or during, the reunion with her family. Rather than reaffirming the connection between Nikki and the Lost Girl, or collapsing the two personae into a single person, the conclusion seems to separate them out from one another.

It seems, therefore, that considering the film's action as neatly wrapped up in the Lost Girl's narrative cannot really account for the film's conclusion (this might perhaps be one reason for Goodwin's perception of the ending as a 'cruel joke', though he does not make this argument). Nikki's fantasy or vision is given an importance that is incomprehensible if she herself is merely a fantasy. The film seems, rather, to present an instance of what Robert Pippin calls 'being bound up in overlapping fantasies' – the fantasies of, at the very least, both the Lost Girl and Nikki (Pippin 2017a: 84). So Nikki must be 'real' – but in what sense? Rourke's claim that '[w]ithin the *fabula*, this final victory is seen by no one and has no discernible effect' (Rourke 2016) is unsatisfactory. Within which *fabula*, or whose *fabula*? Does this not raise the question of how the *fabula* in a film as confusing as this is to be established at all? Should we postulate that Nikki and the Lost Girl exist in parallel worlds of equal diegetic status that fantastically connect? Or is there another way of reading the situation?

One possibility might be to reconsider the relationship between *syuzhet* and *fabula*. Daniel Neofetou has suggested that Lynch's film's 'could often be said to have syuzhets without fabulas' (Neofetou 2012: 11). In this he goes too far; there is no Lynch film where a *fabula* cannot at least partly be reconstructed from its *syuzhet*. Nevertheless, the proposition is not unhelpful because it reminds us that the *fabula* is always a reconstruction, never something we are presented with directly. (This situation exactly parallels the argument in Chapter 1 about diegetic status.) *Lost Highway* might be Lynch's boldest foray into such territory, because the narrative is explicitly paradoxical: its end is its beginning, and Fred Madison (Bill Pullman) is (like the film's Mystery Man (Robert Blake)) in two places at once, both downstairs speaking into the intercom and upstairs listening to it. Perhaps the fundamental trick of linear narrative is to make us willingly entertain the notion that its linearity is merely a way of unfolding something that exists, as it were, outside time, as a consistent totality. Roland Barthes observes that 'rereading draws the text out of its internal chronology ("this happens *before* or *after* that") and recaptures a mythic time (without *before* or *after*)', as if, that is, one could build a physical model of a story, existing all at once, and it is merely a contingent limitation of our condition that it takes us a while to explore it bit by bit (Barthes 1990: 16). But the really startling realisation that Lynch's work can give rise to is not, I think, that the *fabula* is merely a reconstruction – this is easy to realise and accept – nor even that it is sometimes impossible to piece together a coherent one. Rather, the surprise is how easily this is concealed. Or, we might say, how surprisingly little disoriented we are by inconsistency, in the right conditions. *Lost Highway* demonstrates impeccably how well a *syuzhet* can get by without without a consistent (non-paradoxical) *fabula*; how much we rely on the *promise* of a comprehensible *fabula* (the expectation of future explanation and clarification), rather than there being anything in the nature of linear storytelling which requires such a *fabula* to exist in order for the *syuzhet* to be followable at all.

INLAND EMPIRE does not operate quite like *Lost Highway*; its complexities do not result so much from direct presentation of paradox. But it certainly puts into question the possibility of passing from our sense of '*before* or *after*' into a region 'without *before* or *after*'. One of Dern's characters articulates this explicitly: 'I don't know what was before or after. I don't know what happened first. And it's kinda laid a mindfuck on me.'[3] Even so, it is the excess of material rather than its indeterminacy that causes the real difficulties. Rourke puts it well when he argues that '[t]he difficulty results from a surplus of narrative series within the *sjužet*, rather than an incomplete or incoherent *fabula*' (Rourke 2016). In his own reading, however, Rourke still insists on constructing a singular *fabula*, even if this requires going beyond any textual warrant. He suggests that the 'young woman who immigrated to the US from Poland' (about whom 'one can never be certain whether her image appears on camera directly, though she most likely resembles the "Lost Girl"') during her childhood 'enjoyed listening with her mother to recordings of a family collection of old radio plays on a phonograph' (*ibid.*). But this is based on nothing more than imaginative speculation. Dennis Lim, more promisingly, suggests that we might view the film as a kind of metaleptical ghost story, that the various stories it contains can be seen to haunt one another: '[T]he film's queasiest effect is in persuading its viewer that its stories – all stories – have a life of their own, that they are spaces to inhabit, forces that haunt' (Lim 2015: 176). What might happen, then, if we set aside for the moment the quest for a single *fabula*? What other strategies might be open to us?

Strategy 2: Laura Dern and Her Characters

If we read the film with the Lost Girl at its centre, the seance scene in which the Polish husband makes contact with the Lost Girl is absolutely crucial, connecting as it does all of the film's most important narrative threads. These include the relation of the Lost Girl to her husband and of Poland to Los Angeles as well as the notion of the Rabbits as transitional figures facilitating the quest to destroy the Phantom (the three old men present at the seance give the husband a gun which he then places for Dern's character to find and use to kill the Phantom, after which they transform into the Rabbits). And yet the scene is not often commented upon either in reviews or criticism, and I suggest that one reason for this is that Laura Dern does not appear in it. Her performance – in what she herself has described as 'the greatest experience I've had as an actor' (Lynch and McKenna 2018: 425) – so strongly gathers our attention that when a narratively crucial scene appearing almost exactly two-thirds of the way through the film (perfectly placed to supply narrative clarity preparatory to the build-up to the final conflict) does not include her it is hard to feel that the scene *is* genuinely crucial.

A very obvious feature of Dern's performance is that she plays a number of characters. There are at least two, Nikki Grace and Susan Blue, but their relationship is sufficiently obscure that we cannot discount the possibility that there are still others: is the woman who tells her stories to Mr K. (Erik Crary) Sue, Nikki or a third persona?[4] Dern is not the kind of actor to become almost unrecognisable in different roles, but she is able to bring about very different effects via characteristic mannerisms, which prevents them from really being mannerisms. This is true in her work across Lynch's *oeuvre* but here it is concentrated in a single film. There is in Dern's performance a reweighting of an ensemble of devices (a repertoire of gestures, of vocal inflections, and so forth), one example of which is a certain way of speaking with her lips only slightly parted and barely moving. The fact of the mannerisms is hardly surprising – it would be true even for a 'chameleonic' actor if we looked hard enough – but that she is versatile while remaining very recognisable is highly appropriate for the kind of disorientations that *INLAND EMPIRE* produces. An actor more given to virtuosic displays of range – a Daniel Day Lewis or a Jennifer Jason Leigh, say – might have signalled the distinctions between characters *too* clearly, diminishing the sense that each bleeds disorientatingly into one another.

The need for recognition and the desire for consistency of character, or rather the fear of their absence or loss, are insisted on throughout the film; Sue and the Polish Lost Girl both implore others to 'Look at me and tell

Figure 3.1 Sandy, Lula and Nikki: Laura Dern speaks while barely moving her lips, variously conveying concern and curiosity (Blue Velvet (1986)), fear and desire (Wild at Heart (1990)), or sorrow and guilt (INLAND EMPIRE).

me if you've known me before!' A. J. Greimas once discussed another way of getting to a time 'without *before* and *after*' in his analysis of how narrative coherence is maintained across a flashback in Maupassant's short story 'Deux Amis': 'Identification . . . implies the neutralization of the temporal category *present* vs *past* . . . The cognitive operation therefore establishes the dominance of the relation of identity over the temporal category' (Greimas 1988: 26). In conventional flashbacks, the fact that people change over time (and are thus, in a sense, *different people* at different times) is neutralised – or at the very least underplayed – and instead the audience's orientation is facilitated: we are reassured that, even though different times are at issue, we are dealing with *the same characters*. But in *INLAND EMPIRE* neither the viewer nor, crucially, the characters themselves can be so sure that identity takes precedence. Characters often seem in a state of radical doubt as to the consistency of their identity, a doubt that the audience may very well share. This is perhaps best seen in Laura Dern's various accents. When we first encounter Nikki she is a guarded and unsympathetic film star with a nondescript standard American accent; she only lights up when her acting is discussed. As Sue Blue, she has a working-class southern accent. As the film proceeds, these accents cease to be so clearly distinguished. When Nikki and Devon discuss going for an Italian meal after the shoot they use their southern accents. At first this seems part of their flirtation: they are covering what they know to be the actual beginning of an affair with the melodramatic playacting of their film roles. But later in the film Dern's accent ceases to be a reliable guide to which character she is currently occupying, as in Buñuel's *That Obscure Object of Desire* (1977) when it initially seems that Carole Bouquet and Ángela Molina represent two sides of Conchita's personality (coolly Gallic or fierily Iberian), a clarity which the film proceeds to undermine.

Just as a lack of faith in self-consistency ('tell me if you've known me before!') attacks – from within – Nikki's (and/or Sue's) Cartesian certainty in her own existence, a sense that everybody else knows more about her than she does herself attacks this certainty from without. Thus Nikki's disorientation does not only involve Ami Harbin's trio of 'others, environments, and life projects' (Harbin 2016: xi); she also loses her bearings in relation to *herself*. But it is often through her relations to others, to her environments and to her life projects (in the general sense of the directions her life is taking, whether willed or not) that this disorientation in relation to herself is felt. There are repeated indications that everybody apart from Nikki is certain that she will start sleeping with Devon, which disorientates them (presumably because they have not yet admitted their attraction to themselves). When they appear on Marilyn Levens's (Diane Ladd) television show, we join them as they return from a commercial break, after which Levens's first words are: 'Mamas, lock up your daughters' doors! Nikki, really, this news, this shocking revelation by Devon must send a shiver down your spine! Are you going to be able to be true to hubby with a wolf in the den?' From their reactions, it seems as if Nikki is as much in the dark as to what she is talking about as we are. Later, when Nikki's husband Piotrek (Peter J. Lucas once again) takes Devon upstairs to warn him off Nikki, Devon seems equally confused. The two are watched by Nikki, prefiguring the moment when she and Devon do have sex (proving 'everybody' to have been correct), when they are watched by Piotrek. This scene is crucial in the development of the confusion of character: Billy insists that Sue is Sue, while she desperately tries to get him to recognise her as Nikki.

Need we, as viewers, come down on one side or another?[5] When it comes to the film's conclusion, perhaps rather than deciding whether we are watching Nikki or a transfigured version of Sue, the presence of other actresses who do not otherwise appear in the film (Laura Harring – Rita/Camilla from *Mulholland Dr.* – and Nastassja Kinski) might suggest that we should really be concentrating on the fact that we are seeing Laura Dern, whose remarkable skills have focused our attention for the preceding three hours.[6] Taggart suggests as much as a way of consolidating her reading of a series of projections, emphasising both the physical projection of the film and its source in the work of David Lynch: 'We see the source of all the Nikkis (actress Laura Dern), signalling the merging of the final remaining projection residue (transfigured Nikki) into the consolidated Lynch-position' (Taggart n.d.). If, however, *INLAND EMPIRE* is a film centred around a performance (or performances), and the reflexive dramatisation of the means by which that performance (or those performances) are achieved, we might feel that it uses profligate means for such an exploration. If performance is central, why all the explicit repetitions and connections between parts? Why not simply allow for thematic or affective resonances (as happens, for the most part, in *Cloud Atlas*)? Would not that have put the emphasis even more on Dern's performance? Aren't we distracted by our attempts to parse the connections? Perhaps it is a mistake to foreground what is being connected. Perhaps by doing so we are neglecting having a really close look at the connections themselves.

STRATEGY 3: CONNECTIONS

It is clear that, despite its confusing surface, *INLAND EMPIRE* contains an abundance of connections between its various parts. There is, as Freddie says, 'a vast network, an ocean of possibilities', though tracing these possibilities may take us to unexpected places; Lynch has remarked that '[y]ou enter the film in one place and come out in another' (Lynch and McKenna 2018: 436). Perhaps rather than attempting interpretation as a method of unifying sense-making (as I emphasised in my first strategy) or concentrating on the relationship between performance, viewer engagement and coherence (as in my second), we could emphasise pattern-finding by tracing connections, as Nikki/Sue does when she follows the arrow beneath the words 'Axxon N.'. Connections are made throughout the film via similarities and repetitions. These are both visual (the silhouettes of the male rabbit, of Visitor #1 in Nikki's doorway, of Kingsley and Freddie entering the soundstage, the many lamps) and sonic (flickering electricity, drones, finger clicks, particular pieces of music). Most striking are the great many verbal echoes; it seems as if everything mysterious in the film is said at least twice: '9:45', 'after midnight', 'horse to the well', 'just down the way', 'look at me and tell me if you've known me before', 'have a way with animals', 'check the gate'. (John Esther pleasingly – albeit, I would argue, not entirely accurately – describes the film as containing 'much rhyme and very little reason' in Barney (2009: 246).) Subtitles are used to provide exact repetitions even between utterances in different languages.

As well as connections we make because of repetitions, the film is full of corridors, doors, staircases: very literal forms of connection. The combination of hotel corridors with the music of Penderecki might put us in mind of Kubrick's *The Shining* (1980), about which Gilles Deleuze wondered how we can 'decide what comes from the inside and what comes from the outside, the extra-sensory perceptions or hallucinatory projections?' (Deleuze 2013: 212). Physical passage is frequently emphasised, and yet in the projection sequences movement in both space and time is achieved *without* any intervening transition. In fact, in the middle of the film, transitions are often combined with a sense of stasis. Previously, even if the connections are impossible or fantastical (as in the projection shots) we can more or less follow them as part of a linear, if sinuous, narrative. Things get stranger and the connections a little looser after Nikki (or Sue) enters the house that should be merely a theatrical front, disappearing 'where it's real hard to disappear'. The first encounters with the characters known as the Bad Girls give rise to a series of visions which demarcate a clear segment of the film, concluding with another moment where two of Dern's personae look at each other (via a shot/reverse shot), one above and one below. Transitions seem at this point in the film rather more like movements between parallel streams of narrative than anything else. We might move, for example, from Sue's house to a Poland of the past, only to find ourselves back in Sue's house with no explanation and with no obvious development having taken place. We have here no secure means for comprehending the relationships between the narrative threads, whether temporally, spatially or causally. As a result the narrative seems to have stagnated, or perhaps – in yet another form of time 'without *before* and *after*' – to have been spatialised, made geometric: different methods of connection and transition are explored without this implying progress or transformation.

I want to conclude by suggesting two ways of considering the notion of connection which this sense of narrative stasis in the middle of the film might be seen to prompt (because it frustrates or at least impedes narrative/diegetic explanation): connection as parody and connection as allegory. A number of interpreters attempt to use the words of Nikki's first visitor as a key to the film. But there is something hyperbolic about them. In the density of their simultaneous suggestiveness and obscurity they take to extremes the kind of riddle that often commences a fairy story and is eventually explained at its conclusion. Despite the efforts of many ingenious interpreters, is it possible to be confident what she means by her references to a 'little boy', a 'little girl' or the 'reflection', the 'alley behind the marketplace' and the 'way to the palace'? Plausible candidates can be proposed (Hollywood as the marketplace, and the alley behind it as all that goes on 'behind the scenes', in the broadest sense, to make its products possible) but not with the neatness with which fairytale riddles tend to get solved. We return to Visitor #1 at the end of the film but not to her words; they set off the narrative but then recur only in verbal ('9:45', 'after midnight'), visual (the alley down which Sue walks with her groceries before following the 'Axxon N.' arrow) or thematic echoes. Is our tendency to latch onto repetition as indicative of meaning being parodied? Certainly at one point our confusion about the identity of characters in the Polish segment of the film is explicitly mocked. We watch

Peter J. Lucas's Polish character take leave of his wife, of whom we can see only her back. She shouts after him 'I'm not who you think I am!', and then Lanni (Emily Stofle), one of the Bad Girls, pokes her head into the frame, grotesquely uplit and very close to the camera, asking 'Who is she?' There is a dissolve to a dead woman played by Julia Ormand (who also plays Billy's wife Doris Side, and later in the film stabs Sue with a screwdriver), and then Lori (Kristen Kerr), another of the Bad Girls, also leans into the frame and again asks 'Who is she?' Is this evidence that the wife and the dead woman are one and the same, or does it mock our desire for this to be so? Our confusion is parodied; the very repetition of the question pokes fun at our determination to find meaning in repetition.

Alternatively, and very differently, perhaps *INLAND EMPIRE* is about the translations involved in the global sex industry. Hollywood may involve whoring oneself out ('I'm a whore!' Sue exclaims to her audience of prostitutes), as, so some think, does marriage. Here we are dealing mainly with metaphor, but movement from Poland to the USA also involves the literal trafficking of women. Richard Peña, the programming director for the Film Society of Lincoln Center, has been quoted as saying that

> the film includes a Hollywood story about a young actress who gets a part in a film that might be cursed; a story about the smuggling of women from Eastern Europe; and an abstract story about a family of people with rabbit heads sitting around in a living room. (Peña, paraphrased in Blatter 2006)

Joshua D. Gonsalves, in an otherwise hostile essay on the film, agrees: 'the not altogether ridiculous sublime of the brutal, statistical facticities of global sex traffic intimate why many insist that Lynch's films are not about anything' (Gonsalves 2010: 118). They insist on it, that is, to avoid the realities that Lynch intends for us to confront. Jennifer Pranolo's psychoanalytic and allegorical reading of the film grasps the nettle of the role of sexualised violence against women in this film (something which is, as is frequently noted, present in most of his works) and makes a number of interesting observations. But even though it would have fitted in well with my previous interpretive strategy centred on Dern's performance, I remain unconvinced by the way the logic of her argument rests, ultimately, on a claim that the violence extends all the way to the impositions of Lynch (the director and writer) upon Laura Dern the actor: 'Recognising herself as a cliche, Dern is nonetheless trapped in her roles-within-roles in films-within-films – roles and films that alarmingly spill over into reality and vice versa – compelled to perform her own fracturing of identity as stipulated by Lynch's self-replicating script' (Pranolo 2011: 483). This seems to me to be one metalepsis too far and not to leave much, if any, room for Dern's performance of violence *as a performance*.

In addition, the claim that at the end we see Dern's character back with her 'Visitor #1' 'pristinely untouched, poised for the whole apparatus of torture to begin again' (*ibid*.: 490) takes no account of the way the film's rhetoric figures this final sequence as an achievement of a state *beyond* torture, where as the 'Polish Poem' puts it, 'something is happening' and we are, at last, 'on the other side'.

The brutality of the connections of sex traffic and the way they associate sex and death are literalised in Street Person #2's (Nae Yuuki) story about her friend Niko, who looks 'just like a movie star' but is 'on hard drugs and turning tricks' and has 'torn a hole into her intestine from her vagina'.[7] Sex, shit and death are brutally connected in a single image we could even consider as a kind of physical metalepsis.[8] More broadly, the confusing experiences undergone by Laura Dern's characters might be seen to allegorise the relationship between fantasy and reality experienced by trafficked women. Seduced by fantasies of a better life to come – perhaps in the movies – they are (literally) dislocated and suffer both violence and profound disorientation. The connections they need are torn apart, while new connections are formed that all too frequently end up destroying them. On such an allegorical reading, the fantastic aspects of *INLAND EMPIRE* would express the extreme nature of this disorientation. Discussing the clinical judgement of disorientation, Alex Pavey explains:

> [T]he terms in relation to which one is judged to be disorientated are socially constructed – they are a matter of consensus rather than objective reality. The disorientated subject experiences this ambiguity viscerally – the very trauma of disorientation arises from the complexity of doing so. Fictional narratives . . . are capable of exploring the possibility that these 'public reference systems' themselves may in fact be unstable, or unreliable, or hostile. (Pavey 2017: 81–2)

The paradoxical dimensions of *INLAND EMPIRE*'s metalepses could, then, be seen as reflections of this instability and unreliability. The trafficked woman does not merely experience disorientation; her attempts at reorientation compound her predicament and emphasise its irrationality. The bizarre eruption of Little Eva's 'Loco-motion' into one of the sequences of Nikki/Sue and the Bad Girls emphasises the connection between movement ('loco-motion') and prostitution: euphoria gives way to desolation via a truly mad movement ('loco-motion'). This sequence is followed by Sue's announcement that she is pregnant with a baby her partner appears not to want, another peril of sex work, after which the Bad Girls dance again, this time to Etta James's 'At Last', which might now seem bleakly ironic as it fades out on the words 'I found a dream'.

Although accounting for the film's ending would, on such a reading, prove even more problematic (at least if it is not to seem an insensitively saccharine wish-fulfilment, either reversing Goodwin's perception of a 'cruel joke' or making it all the more brutal) I believe such a reading to be at least partially defensible. I also recognise that the 'translational' operation of interpreting allegory leaves largely unaddressed the issues of the film's actual affective treatment of sexualised violence against women. This is not the place for a full discussion of this issue, but suffice it to say that neither a reading of this film (nor indeed Lynch's work in general) as simply manipulating sexual violence to misogynist ends nor as innocent of all charges of exploitation seem to me to be satisfactory. (Pranolo's reference to 'Lynch's pornography of the uncanny' (Pranolo 2011: 492) is, I think, deserving of further investigation.) Be that as it may, and at the risk of turning a reference to something painfully concrete into a cipher for something abstract, I think that the introduction of the theme of the trafficking of sex workers might alter the significance of the many confusions between inside and outside that occur in *INLAND EMPIRE*, in the following way.

At the same time as the reality of people-trafficking can be used to organise the film's abstractions in relation to a desolate reality, the metaphor of smuggling opens out again into an account of a pervasive phenomenon in human experience. Every boundary in *INLAND EMPIRE* (such as those between characters (e.g. Nikki and Sue), between places (e.g. a real street in Hollywood and its recreation on a soundstage) or between nested narratives (*On High in Blue Tomorrows* and *Vier Sieben*, the cursed film of which it is a remake)) might be seen as creating a border across which things can then be smuggled. The ways borders are crossed in the film indicates that literal smuggling is only one instance of a fundamental human phenomenon, in which something crosses a boundary surreptitiously and lies hidden and often unnoticed on the other side. The emphasis on memory might, for example, indicate the smuggling of the past into the present, while the film's multiple impossible projections could be seen as emblematic of what Tony Tanner calls the 'magics' by which different selves overlap and impinge upon one another: 'We smuggle ... ourselves into other people through who knows how many mesmeric and penetrative magics' (Tanner 1987: 207).[9] The fact that we are frequently unsure where the borders might lie in *INLAND EMPIRE* becomes precisely the point: it is less an issue of mapping a whole by tracing connections and more about the way selves and societies are constructed through hidden and often forbidden transitions – or, perhaps, projections.

I do not intend the three reading strategies I have presented to represent a progress from less to more satisfactory strategies for orientating oneself with regard to the film. There is a great deal to be gained from considering it, for example, as in some sense the story of the Lost Girl's release or redemption. I have tried to show that the fact that the strategies I have outlined do not, in the final analysis, add up neatly does not prevent the film from being responsive to the questions one asks of it; one can always ask different questions with each viewing. But if I were to close my investigations of the film with an attempt at some kind of general claim it might be something like this: that the manifold confusions and disorientations that *INLAND EMPIRE* both contains and generates can, ultimately, be seen to indicate that all consistent selves based on a logic entirely free from paradox may, just like consistent stories, only come about as the result of so many acts of smuggling which attempt to conceal that which does not fit somewhere where it is, nevertheless, 'real hard to disappear'.

CHAPTER 4

Achieving Coherence: Diegesis and Death in Holy Motors

Leos Carax's 2012 film *Holy Motors* follows a certain M. Oscar (Denis Lavant) as he pursues a series of 'rendezvous' that involve performing as a great many characters; he is driven from one appointment to the next in an enormous white limousine by his chauffeuse, Céline (Édith Scob). The film is many things – depending on who one listens to it might be a love letter to the cinema, an elegy or even an obituary for film, an exultation in the multi-faceted possibilities of screen performance, or a self-indulgent and only intermittently successful mess of uncoordinated fragments – but neither its admirers (of whom I am one) nor its detractors have paid much serious attention to its diegesis. The strategy of simply assuming that any investigation into the possibility of a coherent diegesis will prove fruitless is encountered from two sides, as it were: for many of the naysayers, *Holy Motors* doesn't even *attempt* to play by the rules, while for some in the yes camp it travels far beyond the trivial straitjackets of narrative logic, leaving them reeling irrelevantly in its dust. In this chapter I will explore this neglected aspect of the film – diegesis – by attempting a reading that largely follows the sequence of events as they unfold. This will provide an opportunity to explore the relationship between orientation and coherence from a different angle than in the previous chapter. There, my focus was on the question of the global coherence of *INLAND EMPIRE* and its relationship to our orientational strategies. Here, I want to look more closely at the impact that these issues have for our relationship with the film as we progress through it, whether on a first or a subsequent viewing.

I want to use the question of the senses in which *Holy Motors* might or might not be said to have a coherent diegesis to explore the proposition that it is less useful to describe a film as being coherent (or as having coherence) than to see coherence as something that is (or is not) achieved by the film in question. Perhaps it is more helpful to say that certain films *achieve* the status of a unified whole (coherence being what unified wholes exhibit) than that they *possess* such a status. Is coherence a *sine qua non* for orientation? Can we only orientate ourselves in the presence of coherence? Orientation is a spatial metaphor, but the experience of watching a film takes place in time. Might there be a sense of coherence which has less to do with a film's patterning, considered in the abstract, and more to do with the drama of its unfolding in time?[1] And if so, what are its consequences for our understanding of orientation? I do not mean to imply that, as we progress through a film, fragments – incoherent in themselves – are gradually added together, so that something incoherent becomes coherent when the final piece is in place. I am thinking, instead, of the way that coherence is – like orientation – something we *expect*, a presumption according to which we organise our experience of a film, and which filmmakers can therefore take into account and manipulate.[2] It is impossible to be oriented in space without knowing how other places (where one is not) relate to one another; we have to be oriented *towards* or *with regard to* something. Perhaps the quasi-metaphorical sense in which we say that we are (or are not) oriented with regard to a narrative has something in common with this. Is narrative orientation not also a form of orientation *towards* – whether towards explanation, resolution or satisfaction in some broader sense? In which case, knowing where we are in a narrative film becomes at least as much a question of process, of development, as it is of whether or not we are in possession of sufficient information to explain the onscreen goings-on. We can, surprisingly, feel oriented with regard to a film even if we don't know exactly 'where we are', as long as we are confident enough in where we are going. In the experience of the viewer, a film is not either coherent or incoherent, once and for all. Instead, its coherence is a function of our continuing engagement with it as we watch and listen; it feels as if films can *become* coherent (or not) and can also *lose* coherence. It might follow from this that we cannot fully demonstrate the coherence of a film without taking account of the spectator's relationship with it. On this account, coherence would seem to have more to do with a satisfying relationship with and between the various aspects of a film (and the way they change) than with a list of logically compatible components. To put it another way, coherence might as easily be seen as a function of orientation (we find coherence when we are orientated) as the other way round (the feeling of orientation is a consequence of coherence).

Holy Motors provides a singular site for exploring these ideas because the ways in which it manifests and manipulates its diegesis dramatise these very issues. Certainly it is difficult to perceive a fully consistent diegesis in the film; probably doing so is close to impossible without speculation that extends well beyond any textual warrant. But far from signifying the abandonment of any aspiration to diegetic consistency, the film's pervasive reflexivity exploits these difficulties. Critics have noted the reflexive treatment of issues such as film production, spectatorship and performance, but *Holy Motors*' reflexivity also extends to the diegetic procedures by means of which films engage and sustain their viewers' interest and engagement (their solicitude, which – as we saw Souriau argue in Chapter 1 – is necessary for the existence of fictional beings). The very variety with which *Holy Motors* generates and addresses its own diegesis *itself* creates a distinctive thread that runs throughout the film. In this chapter I want to show some of the structural means by which the film accomplishes this, and to explore the way its most confusing and disorientating aspects are intimately related to the way it thematises coherence and belief, which it seems to me it does most significantly in its (often allegorical) treatment of death.

WHAT IS COHERENCE?

Films take time to happen. It takes time to watch them, and viewers make judgements about their internal patterning, their narrative, their visual and sonic style, not only when the credits have rolled, but also during the film. In order for us to feel that one sequence in a film has something to do with what follows – or that it does not – we must be continually evaluating its coherence, whether or not we are strongly conscious of it. Judgements about coherence made while watching a film are necessarily provisional, and may be revised in the course of a viewing, or on subsequent viewings, but nevertheless this continual process of evaluation suggests that we might consider coherence as something that is in continuous negotiation during a film's passage, and that, even when achieved, is always at risk of being destabilised or destroyed: not only the judgement but also the coherence itself must remain to some degree provisional. (It is always at least *possible* that a new reading could persuade me that a film I thought incoherent is in fact coherent, and vice versa.) There is, certainly, no coherence without a film being viewed: coherence involves a relationship between the film and its audience. This need not, however, imply that coherence can only properly be said to apply to the reception, rather than to the object of that reception. C. S. Peirce wrote in 1868 that 'men and words reciprocally educate each other; each increase of a man's information involves, and is involved by, a corresponding increase of a word's information' (Peirce 1966: 71). Each increase of a film viewer's information, then, is perhaps also matched by a corresponding increase in the film's information. When a film is seen to achieve (or to lose) coherence, something happens both to the viewer and to the film.

In language, a 'coherence relation' can be understood as 'an aspect of meaning of two or more discourse segments that cannot be described in terms of the meaning of the segments in isolation' (Sanders et al. 1992: 2). By being coherent, two elements of a discourse give rise to more than the sum of their parts. Coherence, in this sense, is distinguished from cohesion:

the latter is focused on 'the linguistic realization' itself, whereas the former is ultimately to do with 'the cognitive representation of a discourse' (*ibid*.: 2–3). This distinction seems meaningful and relevant with regard to other forms of discourse that are either non-linguistic or, like film, include language as only one of their aspects. On this reading, coherence is the more abstract – but also the more powerful – concept, referring to the way that parts combine to make a whole (and not just a collection) in what Sanders et al. refer to as our 'cognitive representation' of the discourse in question.[3] Coherence requires more extensive and thorough demonstration than cohesion, which has to do largely with the connections between surface features. A sequence with little cohesion could, for example, give rise to a coherent cognitive representation, precisely because of the specific form the lack of cohesion takes. On the other hand, showing that a film deploys a limited range of colours, say, would be to show only that the colour scheme of the film exhibits a certain cohesion. To demonstrate that this colour patterning gives rise to coherence would require a more extensive argument.

To many critics, the series of apparently unconnected narratives that makes up Carax's film frustrates the diegetic consistency which grounds the sense of coherence in most narrative films.[4] 'Consistency' is another rather slippery word beginning with 'c' to add to 'coherence' and 'cohesion'. I am taking consistency here to refer primarily to the compatibility of different segments or aspects of a film (logically speaking, that which is inconsistent is contradictory); cohesion has, perhaps, more to do with similarity (because similar things fit together). The distinction between consistency and cohesion is useful because both can be operative at the same time in different ways. Two sequences in a film could, for example, be stylistically cohesive (filmed in the same style with the same kind of *mise-en-scène*) but narratively inconsistent if, say, they portrayed the same event in two incompatible ways; *Last Year at Marienbad* springs to mind. Conversely, these hypothetical sequences could also be narratively consistent (telling a single story) but stylistically incohesive. Cohesion and consistency are both, on this account, less general or global concepts than coherence; judgements about coherence need to take into account the way cohesion and consistency interact. The complexity of these different aspects of a film's coherence is a good indication of how complicated the question of coherence might, in many cases, need to be.

These issues have been notably pursued with regard to narrative in American cinema of the 1970s. In 'The Incoherent Text: Narrative in the 70s' (an article originally written in 1980), Robin Wood usefully notes that '[t]he dividing line between coherent works that register incoherence and works that are incoherent within themselves may not always be clear' (Wood 2003: 41). His focus is, however, on unintentional ideological incoherence and thus very different from mine. To echo Wood's language, I am in a sense arguing that *Holy Motors* is an 'incoherent work that registers coherence', but because I am focused on orientational, narrative and thematic issues rather than on ideology, to say so risks being slightly misleading. Wood's article does not address distinctions such as those between coherence, consistency and cohesion. In his book *Hollywood Incoherent*, Todd Berliner does address them (adding the term 'incongruity' into the mix), but handles them rather differently, declaring his intention to use the word incoherence in what he calls 'the literal sense to mean a lack of connectedness or integration among different elements' (Berliner 2010: 25). Thus Berliner's 'incoherent' parallels my 'inconsistent' or 'incohesive'. Although I am not entirely sure that Berliner's terminology is completely consistent (he does not, as far as I can see, sufficiently articulate the distinction between incongruity and incoherence: coherence, apparently, 'refers to a congruity of elements' (*ibid.*), which doesn't get us very far), I would tend to agree with his conclusion that '[d]isunity oftentimes indicates good filmmaking – filmmaking that is unpredictable and varied, filmmaking that takes us to destinations that we could not foresee but that nonetheless feel, once we make an improbable connection or resolve an incongruity, as inevitably the right place' (*ibid.*: 221).[5] Berliner's logic here echoes Sanders et al. 1992; when two disparate elements are understood as existing in a coherent relationship, there has been a cognitive gain that could not have been achieved by either element in isolation: we have been taken to a destination 'that we could not foresee'.

READING *HOLY MOTORS* IN SEQUENCE

As Adrian Martin has correctly observed, while watching *Holy Motors* 'we are constantly led to wonder about the precise *status* of almost everything we see and hear' (Martin 2014b: 13). What happens if we pay particular attention to *diegetic* status? I do not by any means wish to dismiss thematic interpretations of the film, but rather to supplement them by showing that linearity and questions of diegesis are by no means as irrelevant as some might think. Doing so challenges the approaches taken by some of Carax's critics. Fergus Daly and Garin Dowd's work in what is still, rather surprisingly, the only book-length study of the director is a case in point. Though character motivation is not something I will explore in detail in this chapter, Daly and Dowd's attitude to it serves to illustrate their attitude to diegesis. When discussing another critic's comments on Carax's *Les Amants du Pont-Neuf* (1991), Daly and Dowd challenge the 'assumption . . . that the action needs to be grounded in character motivation in the first place' (Daly and Dowd 2003: 118). *Holy Motors* seems to make this remark all the more pertinent. But one might respond by charging

Daly and Dowd with not even *attempting* to ground action in character motivation (and subsequently, should this prove impossible, drawing conclusions from their failure). They claim that 'what Carax is interested in pursuing . . . is what Maurizio Grande has called "images non-dérivées"' ('non-derived images'), and pursue their argument in terms of the relationship between fate and chance in Carax's cinema (*ibid*.: 114). This relationship is certainly of great importance, but part of its importance lies in the fact that the characters' responses to contingent events are crucial. In *Les Amants du Pont-Neuf* these responses include those to events which characters take to be contingent but which have in fact been engineered, such as when Michèle (Juliette Binoche) thinks she has accidentally knocked the money they have stolen into the Seine, whereas in fact Alex (Denis Lavant) has moved it closer to her precisely to make her more likely to do so. Such sequences simply cannot be fully understood without paying attention to questions of motivation.

Daly and Dowd seem to assume that doing so would risk reducing the film to a conventional fable dressed up with formalist, auteurist fireworks. The critical desire to challenge such a hierarchy is admirable, but they go too far the other way and simply declare, by fiat, that Carax's cinema is far too advanced to have anything to do with such antiquated notions as character motivation. But what might happen if, granting that we cannot assume that everything needs grounding in plausible motivation, we nonetheless seriously enquire into the possibility that it has an important role to play? Not to do so risks grossly misreading films such as *Les Amants du Pont-Neuf* and *Pola X* (1999); indeed the relationship between motivation and artifice in these films – the increased role given to motivational plausibility – seems to me to be one of the things that most clearly distinguishes them from *Boy Meets Girl* (1984) and *Mauvais Sang* (1986). Given this account of the development of Carax's films, we cannot make, at the outset, the kind of assumptions made by Daly and Dowd with regard even to a film as peculiar as *Holy Motors*; Carax generates here a new relationship between motivation and artifice whose power to disconcert comes about precisely because it denies us the certainty about the irrelevance of motivational coherence (or other forms of diegetic coherence) that Daly and Dowd recommend.

It is time to examine the film in more detail. The constructed nature of the fusion between image and sound that is the narrative sound film is underlined at the film's outset, and its history (synchronised sound coming to cinema later than image) is mimicked in miniature. *Holy Motors* begins with silent animated images from Étienne-Jules Marey's photographic studies of movement: image divorced from sound. We then see an audience in a cinema – unremarkable except for the fact that they appear to be fast asleep. (Carax says that he does not know if they are asleep or dead; see Asdourian

(2012).) We can hear the film they are watching but not see it: sound divorced from image. The next sequence involves Carax himself playing a character identified in the credits as the Sleeper. The Sleeper wakes up in what might be a hotel room and finds a secret door into the cinema with the audience of sleepers or corpses. This is relatively easily absorbed as a reflexive, metanarratological commentary; the convention of the introduction means that the beginning of a film is a site where we are open to more abstract sequences before the diegesis properly establishes itself.[6] I would suggest that we do, however, expect to be shown something of the film that is playing before the sleeping audience and the Sleeper: perhaps even that it will prove to be the very film we, the audience, go on to watch (as seems to be the case with the images on the Lost Girl's television in *INLAND EMPIRE*).

This is indeed what we appear to be offered. At the end of the introduction we cut to an image of a girl sitting in the window of a boat, looking out. Except that we have been tricked: the nautical associations are prompted only by the soundtrack, and the fact that the window is round (and hence suggestive of a porthole). Cristina Álvarez López thinks that the continuity of sound at this point tell us that '[e]ven though we never see the images projected onto the screen, we know that it is Carax's film because the sounds we hear (lapping waves, birds, a horn) are stretched out to cover the beginning of the next scene' (López, in Martin and Shambu 2012). But I think this overlap of sound – what Genette would call a sonic metalepsis – serves rather to indicate the opposite. We never see those waves or those birds, and the image that appears to suture sound and image (the porthole) is not in fact a porthole. The girl is in fact looking out of the round window of a large – and admittedly ship-like – modernist house, the sound being merely 'held over' from the unseen film. This figure is a complex riff on what is known as a pre-lap, in which the sound from a succeeding scene enters before the image. This device can be made to serve various purposes; not infrequently the sound is introduced in such a way that the viewer initially assumes it 'belongs' to the scene they are still watching. There is, therefore, momentary confusion when the image changes and reveals this not to be the case. Murray Pomerance has written about this phenomenon, arguing:

> [T]he pre-lap functions as a kind of upholstery to soften the shock of the voyage . . . In the 'voyage' of the pre-lap, the 'upholstering' buffer is a particular nuance in the sound as it occurs in the first shot, one that makes it seem, somehow, obscurely and dimly, not only logical and appropriate but also, and at the same time, *wrong* . . . When the transition is resolved, we have a feeling of release and coherence: yes, *here* is where that voice truly belongs. This is why we are neither exasperated nor utterly confused when the cut occurs, nor displeased, even though we have been, as it were, ripped away from an

Figure 4.1 *The fraudulent porthole.*

integrated whole of picture and sound only to have our world displaced by a temporary transition that may well seem, as it is occurring, relatively loose-jointed and incomprehensible. (Pomerance 2008: 148–9)

What happens at this point in *Holy Motors* takes advantage of our familiarity with the kind of process Pomerance describes, but only in order to undercut it. The fact that the scene before the transition takes place in a cinema means we feel – wrongly, it turns out – more secure than in Pomerance's examples: we hear nautical sounds and ascribe them to something that is, diegetically, a movie; we think we have a clear rationale for the disjunction between image and sound. At this point the Sleeper, standing on the balcony of the cinema, turns his head to look directly at the screen, and there is a cut to what appears to be a porthole.

The apparent eyeline match and the continuity of sound both encourage us confidently to conclude that we have now entered that movie ourselves. But the nautical sounds soon fade away and are replaced by early morning birdsong and children playing. Carax creates a moment of false diegesis, a fraudulent image (what we see is not part of a boat) that, by means of what we can only in retrospect see as suspiciously comfortable 'upholstery' takes advantage both of our desire for orientation and our slightly smug satisfaction at successfully – so we suppose – avoiding disorientation. The 'feeling of release and coherence' that Pomerance refers to is generated only to dissipate almost immediately. The film is so constructed as to give us the feeling of being slightly ahead of it, whereas in fact it is we who have to catch up with it. Reflecting on this might prompt us, very early in the film, both to be sensitive to precise diegetic status and wary of the means by which it is generated.

After this, things relax a little. The banker (the role in which we first see Lavant; he appears to be the father of the little girl in the 'porthole') speaks to Céline about the number of appointments he has for that day, something very reasonable for a rich, successful and busy banker to do. He discusses firearms with a colleague on the phone, apparently believing himself to need a greater level of protection; a thriller might be in the offing. But his first appointment turns out, astonishingly, to be that of spending some time acting the role of an old woman begging on the streets of Paris. This is followed by a sequence in which he takes on the role of a motion capture artist, working on fight scenes and scenes of fantastic reptilian intercourse, presumably for one or more films or computer games. By this point diegetic problems seem to have faded into the background. We think we have cottoned on: the film has a fantastic premise, that of a man whose job is to be a series of others. Narrative – in the sense of a fictional thread running through the whole film, with events at one point in the film having consequences elsewhere – will not be a primary concern. We are perhaps led to expect a series of variations on the idea of acting and performance. The dominant mode might seem to be that of the permutation or series: how many variations on the idea will the film be able to come up with? We might at this point wonder how – or if – the film will manage to sustain interest: will it be essentially a series of vignettes, vulnerable to longueurs if a particular vignette does not interest us? Will even its high points seem disconnected from the body of the film? Will it be possible to present something 'new' each time, and even if it is, will this be enough? Will the film suffer the cinematic equivalent of what the composer Helmut Lachenmann describes as the risk, in new music, of 'withering away in the "sonically interesting" – i.e. boring – no man's land of exotic defamilarisatory acrobatics' (Lachenmann 2004: 66)?

The M. Merde sequence that follows does not disrupt this hypothesis, but does introduce the possibility, which promises to be a means of avoiding some of the possible pitfalls just outlined, of more extensively drawn characters and the presence in the 'appointments' of mini-narratives, however bizarre and oblique. The narrative in this sequence is clear, even if its exact import is not: M. Merde (a character who first appeared in Carax's contribution to the portmanteau film *Tokyo!* (2008)) emerges from the sewers, stomps through a graveyard munching flowers and terrifying passers-by, before coming upon the model Kay M (Eva Mendes) being photographed by Harry T-Bone (Geoffrey Carey). This prompts T-Bone to move from expostulations of 'Beautiful! Beautiful!' to 'Weird! Weird' – which could easily be taken as reflexive, as Carax's sarcastic portrait of enthusiasts who can say nothing more about his films than that they're 'so weird' – and insist that his assistant (Annabelle Dexter-Jones) ask if Merde is willing to be photographed. This results in some violent slapstick: Merde bites off the assistant's fingers and abducts Kay M, throwing her over his shoulders. Back in the sewers he removes some of her clothes and fashions them into a makeshift burka, in a kind of dance of the seven veils in reverse,[7] before finally falling asleep in her lap, with a prominent erection, while she sings him a lullaby (albeit a rather disturbing one, a version of 'All the Pretty Horses' that makes reference to a lamb having its eyes pecked on).

This sequence is immediately followed by a deliberately 'normal' narrative, that of a father and his shy teenage daughter who pretends to have had a good time at a party when in fact she has been hiding in the toilet. The scene is a remarkable exercise in narrative economy, presenting rounded characters with emotional plausibility and power in a brief span of time (the sequence lasts about nine minutes). But it also plays with our wish, perhaps not fully extinguished, that the film might present some kind of diegetic reality. Though we can certainly read this sequence as presenting a variation on the previous sequence (and hence developing a coherence through contrast: the Merde sequence is extremely unusual, almost aggressively unfamiliar, while the story of the father and daughter could come from any number of other films or television series), does it not also activate our wish to know more about M. Oscar? Are we wrong to hope that perhaps the diegesis of the frame narrative, or conceit, is not so loose as it seems? Could it be that this is really M. Oscar's daughter? It is soon indicated that she is not (Oscar is made up for this role, complete with wig, just as he is for all his others), but that we might feel this way is not accidental or based only on importing inappropriate expectations into a film which has given us plenty of clues that they have no place here. Instead, the film encourages such speculation: we do not see Céline give Oscar the dossier for this appointment, as we have for all the previous appointments; the father tells his daughter that he's had 'appointments all day long'; and Oscar seems genuinely angry and frustrated when he returns to his limo. Is this more acting, the emotions awakened by the scene bleeding – in a kind of metalepsis – into the actor's real life, or something else? Immediately afterwards comes an entr'acte, a musical sequence in which Lavant (is he or is he not Oscar at this point?), playing an accordion, leads a group of ambulatory musicians around a church playing an exhilarating version of R.L. Burnside's 'Let My Baby Ride'. The sequence certainly furthers the film's thematic interest in the body, movement, and the relationship between sound and image but also reinforces the power of conventional formal designation: precisely because this sequence is marked as an interlude, its diegetic status is unlikely to concern us.

After the entr'acte, however, we are presented with a host of sequences that force us to ask questions about the film's diegesis. Jeremy Biles claims that '*Holy Motors* thus has no discernible plot, but rather proceeds through a chain of episodes, each requiring Oscar to adopt a different persona' (Biles 2013: 3), but this is not the case. It is, rather, the film's wager to make this *seem* to be the case at the beginning, but then to undercut this conclusion. One of the deleted scenes included on the Artificial Eye DVD and Blu-ray editions of the film supports this idea – namely, that the film *deliberately* runs the risk that we will come to Biles's conclusion. In the deleted scene, we see M. Merde and Kay M emerging from the sewers, thanking each other and each getting into their own separate limousines. To have included so early the idea that there is a whole world of Oscars, as it were, each with their own limo and series of roles to play, would have drastically altered the drama of the film. It is crucial that this revelation occurs later in the film, precisely so that it can be a striking, even shocking realisation.

Absorption and Inconsistency

The second half of *Holy Motors* makes part of its project a testing of the possible tensions between viewer absorption and cinematic inconsistency. James Naremore is right to point out that 'most movies contain a heterogeneous mix of performing styles and skills' (Naremore 2014: 51), but it is of course rarer for a single actor to express such a 'heterogenous mix' in a single film. When this does happen it almost without exception draws attention to itself and becomes a *tour de force* of performance: think of Alec Guinness's multiple roles in *Kind Hearts and Coronets* (Robert Hamer, 1949) or those of Peter Sellers in *Dr. Strangelove* (Stanley Kubrick, 1964). And so it is with Lavant in *Holy Motors*. The second half of the film draws out various paradoxes from this situation by means of metaleptical entanglements between Oscar and the characters he performs. In one of the few readings of the film seriously to take account of the way it develops, Daniel Morgan observes:

> Starting from the postulate of a robust account of absorption, *Holy Motors* strips away seemingly necessary features, revealing them to be irrelevant to the creation of an immersive fictional world. It takes some time for this project to emerge. While the first half of the film contains a number of extraordinary and strange sequences, by and large there is a fairly clear distinction between Oscar and the characters he plays . . . it's only with the pivotal scene in the warehouse that the complications really begin to arise . . .

> The ontological border between character and actor, seemingly intrinsic to narrative feature films, is increasingly porous. (Morgan 2015: 7)

The first of M. Oscar's appointments after the entr'acte involves him playing (or becoming?) an assassin. Lavant, however, plays not only the assassin but also his victim. What begins as perhaps the most explicit genre pastiche in the film thus far (of a Hong Kong crime drama) descends into the realms of the diegetically weird, or even impossible. Oscar's character, Alex, reclothes and shaves his victim, Théo, so that they will look identical (even giving him an identical scar above the eye). But Théo proves not to be dead and gives Alex an identical wound to that which Alex gave him. *Had* this been a Hong Kong crime drama the narrative might, perhaps, have been that Alex and Théo are twin brothers and that Alex wishes his enemies to think it is he, not his brother, who has died. But when Théo proves not to be dead and wounds Alex, identity is more profoundly challenged. Morgan's account of this is as follows:

> The physical care involved in this transformation contrasts with the absence of work involved in the motion-capture process shown earlier, and it occasions what seems to be a kind of pun: whereas Oscar and the woman are turned into animation, Alex's victim is literally animated – made to resemble Alex, he then comes to life as Alex, stabs him, and then, confoundingly, staggers out to be rescued by Céline and resume his schedule of appointments. (Morgan 2015: 4)

The point about the pun is excellent and anticipates some of the notions of figuration covered in the next chapter, but Morgan is a little too sanguine about identity here. When a wounded man emerges and collapses before he can get back to the limo and has to be assisted by Céline, we have *no way* of knowing whether it is M. Oscar or not. For the first time, Oscar seems to be in real (diegetic) danger, and yet at the same time his identity is made a matter of – perhaps unresolvable – doubt.

Characteristically, this doubt is then undercut by simply being ignored: the next sequence shows Oscar (or his double) as hale and hearty as before, talking to the character known as the Man with the Birthmark (Michel Piccoli). Morgan is, I think, quite right when he argues that:

> The great achievement of *Holy Motors* is to show us that despite what we know about the film, what we cannot help but knowing about it [*sic*.], each time a scene begins we are drawn in, absorbed by and engaged in its actions. We are helpless, rapt as much as the spectators in the film's opening scene. (Morgan 2015: 8)

As we have seen, however, far from being 'rapt', the cinema audience is either asleep or dead! The projected light from the screen reflects back on the bodies of the audience in a kind of 're-projection' which links to all the film's varied explorations of repetition and afterlife. Projecting a film is to bring it *back* to life, which is not quite the same as having a life after death. Perhaps, in its allegories, *Holy Motors* tries to show how the cinema has been more concerned with resurrection (a return to how things were) than it has with the afterlife (a new state of being). The question of the afterlife of cinema itself can be raised now given that the notion of the death of cinema is conceivable, but this does not mean that the only death that the film is concerned with is that of cinema; immediately following the discussion with the Man with the Birthmark is a sequence which initiates a series of narrative investigations of *human* death.[8]

Oscar sees his banker persona sitting at a roadside cafe, insists that Céline stops the car, and gets out and shoots him. Some kind of metaleptical entanglement seems to have taken place, but what kind? During the phone call in his limousine at the beginning of the film the banker mentions a meeting to take place 'tonight at Fouquet's', and it is indeed at a cafe called Fouquet's that he is found and shot. Our sense of diegesis is severely challenged – not just because Oscar himself, shot repeatedly by the banker's bodyguards, is apparently killed for a second time and again suffers no lasting ill-effects, but because we had assumed that Oscar's performances had no life outside his engagement with them. But here it appears that they do: is Oscar taking on the role of people that *do* otherwise exist? Or perhaps that *did*? The diegetic confusion is directly connected to the theme of death. Céline, in yet another reflexive moment, links the audience's state of mind with Oscar's, telling the crowd to 'excuse him; there's been a mix-up [confusion]' ('excuser-le, il y a eu un confusion'). Are all Oscar's roles meant to be of the dead, meaning that the banker is breaking the rules by being alive?[9]

These scenes absorb us – puzzle and intrigue us – precisely because they *break* the ground rules of diegetic consistency (which is to say the presumption of its irrelevance) we had assumed to be in operation.[10] The rules are broken is such a way as to comprise a sequence of metaleptical, or quasi-metaleptical, transgressions of the boundary of death which demonstrate that (as I argued in my first chapter) metalepsis can be more productively considered as a rhetorical instrument than as a logical category. Both 'Alex' and 'Théo' seem mortally wounded, but somebody survives; we do not know which one – or is the answer simply that it is Oscar who survives? Does he play both parts? (Denis Lavant certainly does!) Then both the banker and Oscar appear to die, and yet Oscar is not dead. In the next sequence an old man dies and his young niece weeps, but since this is only a performance they are able to speak to each other and express the wish that they will meet again. The niece is called Léa but the actress is Élise; the fact that the *actual* actress is also called Élise suggests a metaleptical connection with the world outside the film. The following sequence reverses this structure. It is revealed that there is more than one performer travelling between appointments in a limousine when Oscar encounters a woman from his past called Jean (Kylie Minogue). We might think that Jean's apparent suicide would be easily explained away as another performance. However, Oscar – even though he is not at this point on one of his 'rendezvous' and hence presumably not performing – reacts as if her death were real, dashing into the limousine with a cry of horror and grief. In *Holy Motors*, death does not only cause emotional confusion but is treated allegorically via a range of narrative or logical confusions, in Baumgarten's sense. The film's metalepses are the rhetorical instruments by means of which its allegories are generated.

I shall discuss death and allegory in *Holy Motors* in more detail to conclude this chapter. For now, I want to continue our passage through the film. The scene after the shooting of the banker is a deathbed scene (deriving from the conclusion to Henry James's *The Portrait of a Lady*) where it is first confirmed for us that (at least some of) those with whom Oscar interacts are themselves performers like him.[11] We might note that when Oscar, as M. Vogan, is lying delirious in a fever he connects the worlds of his appointments: 'You should have deliberately not done it, Théo', he says, which is one of his lines from the preceding Hong Kong gangster murder appointment. Who exactly is suffering from delirium: Vogan, or Oscar as well? There is in this scene a very meticulous but yet puzzling treatment of diegetic and non-diegetic sound. Shostakovich's 15th string quartet begins non-diegetically, but it also functions to signal the beginning of the scene proper: the music does not start until after Oscar has sprayed on fake sweat and climbed into bed. It seems to signal the real beginning of his existence as M. Vogan (even though the hotel staff had earlier greeted him as such). Like the music in the shower in *Psycho* (see Cecchi 2010) this clearly non-diegetic music has a diegetic significance: it cues the audience to the shift of diegetic level from the performance of performance to the embedded narrative itself. There then follows, however, a great show of reintroducing the same music diegetically. Léa switches on the CD player. The music begins again, and it continues as she goes into the next room to change, but it then continues undisturbed when there is a cut to her sitting by the bedside – so it cannot now be diegetic. Is this a deliberate inconsistency? Or were we perhaps too hasty in our assumption that the scene proper had commenced? It seems more plausible that it is Éliane, the performer, not Léa, the character, who switches on the music. Does she only become Léa after she has changed her clothes, despite having earlier mopped Oscar/Vogan's brow? Is she in fact switching on *non-diegetic* music? After all, a CD player would be an odd prop in a Henry James adaptation, and we do not see it during the two characters' dialogue. How do we distinguish performance and the performance of performance?[12]

The next scene is the meeting between Oscar and Jean. The film enters another genre pastiche, this time of a musical. The lyrics to the song satirise both the audience's feeling that diegetic explanation would render things intelligible and the film's tendency toward the elliptical. Jean sings 'we once had a child / we called her / but then she'; a backstory to the relationship seems to be offered, but any further information that might actually explain things is withheld. Or is the withholding merely an obvious euphemism for the daughter's death? What else could have happened to the child to cause her parents to 'wander so very far apart', to make 'lovers turn into monsters'? Enigma and melodramatic predictability coincide, and we are led to wonder whether the explanation we think we want *would* be any kind of satisfactory explanation. The scene could merely be the latest in the film's series of variations: having learnt that there are other performers, an obvious variant is for two of them to meet outside of the arena of performance. And yet, though Jean tells Oscar that she is about to play an airline hostess called Eva Grace, when her lover comes to meet her (while Oscar slips away unseen), he calls her Jean, not Eva. Is a real betrayal of some kind taking place? To further complicate matters and further destabilise our sense of the distinction between authentic and inauthentic personae, Jean *removes* her wig to become Eva, rather than putting one on.

The film is nearly over. There remains what seems to be a satire on the nuclear family, albeit one executed with a peculiar degree of pathos, when Oscar's return home turns out to be just another appointment, this time as the husband and father of a family of chimpanzees. Céline then returns the limo to its garage, where she puts on the mask Édith Scob wore fifty years earlier in Georges Franju's *Eyes Without a Face* (1960), after which the group of limos in the garage have a brief, sleepy conversation. The latter parts of the film constantly pose challenges to our sense of its consistency, in a manner that verges on the exhaustive. We could consider consistency of genre (drama, musical, melodrama and comedy all make an appearance), consistency of tone, consistency of register, consistency of plausibility and consistency of diegetic level. Inconsistencies in all these departments disrupt the diegesis, or have the possibility to do so, but they coexist with affective phenomena which affirm it, in its absorptive sense. Concurrently, there are also bewildering and paradoxical *connections* which cause diegetic problems, but also negatively underline the importance of narrative diegesis; if diegesis were not important, the connections would not cause problems.

Throughout *Holy Motors*, then, questions of diegetic cohesion, consistency and ultimately coherence are all raised, varied and developed in a manner whose sequence is crucial to their effect. These effects are often in tension and at times paradoxical, but the film achieves a singular coherence precisely via the way in which it reflexively manipulates the cohesion and consistency of its own diegesis. Like *INLAND EMPIRE*, *Holy Motors* demonstrates that cohesion and consistency – connections in general – do not automatically reduce disorientation; in fact, if we are led specifically *not* to expect them, they can lead to profound bewilderment. The film also demonstrates how near to paradox are many features we often take for granted in narrative films. Enigmas only make sense because for most of the time they do not make sense (if they did they would not be enigmas); performances are only absorbing because we are aware that they are performances and thus not wholly absorbed by them.[13]

LOVE AND DEATH

Just as I argued in my chapter on *INLAND EMPIRE* that the possibility of mutually incompatible interpretations need not result in a meaningless free-for-all, I want to conclude this chapter by showing that the formal self-awareness and ludic manipulation of the viewer's responses that permeate *Holy Motors* need not preclude serious treatment of matters that extend far beyond the film itself, in particular of one of the most serious matters of all – namely death. I argued above that the film's paradoxical metalepses involving death help generate its allegories. Gilberto Perez has persuasively argued against the notion that allegory is 'abstract and lifeless – "incompatible with modern poetry"', as Erich Auerbach calls it; of course it *can* be lifeless, but so can any other mode of representation (Perez 2019: 106). Perez discusses Auerbach's influential essay on *figura* and claims that Auerbach attempts to distinguish allegory from *figura* (which involves real historical personae and events foreshadowing one another) precisely because of the widespread notion that allegory must be sterile. On the contrary, says Perez, '[w]hat Auerbach's figural mode demonstrates is that allegory need not retreat into thin abstractions but can marshal a living concreteness to its purposes' (*ibid.*).[14] Perez attempts to demonstrate this by showing how it can activate real, urgent historical situations; he discusses allegories of independence and Islam in Ousmane Sembène's *Ceddo* (1977) and of American nationhood in John Ford's *My Darling Clementine* (1946). Although *Holy Motors* might seem very far removed from the 'living concreteness' that Perez argues allegory can 'marshal . . . to its purposes', it might well put us in mind of his speculation that 'allegory is necessary when you can't get there from here, when no part of experience, no laborious recounting of many parts of experience, can adequately stand for the whole and comprehend its meaning' (*ibid.*: 107). Death surely fits these criteria perfectly; what possible coherence could there be between the world of the living and that of the dead? It is no accident that the religious allegories Auerbach discusses so often involve looking forward to life after death: Perez cites the examples of the figural connections between Joshua leading the Israelites into the promised land and Jesus's promise of eternal life, or 'between Cato the free man who preferred death to life in servitude and the freedom from bondage to sin enjoyed by souls in heaven' (*ibid.*: 106). Religion does, in fact, have a presence in *Holy Motors*; the film's final word, spoken in ragged chorus by the limousines, is 'Amen'.

The first part of the film's credits pass in silence, ending with one final brief sequence from Marey, of a young boy playing with a ball, followed by the words 'un film de Leos Carax' and then a photograph of Yekaterina Golubeva, Carax's partner, and the dedication 'Катя, – тебе' ('Katya – to you'). The girl we see in the circular 'porthole' as the film proper commences is in fact the daughter of Golubeva and Carax; Golubeva died in 2011 during the production of *Holy Motors*.[15] Perhaps we should take the role of actual human death in *Holy Motors* more seriously than is sometimes done; or rather, because nobody doubts the sincerity of the dedication, consider it to be more than incidentally and biographically relevant to the film. A number of critics have noted that Carax says that it was Golubeva who gave him the E. T. A. Hoffmann short story that inspired the scene with the Sleeper (see Asdourian 2012). We might also note what Carax has said about Golubeva's role in *Pola X*, where she plays Isabelle: 'one could think of Isabelle that she comes out of one of those bombed tombs and she walks towards us like in Abel Gance's film *J'accuse* wherein the dead of the First World War walk toward the camera, walk toward us . . . She is somewhat like that phantom' (quoted in Daly and Dowd 2003: 153). In her only acting role in Carax's films, Golubeva played a kind of ghost, before becoming as it were a 'real' ghost in *Holy Motors*. Viewed in this way the explorations of different kinds of deaths, non-deaths and not-not-deaths in the second half of the film seem much more emotionally intense, as does Oscar's return to the chimpanzee family (not to mention the use of the Sparks song 'How Are You Getting Home?' in the father and daughter sequence).[16] Perhaps the film's more surreally light-hearted touches should be interpreted along the lines of Albert Camus's recommendation, cited by Geoff Dyer at the beginning of his book *Zona*, that 'the best way of talking about what you love is to speak of it lightly' (Camus, 'A Short Guide to Towns Without a Past', quoted in Dyer 2012: n.p.). This might help explain the film's distinctive brand of gentle black humour that treats death as something of a social embarrassment. When the banker's bodyguards have shot Oscar, for example, Céline whispers to him – so that the crowd of onlookers can't hear – that they'll be late, and when M. Vogan has died and his niece is weeping with her head on his chest, Oscar gently moves her head as he gets up, saying 'pardon' and explaining that he has another appointment to get to.

James Naremore has made the following observation about Stanley Kubrick: 'the key to his style lies in his anxious fascination with the human body and his ability, which he shares with all black humorists and artists of the grotesque, to yoke together conflicting emotions, so that he confuses both our cognitive and emotional responses' (Naremore 2007: 35). Particularly if we consider Naremore's use of 'confuses' in the light of the double senses of the word (pejorative and technical) which I outlined in my Prospectus, this passage suggests a perhaps unexpected but I think illuminating affinity between Kubrick and Carax. The grotesque links the body and the intellect, emotional reactions and considered conclusions: hence Kubrick's interest in 'confounding the animate with the inanimate – a type of confusion that Wolfgang Kayser specifically connects with the grotesque' (*ibid*.: 31).[17] The relationship between the animate and the inanimate is at the heart of *Holy Motors*. The passage of time brings about the end of biological life, and yet it tends to animate old technology: just as the analogue film that once seemed mechanical and alien now seems idiosyncratic and organic in comparison with digital media, analogue electronic music that once seemed cold and alien (in Bebe and Louis Barron's soundtrack to *Forbidden Planet*, say) now seems positively warm and alive compared with some digital electronics. Carax highlights the way that the obsolete is so easily viewed as dead or dying; obsolescence itself blurs (or 'confuses') the boundary between the animate and the inanimate. The apparent immateriality of the new virtual world, which is really an occlusion of materiality (an Internet search involves real computer servers doing real work, but distant and hidden from the searcher) makes the very physical presence of machines, whose qualities once served to emphasise their difference from living beings, into a point of connection with non-machinic bodies. We might consider the film an allegory for death that is seen as much from the perspective *of* the dead, or at least of those – like the cars – poised precariously between death and life, as it looks forward to death as the uncrossable horizon. Carax, the Sleeper, is alive, but the film he sees or dreams is in a sense the world of the dead.[18] This, in one more paradox, is true even though at the same time it is also the world of life, of bodies and machines in motion. This particular paradox is, of course, one of the most familiar in film: the bodies Marey photographed seem as alive as they did more than a hundred years ago when they were first filmed; *are*, in fact, as alive as any other body on film, even though the bodies we see have long been dead, many of them – in all likelihood – for a hundred years or more.

Holy Motors brings these paradoxes vividly to life even when they concern death; its confusing allegories, reflexivities and contradictions put to the test our understanding of the relationships between coherence, cohesion and consistency. In doing so, however, the film brings these elements into closer, more complex relationships ('confuses both our cognitive and emotional responses', as Naremore puts it) rather than separating them ever further from one another. Ultimately the film does, it seems to me, achieve coherence. Even if we are often puzzled or unbalanced by it, the extent to which the film does *not* fundamentally disorientate us – despite its many contradictions, inconsistencies and moments of apparent incoherence – is remarkable; this might in fact be one of its most significant achievements. James Walters has speculated that 'those moments in films when events occur inconsistently to the potentials and possibilities of the fictional world that the film has created' might turn out to be 'ultimately . . . the times when viewer disappointment sets in as a film's credibility dissolves' (Walters 2008: 101). On my reading, *Holy Motors* indicates that this is rather too broadly stated; many other results are also possible. Stephanie Van Schilt observes that '[t]he path that *Holy Motors* led me down was often murky, rough, violent and puzzling. But I never felt lost because, while at times disorienting, it never became obtuse' (Daly and Van Schilt, in Martin and Shambu 2012). This achievement has its roots, I suggest, in a love both for the cinema in general and for one woman in particular; this love is something that, for once, the film expresses both consistently and coherently.

Part 2

Disorientating Figures and Figures of Disorientation

CHAPTER 5

Figuring (Out) Films: Figuration in Narrative Cinema

Writing about films involves choosing appropriate words. This is necessary both in order successfully to reduce confusion, where appropriate, as well as accurately to convey disorientation, where that is appropriate. This is, of course, not only a question of language; the distinctions between abstract and concrete, between literal and non-literal, and between implicit and explicit, may (strictly speaking) be intralinguistic, but they also have ontological and epistemological significance.[1] In what follows I aim to make some remarks which will be both clarificatory and stimulating with regard to what (and how) films mean as well as what (and how) we can productively write or say about it. These are, of course, questions that might be raised by any film but that disorientating films can render unavoidable. In places this chapter is somewhat abstract because this seemed the most efficient and uncluttered way of presenting my ideas, but elsewhere (as well as in the chapters that follow) I have tried to present sufficient numbers of concrete examples as to tether any abstractions to the details of actual films.

This chapter takes, then, something of a step back in order to clarify and defend some theoretical positions that implicitly underlay Part 1 of this book, and that will come more to the fore in Part 2. *The Cinema of Disorientation* contends that confusion and disorientation are not merely the result of encountering shapelessness, but that different filmic forms may prompt different kinds of disorientation, all of which have their own shape; I attempt to trace some of these shapes in the chapters devoted to specific films. Another word for shape is figure. The concept of *figuration* can, I claim, contribute to this process of tracing, as well as to a critical approach to films which offers the possibility of tailoring one's methods and interpretations to the film in question and does not require one to either select a rigid methodology or succumb to eclecticism. Because of the concept's complexity and pervasiveness, I will not attempt to define figuration at the outset. Instead, the first part of this chapter will work towards a provisional definition, which will then be explored through the recent work on figuration in film that I find most stimulating. Finally, I will set up the chapters that follow with a very short exploration of the ways some theorists have used figuration to investigate extreme situations of disintegration, short circuit and overload – which is to say precisely some of those situations in which disorientation or confusion seem likely to result.

What Is a Figure, or What Is It That Is Figured?

Certain words are so central to our thinking that a rigid division into literal and figurative is not desirable. *Shape* is one of those words. A shape drawn on a wall is a literal shape, while an argument has a shape only metaphorically; I would not contest this. But the way an argument has a shape is very close to the way our notional graffiti does: it has parts that relate to each other in a particular way. Not all concepts fall neatly on one side or the other of the distinction between the literal and the figurative. (If we were to say that both the image and the argument had a *form*, would one instance be literal and the other metaphorical?) Talk of shape in a film readily takes on both literal and figurative senses. What shapes are on the screen? What is the shape of a film's plot? The study of figuration represents a prime site for demonstrating the way that certain distinctions can be problematised without being superseded. We can deconstruct the distinction between the literal and the figurative but we do not have to discard or destroy it.

The word figure, from the Latin *figura* (shape, figure, form) has almost exact cognates in a great many European languages (Dutch *figuur*, English and French *figure*, German *Figur*, Italian and Spanish *figura*, to name but a few), all of which deal with roughly the same constellation of meanings, which are many and various. A figure can be, for example, an abstract shape; a number; a representation of a human being ('a figure appeared in the doorway' or 'the police chief seemed rather a suspicious figure');[2] an instance of non-literal language (figurative language being, precisely, that which is not literal);[3] a musical motif; or, at the most abstract, anything isolable as an object (as in the Gestalt notion of figure and ground). As developed in criticism and philosophy, even if we restrict ourselves to instances that have been put to use in film theory, the range of senses seems, if anything, even more bewilderingly broad, as Chang-Min Yu indicates: 'Figures can be an interpretive structure (Erich Auerbach via Hayden White), libidinal events (Jean-François Lyotard), formal and corporeal subversions (Gilles Deleuze), semiotic short circuits (Dudley Andrew), and units of cinematic economies (Nicole Brenez)' (Yu 2016).

Yu's list indicates that there will be no possibility, in the space available, even to outline the full compass of the different notions of figure. As I noted in the Prospectus, the primary meanings of figuration in visual art and in literature could be seen to pull in opposite directions. In both cases they relate to representation, but in visual art figuration moves *towards* direct 'replication' while in literature it pulls *away* from it – away from direct, literal, factual statements. Figurative painting represents people and objects from the 'real world', or at least things similar to them (gods, heroes, etc.), while figurative writing exists in contradistinction to literal writing. It can at times even seem as if the word is used in diametrically opposed senses. Compare, for example, the notion of the figurative as it is often used in studies of language and literature (namely to refer to that which is not literal) with Jean-Louis Comolli's reference to the way films have deployed 'the initial impression of reality (figurative analogy + movement + perspective)' (Comolli 1980: 133). Comolli means to indicate the way that images of people and objects on screen resemble those we see in our everyday lives, which is perhaps as close as an image can get to being 'literal'. If this (literal) resemblance can be called 'figurative' it is not far from being the opposite of the sense of 'figurative' that would be in play were we to say that calling our history teacher a fossil is a figurative (i.e. non-literal) use of language.

Specifically, of course, calling a teacher a fossil is an example of a metaphor. The debate in literary and linguistic studies about which form of figuration is dominant is too intricate to rehearse here (but see Matzner 2016: 25ff. for an excellent discussion). Suffice it to say that I do not take the position that all literary figuration is ultimately a kind of metaphor; for one thing, metonymy, irony and synecdoche have all been credibly argued to be distinct forms of figuration of equal conceptual status (see Perez 2019, in particular pp. 51–64, for a recent film-focused discussion of this topic). I suspect that taking metaphor to be more or less synonymous with figuration has discouraged some critics from pursuing the notion of figuration in film, because it makes it seem too fundamentally literary a concept to be truly helpful. The discussion that follows will, I hope, go some way to indicating the potential richness and usefulness of considering figuration as covering a much wider territory than metaphor alone. Metalepsis is, of course, part of this territory; this book has been structured in the way it is partly in order to give readers a concrete grasp of some of the ways one particular kind of figure can operate before entering the more general theoretical landscape.

But does considering figuration as covering not only the whole range of its literary meanings (metaphor and beyond) but also the plastic sense used in visual art risk rendering it so general as to evacuate its usefulness? Does it simply confuse, in the pejorative sense, the word's different meanings? The apparent incompatibilities between the different senses of figure have to do, as we have seen, with problems of the literal versus the figurative or the abstract versus the concrete, as well as the ways that these oppositions cross-pollinate, so that the literal can, for example, seem to be in opposition to the abstract. This kind of overlap, and the tensions that underlie it, indicate something of the possible resources that thinking about cinema in terms of figures can help generate, precisely because films are so reliant both on actual, physical shapes and a wide variety of more abstract types of patterning (narrative, symbolic and so forth).[4] I want in this chapter to clarify the notion of figuration in film (to reduce confusion in the pejorative sense) because it has the potential to be such a helpful concept for discussing some of the cinema's fundamental confusions, in Baumgarten's sense.

Discussions of figuration in film frequently hinge on its relation to ideas of language, of representation, of narrative. But such ideas are all too often seen only as restrictive, as things which cinema has the power to do without, or even to explode, a viewpoint that William D. Routt characterises, without endorsing it, as thinking 'that there is a special, visual dimension of communication ("the figural") where verbal meanings become fuzzy and inadequate or where the symbolic is confounded by the real' (Routt 2000).[5] Rather than using the concept of figuration to gesture towards a supposedly liberated realm beyond the reach of language, it seems to me more productive to attempt to express the complicated ways that films combine the literal and the figurative, the abstract and the concrete. I have difficulties, for example, with Jennifer M. Barker's claim that '[t]o say that we are touched by cinema indicates that it has significance for us, that it comes close to us, and that it literally occupies our sphere' (Barker 2009: 2). Despite its proximity to the claim that cinema 'literally occupies our sphere', the word 'touched' remains metaphorical here. The literal is implicitly equated with the real, which leaves no way of insisting on the importance of a particular metaphor other than to carry on as if it were not a metaphor: 'These terms [skin, musculature, viscera] are not used metaphorically, but are stretched beyond their literal, biological meanings to encompass their more phenomenological significance' (*ibid.*: 20–1). Stretching something beyond its literal meaning, besides being itself a metaphor, is also a pretty good definition of metaphor; far better, I suggest, to explore the nature and value of metaphor both in films and in talking about them than rhetorically to insist on its absence.[6]

But if studying figuration in film is, among other things, a way of addressing the intersection and interaction of the figurative and the literal, we might reasonably ask ourselves what it is that is figured. Is figuration just another word for form, for the shape that content takes? On the contrary, Genette indicates how attention to figuration can move us beyond sterile notions of form versus content:

> For Louis Hjelmslev . . . the opposite of form was not, as in the academic tradition, *content*, but *substance*, that is to say, the inert mass, either of extralinguis-

tic reality (the substance of the content), or the means, phonic or otherwise, used by language (the substance of expression) . . . If the relevant opposition is not between form and content, but between form and substance, 'formalism' will consist not in privileging forms at the expense of meanings – which is senseless – but in considering meaning itself as a form imprinted in the continuity of the real, in accordance with an overall segmentation that is the system of the language: language can 'express' the real only by *articulating* it, and this articulation is a system of forms, just as much on the level of the signified as on the level of the signifier. (Genette 1982: 70–1)

Genette uses 'articulation' in a way that is almost a pun on the word in the sense of *conveying meaning* ('I tried to articulate what I was feeling') and in the sense of *made up of connected parts* (as in an articulated lorry). In his essay 'Shelley Disfigured' Paul de Man also relies on the notion of articulation, declaring that 'it is the alignment of a signification with any principle of linguistic articulation whatsoever, sensory or not, which constitutes the figure' (de Man, in Bloom et al. 1979: 61). The crucial point, as I understand it, is that figures do not arise only through the representational elements of poetry but that it is via patterning *of any kind* that figuration can come into being, because meanings have to be patterned and hence pattern (whether of something that can be sensually imagined or not) implies the presence of meaning – even though this might turn out to be only an 'illusion of meaning' (as de Man, being a good deconstructionist, wants to insist). Meanings and patterns reciprocally rely on and inform one another, hence both the interest and the slipperiness of figures. What does it take for a pattern to be meaningful? Does it rely on existing structures of meaning or can it bring new such structures into being? Dudley Andrew puts it this way: 'Figures alter, but don't dispense with the dictionary'; he argues that they have the power 'to reorient not only the discursive event but the system itself' (Andrew 1983: 137 and 140). Therein lies much of their power: a figure that initially seems to *dis*orient may intervene in our understanding, may come ultimately to *re*orient us instead.

Following this line of thinking, it would not, I suggest, be too cavalier to elide 'linguistic' in de Man's reference to 'any principle of linguistic articulation'. We might then be able to risk a definition of the kind of figuration that is relevant here and declare that figuration, in any artistic medium, can be understood as *signification that is significantly aligned with articulation*. I am here retaining de Man's terminology; his use of 'articulation' is close to the broad sense of 'shape' or 'shaping' that I have used already. This definition has the consequence that figuration in film can, certainly, be linguistic, but it can also be chromatic or durational or perspectival or any number of other things; any aspect of the way an artwork is articulated or shaped is potentially available for figurative deployment. In other words, any articulation that is aligned with signification (we might even say confused with, in Baumgarten's sense) is a candidate for being described as figurative, as long as this alignment can be shown to be significant or meaningful. Cinematic figuration refers to any aspect of any way that a film is shaped (in any sense), insofar as it can be demonstrated that the shaping is significant. Such demonstrations are accomplished by showing *how* the shaping (or articulation) is aligned with signification and what the consequences of this alignment might be. This, of course, is largely a task for film criticism (though it may involve film theory and, potentially, film history as well).

Quintillian wrote in the first century that 'nihil non figuratum est' ('nothing is not figured'), though he was aware that this was true only in a certain sense (see Matzner 2016: 33).[7] We have already seen Genette claim that all language (or, we might say, all discourse) is shaped. This is certainly true but it threatens to evacuate the idea of figures of all usefulness. If everything were a figure there might be no criteria of recognisability for figures. Niklas Luhmann, in this context, makes extensive use of the distinction between form and *medium* (rather than 'content' or 'substance'), arguing that it is only forms that are ever perceived directly; because everything is 'shaped' – figured – we have no access to media 'in themselves':

> The medium can be observed only via forms, never as such. The medium manifests itself only in the relationship between constancy and variety that obtains in individual forms. A form, in other words, can be observed through the schema of constant/variable, because it is always form-in-medium. (Luhmann 2000: 106)

This argument can be used to help construct a case that claiming that everything is 'figured' need not entail that there are only figures. Everything manifest must be a form, but the discovery of figures is not thereby rendered critically vacuous because we can distinguish between form and figure via the notion I argued for above, namely that figures are forms that repeat and/or transform ('are aligned with articulation') *in a significant way*. Thus studying figuration necessarily involves evaluation. There is a transition from signification, in a general semiotic sense, to significance in a more evaluative sense: signification is how meaning is produced, but to claim something is significant is to claim a particular value for it. (The distinction between signification and significance in this sense could be seen to parallel that between *meaning* and the *meaningful*.) If a pattern or an articulation can be shown to be meaningful *in any way*, then it constitutes a figure; how significant this figure is within our interpretation of the film as a whole is a separate question. Demonstrating that the transformations of a particular figure are significant is, as I said above, a critical task; it cannot be accomplished according to a foolproof method or algorithm. A segment of a film either is a dissolve or it is not. Anybody who understands the definition of 'dissolve' will be able to identify it as such, but showing whether or not this dissolve is a figure, and if so what kind of figure, is – once again – a task for criticism.[8]

In the remainder of this chapter I shall cover two issues in more detail, which are more obviously related to questions of orientation and disorientation than the first part of this chapter because they concern the questions both of what, in a film, we are oriented with regard to, and how we are so oriented. I want first to look in more detail at the treatments of filmic figuration which I find most helpful, as well as some of the pitfalls they help point out. Secondly, I will briefly discuss some ways that the notion of figuration might help us articulate how films handle difficult, disorientating relationships between the meaningful and the visible.

FIGURATION IN RECENT FILM THEORY

George Bluestone's pioneering 1957 book *Novels into Films* has some interesting things to say about the ways that successful cinematic metaphor has a different relationship to the constraints of diegetic motivation and plausibility than does literary metaphor. The relationship between the literal and the diegetic assumes a distinctive importance. Sounding not unlike V. F. Perkins, Bluestone argues that 'a special kind of film trope is possible, but only when it is confined to cinematic terms: it must arrive naturally from the setting (as Lilian Gish's knitting in *Way Down East*, or Marlon Brando's horse in *Viva Zapata*)' (Bluestone 1957: 22). This claim might have allowed Bluestone to develop an argument around, say, the relationship between cinematic metaphor and irony (see his remarks on ironic contrast on p. 25) which would have directed him towards the wider territory of figuration, as I understand it, but any such possibility is, unfortunately, obscured by his dubious insistence on a fundamental distinction between literature and cinema that rests on 'the contrast between the novel as a conceptual and discursive form, the film as a perceptual and presentational form' (*ibid.*: ix).

Kamilla Elliott has done useful work unpicking this supposed dichotomy, while also agreeing with Bluestone's sense of the necessary conditions for effective filmic metaphor: 'For figures to be effective in realist film, the connotative, nonliteral element of the figure must also hold its own in the realist filmic world' (Elliott 2003: 235). Unfortunately, her own arguments also exhibit significant confusions. For example, when discussing Roman Polanski's *Tess* (1979), Elliott claims that the director 'creates a highly effective adaptation of Tess's "peony lips" [from Hardy's novel] in a filmic metaphor on "lips" and "strawberries"' (*ibid.*: 235). That things are becoming a little strained is indicated by the oddness of her phrasing; we don't ordinarily refer to metaphors 'on' things. Rather ironically, given Elliott's dismissal of those who apply a literary perspective too strictly (N. Roy Clifton's work on filmic figures 'has had little impact largely because it applies verbal paradigms, which rest uneasily on film' (*ibid.*: 273, n. 60)), she insists on finding a strict structural parallel between linguistic and filmic metaphors, directly carrying over I. A. Richards's distinction between tenor and vehicle. Tess (Nastassja Kinski) receives a strawberry from Alec (Leigh Lawson): '[L]ips and strawberries are similarly colored and shaped, so that the strawberry visibly enhances and modifies Tess's lips just as the word "peony" enhances and modifies the word "lips" in the novel. The tenor (mouth) is briefly juxtaposed to and enhanced by the vehicle (strawberry) before the vehicle vanishes' (*ibid.*: 235). When Elliott argues that '[t]he strawberry-lip metaphor avoids confusion because the strawberry is a diegetic part of the scene, with realist and narrative as well as metaphorical significance' (*ibid.*), this contradicts the claim, only two paragraphs before, that it is essential that there is 'clear signalling of which is the figure's literal and which is the figure's figurative part' (*ibid.*: 234). The notion that because 'the vehicle (strawberry)' is 'diegetic' this, somehow, contributes to 'signalling' that the strawberry is 'the figure's figurative part' – and that because of all this confusion is *avoided* – is profoundly muddled. We might ask whether the sequence is not most straightforwardly seen as an instance of comparison, as a filmic simile rather than a metaphor at all; to reiterate, metaphor is not the only kind of figure.[9]

The understanding of figuration that Jacques Rancière displays in his chapter on Nicholas Ray's *They Live by Night* (1948) in *Film Fables* appears to me to be much more fruitful, and very much in accordance with the view I have been arguing for in this chapter. A perfect instance is his discussion of the early scenes that convey the birth of the love between the young Bowie (Farley Granger) and Keechie (Cathy O'Donnell). The scenes take place in the garage run by Keechie's father, in which Bowie and his fellow bank robbers Chicamaw (Howard Da Silva) and T-Dub (Jay C. Flippen) take refuge. Unfortunately the English translation, through a very minor error, obscures this. There, we read that 'Ray needs more than a cinematographic trope to get this body removed from resemblance to materialize before us' (Rancière 2016: 96). The French, however, reads: '[I]l aura fallu plus d'un trope cinématographique pour faire consister devant nous le corps sans ressemblance de Keechie' (Rancière 2001: 128). The point is not that Ray needs 'more than a cinematographic trope' – which suggests that he needs something *other* than a mere trope – but rather that he needs *more than one* such trope. This makes sense of the subsequent declaration that '[w]hat he needs, first of all, is a synechdoche' ('all we have at first are this voice, these cheeks, and these hands floating in the night as if severed from their body'), which is to be combined with 'a second operation of subtraction that isolates the two lovers in the thieves' hide-out' (Rancière 2016: 98), and also 'a new operation that imposes two overlapping yet incompatible spaces onto the homogenous sensorium created by the "cinematographic" prose of the novel' (*ibid.*: 98–9). Rancière is arguing that Ray needs *three* cinematic tropes (a synechdoche, an 'operation of subtraction' and the imposition of 'two overlapping yet incompatible spaces') to achieve his aims.

The 'operation of subtraction' is an example of what Sebastian Matzner would call a trope, a deviation from ordinary or expected procedure: the growing love between Keechie and Bowie is represented by, in the main, *avoiding* showing them looking at one another.[10] Instead, for the most part one of the pair *looks* while the other *does*:

> Keechie's absent presence cuts right through Deleuze's very neat opposition between the functionality of the action-image and the expressive power of the affection-image. The film captures the different intensities of sensation in the execution of ordinary, daily tasks like fixing a heater, pulling out a jack, changing a car wheel, or massaging a wound. These are actions that two people do together, or that one does while the other looks on, actions whose proper gestures and time are much better suited to indicating the love budding between two people who don't know what love is than any ecstatic exchange of glances or conventional approximation of bodies. (*ibid.*: 98)

The third figure consists of superimposing the 'incompatible spaces' of Bowie-Keechie-Chicamaw-T-Dub and Bowie-Keechie. This is achieved by framing. When Chicamaw and T-Dub disappear from one shot to the next, 'it is as if they had never been there, as if there never had been enough space for the two of them in this room' (*ibid.*: 99). This is the case even though '[t]his instant when they are alone doesn't last even five seconds. By the next shot the camera has already moved back to frame Keechie and Bowie squarely between the two other thieves' (*ibid.*). We are aware that, diegetically, all four characters are present throughout the entire scene, but Ray's handling of the *mise-en-scène* gives us the feeling that this is not the case. The ordinary procedure whereby not every character present in a scene is visible in every shot is figuratively amplified to give the feeling that when we can only see two characters – two characters who are in the process of falling in love – they are the only people there, the only people who *could* be there.

Rancière is interested in how cinema presents without representing, in 'the construction of a completely novel individuation, of a love object that is one precisely because it has been stripped of the identifiable sexual properties that make it an object of desire' (*ibid.*: 95). Ray manages, in Rancière's eyes, to present an object of desire directly *as an object of desire*, rather than presenting that about it which is desirable so that the audience can infer that it is such an object (potentially so for us, and hence plausibly so for a character or characters). This example exemplifies the kind of complex entanglement films can achieve between what figures show and how they show it. It also demonstrates that cinematic figuration in no way requires us to ignore our everyday knowledge of the world. We need to 'inhabit' the scene in the garage imaginatively (as V. F. Perkins would insist) in order to understand the figurative logic of its gazes and non-gazes. But note that Rancière only needs a specific rhetorical name (synechdoche) for the first of his three figures: the study of figuration should by no means be reduced to searching through films for equivalents to classical rhetorical figures, but neither are they ruled out as irrelevant. Specific, named figures are particular examples of a much wider phenomenon, a great many of whose manifestations cannot be pinned down so neatly.

Some of the most extensive work on figuration in cinema has been undertaken by Nicole Brenez. In 1990 she edited a three-issue run of the journal *Admiranda* devoted to 'Figuration Defiguration' including a glossary prepared by Brenez and Luc Vancheri, which defines figuration as the:

> symbolic game or process aiming to establish a fixed, evolving or unstable correlation between the plastic, aural and narrative parameters able to elicit fundamental categories of representation (such as the visible and invisible, mimesis, reflection, appearance and disappearance, image and origin, the integral and the discontinuous, form, the intelligible, the part and the whole . . .) and other parameters – which may be the same parameters, depending on the particular type of determination effected – relating to fundamental categories of ontology (such as being and appearance, essence and apparition, being and nothingness, same and other, the immediate, the reflective, inner and outer . . .). (Brenez and Vancheri 1990: 75, trans. Adrian Martin, in Martin 2012a: 8)

Although the attempt to produce a general definition produces a tangle of subclauses and confusing qualifications we can see immediately that, although they do not define figuration as pertaining to any kind of significant shaping whatsoever, Brenez and Vancheri certainly *do* see it as a profoundly pervasive concept.[11] That it involves change or transformation is clear, but it also has (or creates) rules or regularities by which it operates. It is a 'game or process', one which involves a relationship between representation and ontology or, more precisely, between whatever parameters can elicit [*relever*] or relate to [*relevant*] the categories involved in representational and ontological questions. We could sum up their position very roughly as the claim that figuration is the way – or, rather, the particular ways – in which representation and ontology (what things are and how they are conveyed) are related.

We should not, therefore, be misled by the fact that the article by Brenez that opens the issue includes a table comparing and contrasting the notions of representation and figuration that she finds in Eisenstein and in Barthes (Brenez 1990: 11). Figuration is not, according to this definition, an alternative to representation, but something that involves it: 'It will be argued here that representation concerns the set of the filmic text *as a set*, whereas figuration introduces ruptures, sutures and divisions by means of which the text organises its elements, including, of course, the rigidity or the wavering of its own categories' (Brenez 1990: 10; my translation).[12] It is not so much that representation is global and figuration local (which appears perhaps to have misled Adrian Martin, as we shall see below), as that representation is to do with consistency (or, we might say, is threatened by inconsistency or discontinuity), whereas figuration is often concerned, precisely, with rupture or, we might say, with disorientation. It is often when a film's representational activity appears disrupted that we need to think in terms of figuration in order to account for its meaningfulness.[13] Figuration is not merely concerned with conveying relationships but, as Brenez and Vancheri's definition has it, with 'aiming to establish' them, with *forming* relationships – or indeed with dissolving them, which is why the three issues of *Admiranda* are titled 'Figuration Défiguration'. Brenez thus seems entirely in agreement with Dudley Andrew's sense of figures as things which 'have the power to disrupt the relation of context to sign and reorient not only the discursive event but the system itself which will never be the same afterwards' (Andrew 1984: 170). If figures can 'reorient . . . the system' this process must, I think, also involve at least a degree of disorientation. This definition is also compatible with the notion of figures as involving articulation aligned with signification; we might say that such alignments are how the correlations between representation and ontology that Brenez and Vancheri refer to are established.

Brenez has, then, led us to a general notion of figuration which is more useful than the notion that 'nihil non figuratum est', but remains profoundly abstract. How can we connect it to the kind of concrete analysis we saw in Rancière's discussion of *They Live by Night*? And to what use has Brenez's work been put by other critics? Adrian Martin, who has been greatly inspired by Brenez's work on figuration, shows, I think, both the strengths of Brenez's line of thinking and some of the traps it lays. Martin argues in an interview with Anna Dzenis about his book *Last Day Every Day: Figural Thinking from Auerbach and Kracauer to Agamben and Brenez* that *Holy Motors* is a '100% figural film, in that it's all about, literally, a body which transforms from scene to scene, with make-up, with acting, with voice; every resource of the cinema is devoted to the mutation of a central character from one scene to the next' (Martin 2012b). The figural is, for Martin, concerned with the representation of bodies (with figures in the visual art sense of the word) and with transformation (which is perhaps closer to the literary notion). Elsewhere in the same interview it becomes apparent that one of the strengths of 'figural thinking' for Martin is the licence it gives for a certain release from plausibility: 'If you plunge in with the idea that every film is a cartoon, every film is unreal, and every film is implausible, then you can actually go somewhere with it' (*ibid.*). If we take this as a recommendation not to be unduly restricted by critical hierarchies, to remember that there exists no necessarily prefixed sequence of critical priorities – 'get the story straight, and *then* we can start looking at themes or visual patterns' – then I think it is sound.[14] But there is also a potential problem. It would be regrettable to end up repeating certain rather brittle forms of avant-gardism that saw the unrealistic as necessarily superior to the realistic or considered it always productive to emphasise artifice as artifice. One could just was well turn the argument around: just as implausibility need not destroy, say, psychological interpretation, so diegetic interpretation need not destroy any insights derived from 'figural thinking'. My analysis of *Holy Motors* was aimed at showing this: it was not my intention to argue, exactly, that the film has a diegesis that has been missed, but that certain transformations (precisely, *figures*) will remain imperceptible unless we are prepared sometimes to think in terms of diegesis.

The danger of which I am warning can be seen even more clearly in an introduction to Brenez's work written by Martin: 'In a figural model . . . the cinema leaves behind its last vestiges of mimesis, copying, or resemblance to the real: the cinema traces, figures, weaves *ex nihilo* its fully imaginary, endlessly renewed repertoire of spaces, places, movements, gestures, worlds and bodies' (Martin 1997). Granted, the notion of removing even the 'last vestiges of mimesis, copying, or resemblance to the real' is an obvious hyperbole; it is nonetheless an unhelpful one. It may well, as Martin goes on to say, be a question of 'corrod[ing] all of our common-sense, facile assumptions about analogical resemblance in film', but this certainly does *not* equate to saying that film has nothing to do with analogical resemblance. I think William D. Routt's summary, already partially cited above, is more helpful:

> What is *not* being asserted, as I understand it, is that there is a special, visual dimension of communication ('the figural') where verbal meanings become fuzzy and inadequate or where the symbolic is confounded by the real. On the contrary, figuration is everywhere – in language, in sound, taste, smell and touch as well as in what we see. It is the common currency of experience. (Routt 2000)

Martin does, it is true, develop a related point in the introduction to his book *Mise en Scène and Film Style*: 'We should be careful not to depart, too brusquely, for the "higher order abstractions" that we regularly translate the evidence of our senses into: meanings, symbols, metaphors, allegories, directorial intentions, "world views"' (Martin 2014a: xvii). The intent of this statement is laudable, but I want to insist on the impossibility of any kind of clean break between sensation and signification, whichever aspect we are inclined to put the emphasis on. What we should really avoid – or at least treat with great care – is 'translational' thinking: thinking that '*this* [image] signifies *that* [meaning]', and hence that, in interpreting the image as such, '*this* has been transformed into *that*' (or has been revealed as 'really' being *that*) and that we can now, therefore, get on with talking about '*that*', leaving the details of '*this*' behind. (This might sound like a recommendation to have nothing to do with metaphor, but only according to an account of metaphor I would reject. It is precisely the *interaction* between what I. A. Richards would call 'tenor' and 'vehicle' that makes a metaphor the metaphor it is. And of course, as I have been insisting, metaphor is only an aspect of figuration, not a synonym for it.) We cannot, in fact, concentrate on the evidence of our senses without being connected to the world of meaning.[15] Saying about Brian de Palma's *Passion* (2012), as Martin does in the very first paragraph of his book, that 'Isabelle (Noomi Rapace) is sitting expectantly in the audience' (*ibid.*: x) is to introduce a great many 'higher order abstractions': that this image is that of a woman called Noomi Rapace; that she is an actress representing – in a fictional world (another abstraction) – somebody called Isabelle; that we can tell from the image that this person is sitting in a theatre as an audience member; and that we can gauge something of her emotional state from her appearance (that her mood is expectant). The question is really *which* abstractions we deal with, and how we handle them – which returns us, as film critics and theorists, to the question of choosing appropriate words with which I opened this chapter. The idea of figuration provides a helpful framework for thinking about the relationship between the way sensory material is shaped and the patterns of the 'abstract' inferences that this shaping allows us to draw, a way of considering the relationship between the concrete and abstract that neither dissolves the distinction between the two nor renders it absolute, final and non-negotiable.

Disorientating Figures

Gesturing towards that which entirely escapes language, in the way that Routt criticises, paradoxically risks leaving us all the more trapped by it, unable to articulate the way that films, like figures, are 'both without and within' language. For the art historian and theorist James Elkins, '[a]n interpretation of a picture that stresses its "visual language," its linguistic structure, or its semiotic system, is not a reading made from somewhere "within" language and "outside" pictures, but simply an interpretation that lists only some of the qualities of the image' (Elkins 1998: 161). I want to reiterate this claim, without qualification, with regard to film. Elkins, sounding very reminiscent of Jean-François Lyotard's influential book *Discourse, Figure* (Lyotard 2011) also observes that 'images are complex in the only ways that a structure can be truly complex: they are partly inside and partly outside systematic, linguistic, logical, and mathematical structures of meaning' (*ibid.*: xii), and follows this up by noting that 'disorder is not a simple absence, but a structured field of possibilities' (*ibid.*: xvii). To return to my overarching theme, disorientation might be described as an experience of disorder, but it is not simply the absence of knowing where one is; it too is a 'field of possibilities' with its own characteristics.

In a 2011 lecture, Brenez outlined her intention to 'consider three major figural operations', all of which refer to situations of extremity and breakdown. They are: 'figurality by disintegration' (exemplified by Antonin Artaud and Philippe Grandieux), 'figurality by overload' (Godard) and 'figurality by short circuits', which she claims to be 'the innovation of Jean-François Lyotard' (Brenez 2011). The experience of such deviations and distortions is very likely to be one of difficulty at the very least (and frequently of confusion or disorientation). For Elkins, 'too often, reading the art historical literature, it can seem as if pictures are relatively easy to write about, to put into words', and thus he has:

> no global objection to contemporary semiotics except perhaps for the occasional claim that it is an optimal, transparent, or transtheoretical approach to visual artifacts. Instead, I am concerned with those places in pictures where the inevitable linguistic or semiotic model stops making sense, becomes counterintuitive, or begins to contradict what is actually happening. (Elkins 1998: xi)

Brenez's 'disintegration', 'overload' and 'short circuit' are not so far from Elkins's moments when linguistic models stop making sense (because they are disintegrating?), become counterintuitive (because our intuitions are overloaded?) or begin to contradict what is happening (because there has been a short circuit?). By no means all instances of figuration are difficult in exactly these ways, but those that are – or that operate according to comparable logics – represent very rich sites for investigation. The remaining chapters of this book explore some of those sites.

CHAPTER 6

Distinguishing the Indistinguishable:
Figures of Imperceptibility and Impossibility in
Lost Highway *and* Caché

This chapter aims to make the theoretical discussion contained in the previous chapter a little more concrete by investigating a few specific instances of figuration. To this end, it consists of an enquiry into some particular filmic figures that have been constructed so as to disorientate the viewer, with a view to 'figuring' that which cannot be directly represented (which I will refer to generally as 'impossibility' or 'the impossible'). More particularly, the chapter focuses on instances wherein disorientation is deliberately courted by images that can easily be confused either with one another, or taken for something they are not (which is another form of confusing one thing for another).[1] This chapter, then, concentrates on the nature and function of images that verge on the indistinguishable or imperceptible; I want to suggest that there is another rich collection of figurative operations to add to Nicole Brenez's notions of disintegration, overload and short circuit (which we encountered at the end of the previous chapter) that we might call 'figurality by indiscernibility'. I will demonstrate the crucial role of diegesis in the creation of these effects, emphasising once again the importance in narrative film of the intersection between the plastic and rhetorical senses of figuration, which is to say between the characteristics of certain images *as images* (what they look like) and how they contribute to a film's rhetoric in the largest sense (narration, mood, affect, theme and so forth). Crucial to the examples that will be discussed here are narratives of trauma and its aftermath – or, to put it more specifically, of attempts to avoid coming to terms with the infliction of trauma – which is to say that the films covered in this chapter not only produce disorientation but represent it; they concern disorientated characters as well as produce disorientated viewers.[2] But I hope to be able to make some claims that are more nuanced than simply explaining away instances of audience confusion as motivated by the way they echo the disorientation of the characters onscreen; confusion, I will argue, may have important consequences for any aspect of a film's meaning.[3]

The chief examples in this chapter will be taken from David Lynch's *Lost Highway* (1997) and Michael Haneke's *Caché* (2005) – and I want to reiterate that this chapter aims only at exploring a few specific figures rather than giving adequate accounts of these films in their entirety – but to set up the issues under discussion I will begin by briefly considering Jacques Tourneur's *Night of the Demon* (1957).[4] Chris Fujiwara has argued that the editing and treatment of space in Tourneur's films often have crucial disorientating functions, as well as that these functions are closely bound up with a preoccupation with that which cannot be shown: 'The cutting in Tourneur's films gives a sense of dislocation and disorientation to spaces that characters inhabit precariously . . . Tourneur's cinema, obsessed with the unshowable and with the conditions of its own impossibility, is the antithesis of the cinema of spectacle' (Fujiwara 1998: 11 and 12). This is demonstrated by Fujiwara's analysis of a well-known sequence – one which he calls 'a model of Tourneurian cinema' (*ibid.*: 251) – in *Night of the Demon* that is brief but extremely disorientating. In this sequence, which begins nearly forty minutes into the film, the sceptical psychologist Dr John Holden (Dana Andrews) has an unsettling experience in a hotel corridor in which he hears strange music and, perhaps, senses some kind of evil presence. As Fujiwara demonstrates, a use of spatial direction that confuses the viewer's sense of which way the camera is pointed contributes greatly to the disorientation the sequence produces.

Fujiwara's full analysis of the sequence occurs on pp. 251–3 of his book; I only have space here to refer to a few of the features he points out. There are eight 'ruthlessly logical' (*ibid.*) shots in the sequence, which Fujiwara refers to by number (see Figure 6.1 for images of shots (2) to (5)). He writes that '[t]he cut from (2) to (3) is disorienting because (3) is not a true reverse angle from Holden's point of view: the angle of the corridor proves that the shot is taken from a point across the corridor from Holden', whereas in (4) 'the camera has crossed to the other side of his look – and simply doing so has thrown the scene into spatial confusion because it unmoors the space from Holden's look' (*ibid.*). The sequence, that is to say, both relies on and scrambles the conventions of point-of-view editing. Shot (3) is like a point-of-view shot from the perspective of the Holden we see in shot (2) but, as Fujiwara says, if it is a point-of-view shot, it is disorientatingly disjointed from Holden's actual position in space. Then, in shot (4), 'Holden suddenly appears in the foreground of a shot approximately the same as (3)' (*ibid.*: 252). In shots (3) and (4) we are looking in roughly the same direction, *not* looking in diametrically opposed directions as we would with shot/reverse shot, but the expectation that we 'should' be – the expectation that (3) will be followed by a return to something similar to (2) – lingers disorientatingly.

As well as these directional and perspectival dislocations, Fujiwara also discusses the way that camera height, music and other elements contribute to the sequence's effect. Particularly pertinent to my purposes here, however, is the way that Fujiwara's analysis helps us to realise the extent to which the

shot (2)   *shot (3)*

shot (4)   *shot (5)*

Figure 6.1 *Fujiwara's shots (2), (3), (4) and (5) from the corridor sequence in* The Night of the Demon.

sequence relies on an inability sufficiently to distinguish images from one another in order to be able to comfortably orient ourselves. Tourneur's film-making amplifies the sensations of uncertainty and dislocation that the anonymity and indistinguishability of hotel corridors have probably, at one time or another, generated in most spectators. For example, the scene does not use the direction in which the corridor recedes onscreen (left or right) as a clue to help us distinguish in which direction Holden is looking. As Fujiwara notes, both (3) and (5) – which look in opposite directions, (5) being a point-of-view shot from Holden's position in (4) – show the corridor receding to the left, whereas (2) – which looks in the same direction as (5) – *does* show the corridor receding to the right. (There are also echoes of this 'left-right corridor' confusion at the end of the film as Holden searches for Julian Carswell (Niall MacGinnis), the magician who has cursed him by means of a runic script, on a train and as Carswell later frantically tries to chase down the runes on the train tracks.) This sequence is, then, an example of 'productive' or 'effective' spatial disorientation. I referred in my introduction to 'poor editing that leaves an audience pointlessly muddled about spatial relationships'; what we have here is very careful editing and *mise-en-scène* that leaves an audience *purposefully* muddled about spatial relationships, so as to echo Holden's growing confusion and discomfort while simultaneously making it very difficult to discover the precise source of this confusion. As I have already indicated, it is crucial to the effect of this scene is in fact that what we might suppose to be, in a sense, opposites (looking down a corridor in one direction or in the diametrically opposite direction) are (almost) indistinguishable from one another; this approach to the edge of indistinguishability at once contributes a great deal to the disorientating effect of the sequence and makes its source hard to pin down. This question of distinguishability runs through all the films I discuss in this chapter. Films can, it seems, attempt to represent the 'impossible' by means of something similar to what, as I cited in my Prospectus, Nicole Brenez calls a 'passage between altered images' (Brenez 2007: 21), but where what is disorientating is precisely that the images are (or at least appear to be, or come close to being) *unaltered* – and this even though we know, or come to know, that they are not identical, that we 'should' be able to distinguish them. This indistinguishability, or 'figurality by indiscernibility', of course leads to us confusing one thing *for* another. Or rather, to be more precise, it leads to us being confused by the fact that we *can* confuse one thing for another, when we would have expected to be able to avoid so doing.

We understand films by means of both what we see in them and what we do *not* see.[5] That this is the case gives rise to the curious possibility that a film might even contain images that, like identical twins, we know to be different from one another, but whose difference does not lie in their visual content. An example of this can be found in the opening shot of *Caché* (see Figure 6.2). We begin with a shot of Paris's 13th arrondissement. There is nothing in the image to indicate that this is anything other than an establishing shot to begin the film, to introduce us into its world. It is only when the soundtrack of ordinary quiet urban noises is supplemented by voices discussing the image and then eventually by the tell-tale signs of a video being fast-forwarded that we realise that the image *itself* is in fact diegetic, in the sense that it is an image not only for the audience in the cinema but also for the characters in the film. The images on the videotape exist *as images* in the world of the fiction. (Later shots in the film showing a very similar scene are sometimes, but not always, also confirmed as, diegetically, images on video.) Without the visual and sonic features that indicated our 'mistake' with regard to the

Figure 6.2   *From the opening of* Caché.

opening scene, we would have no resources by which to confirm their status; as Catherine Wheatley remarks, recalling my argument about the function of the 'porthole' in *Holy Motors*: 'The tell-tale white lines that announce the film's first fast-forward simultaneously offer a warning that none of the images that follow can be taken at face value' (Wheatley 2011: 80). This opening shot confuses inside and outside, since the film's protagonists Anne (Juliette Binoche) and Georges (Daniel Auteuil) are in fact watching the video *of* their house from inside the very house that is shown *on* the tapes.[6] When we first see Anne leave the house we are, in fact, in a sense watching her watch herself, but we can't know this on a first viewing of the film. *Caché* could be seen as an investigation into the convention of the camera's invisibility (or rather non-existence) in the diegetic world and the question of the viewer's placement. Until we hear the voices of the characters, is there even an answer to the question as to whether we, the viewers, are 'located' outside or inside? I reiterate my claim, from the end of Chapter 1, that diegetic status is a production, not a fact.

That this quandary about what exactly we are watching, and how, can arise is a consequence of the fact that in narrative films images are never 'merely' images – whatever that might mean – but are instruments of narration. By withholding any visual clues that we are looking at an image on video – by making the diegetic image indistinguishable from a non-diegetic image – the film indicates that the very distinction between an image *of* the film world and an image *in* the film world is itself a diegetic distinction; it only has meaning if we engage with the film's diegesis. But, nevertheless, it is hard here to avoid the feeling that we are dealing with some kind of failure of vision, or perhaps a failure of visibility. To explore the conjunction of various kinds of indistinguishability and how they might figure conditions of impossibility I want briefly to sidestep into the theory of art in order to present the idea that there is more than one way in which images may be rendered 'impossible'. In his book *On Pictures and the Words That Fail Them*, the art historian, critic and theorist James Elkins, whose work we also encountered in the previous chapter, offers a taxonomy of four different modes in which pictures – in a broad sense – can be or become impossible, which I shall now briefly survey.

Elkins's first category is that of the *unrepresentable*. This refers to 'whatever is forbidden or considered dangerous for the eye, as well as whatever is thought to be beyond technique at any given moment or for any given medium' (Elkins 1998: 252). The unrepresentable is whatever is either *prohibited* or is beyond the reach of current technique. We might perhaps be tempted to divide the category further, possibly reserving 'unrepresentable' for what is beyond current ability and calling what is prohibited by another name, but what unifies these two categories, for Elkins, is that they both refer to things that *can* be 'specifically imagined *as a picture*' even if actually making such a picture is currently impossible (*ibid.*; italics in original); '[u]nrepresentable images are censored, either in the usual sense or in the Freudian one: in its broadest use censorship includes both voluntary acts of self-prohibition, as when I refuse to see some illicit image, and unconscious acts, as when I turn away from a horrifying scene' (*ibid.*: 254). From this follows the usefulness of reference to such images in film: as a means of *representing* phenomena of censorship, in a broad sense, as they pertain to characters. (This will, I hope, become clearer via some of the examples I discuss below.) Elkins's second category is that of the *unpicturable*, which refers to 'whatever does not present itself to the imagination as an image' (*ibid.*: 255). We cannot even *imagine* the unpicturable as an image; we cannot *picture it* even to ourselves, but we can imagine it in *some* way. Elkins's third category moves logically on from here; it is the *inconceivable*, that which we cannot even imagine. We might think that this means we have no access to it all, but in fact, Elkins argues, by thinking of the logical culmination of a sequence, we can at least get some kind of purchase on what was inconceivable in the image's production: 'any layered structure in an image (from one schema to another, from word to image, from low to high genre, from line to color, from the image of God to God) makes it possible to deduce what must have remained inconceivable in the making of a given image' (*ibid.*: 259). The sequence from the unrepresentable, via the unpicturable to the inconceivable might seem to exhaust the possible categories, but Elkins in fact adds one more, in a sense simpler than the others, but also – if anything – even more pervasive, which he calls the *unseeable*, by which he means 'whatever is physically present, but induces blindness, hiding itself 'in its own medium.' Once they are uncovered, examples of the unseeable (which would then have to be called the *unseen*) effect radical changes in the way we experience such pictures' (*ibid.*: 260). This is, more or less, the familiar notion of hiding in plain sight: 'Any hidden image, while it is still hidden, is an instance of the unseen' (*ibid.*).

I think these categories are immensely interesting, and I shall have cause to employ them in what follows. But they are not necessarily exhaustive, particularly if we think about what happens to them when we encounter movies, *moving* pictures (which Elkins does not discuss). I think one of the categories' chief virtues is the way they indicate how rich this territory is, when we might have thought that if something cannot be made into an image, it is simply unrepresentable – end of story.[7] It's worth noting, for a start, just *how many* words we have for a failure of vision, or of visibility. It's also worth noting how frequently these words are in fact *cancelled*, but in a way that does not actually cancel them, by bringing them close to, but not below, the minimum threshold necessary for them to be operative. We readily speak of the 'almost imperceptible', the 'almost indistinguishable' – when of course, strictly speaking, something that is 'almost' either of these things is therefore not it; the almost imperceptible *is* perceptible and the almost indistinguishable *is* distinguishable. It seems that with words that denote a failure of vision or of visibility, it is very frequently via a particular state of visibility that we gain a sense of this failure. If we want to *figure* imperceptibility we have to use something perceptible – but also, perhaps, to take the risk of its not being perceived. This is extremely pertinent to the kind of 'figurality by indiscernibility' that I am exploring in this chapter.

A case in point is David Lynch's 1997 film *Lost Highway*. Like the later *Caché*, the narrative of Lynch's film centres on a couple who receive mysterious anonymous tapes that, to begin with, show only the outside of their own house.[8] Lynch's film, however, is much more explicitly fantastical. The second tape the couple receives not only shows the outside of their house but moves inside and shows them asleep. The third shows the husband, Fred Madison (Bill Pullman), surrounded by his wife's dismembered body. Fred is then imprisoned for his wife's murder, which he swears he did not commit, and sentenced to death by electric chair. But in prison he mysteriously transmutes into a completely different person, Pete Dayton (Balthazar Getty), who the police are forced to release. Pete's ensuing life contains various uncanny echoes of Fred's, most significantly the presence of Alice Wakefield, played by Patricia Arquette, who is a blonde version of Fred's wife Renee, also played by Arquette. At the film's conclusion Fred returns again, and the film ends with him pursued by the police, his face distorting weirdly and painfully. It has been suggested that this film, like a number of Lynch's subsequent works, might be interpreted as a version of Ambrose Bierce's 1890 story 'An Occurrence at Owl Creek Bridge', in which a soldier is sentenced to death by hanging. The rope, however, breaks, he escapes, and various events ensue, only for the story to end with a blow on the back of the soldier's neck, a loud noise and a flash of white, succeeded only by 'darkness and silence' (Bierce 2000: 19). The noose has tightened and his neck has broken; the entire narrative was something that flashed before his eyes, in the proverbial fashion, in the final moments before his death. I think it is certainly plausible to see *Lost Highway* as a version of this narrative structure; the film would then represent a man's final moments in the electric chair. But other interpretations are certainly possible, and I'm not going to present a case for this one here, but merely ask for the reader's indulgence in provisionally accepting it. The reason that this account particularly interests me is that it has the consequence that we cannot divide *Lost Highway* into 'fantasy' and 'reality' segments; cannot distinguish one from the other. The 'Fred' section of the narrative has as much that is fantastical and paradoxical as the 'Pete' segment;

indeed, the whole film is bookended by the paradox that the message Fred receives over his intercom at the beginning of the film turns out at the end to have been spoken by none other than himself. This means that Fred's reality is no more secure than Pete's. On the 'Owl Creek Bridge' interpretation, we are watching the imaginative spasms that occur during the final moments of life of a man who murdered his wife out of pathological jealousy, but beyond this we know almost nothing about him. Thus, on this interpretation, the 'real' diegesis of *Lost Highway* is presented exactly *nowhere* – all we see are events that are, diegetically, disorientating hallucinations or traumatised fantasies.[9]

This seems like it might be a dangerously irresponsible interpretive path to follow. If we are never shown 'reality', how can we say anything about it? One possible answer to this question would involve emphasising that, on this interpretation, a number of Elkins' categories apply to the man in the electric chair, who cannot bear to represent his guilt to himself – it is *unrepresentable* to him – and therefore he spins elaborate narrative fantasies around the facts. Still less can he bear to *picture* it to himself, except in the rarest of horrific instances, and even then he tends to distort it (as in the grainy black and white video images we see from time to time). But he is also confronting the fact of his own death, something that we might say hovers between the *unpicturable* and the *inconceivable*. What I want to suggest is that *Lost Highway* frequently figures these narrative elements – phenomena that are unrepresentable, unpicturable or inconceivable *for a character in the diegesis* – by means of images that are (almost) *indistinguishable* for us as viewers of the film.

The idea of the indistinguishable naturally evokes notions of *comparison*, and *Lost Highway* exploits this fact by means of images that emerge from Elkins's category of the *unseeable*, becoming then (retrospectively) what he calls *unseen*. One particular such figure is used in both the 'Fred' and 'Pete' sections of the narrative (see Figure 6.3): we see a shot of our protagonist standing alone, after which they step into the frame and we realise that we were previously looking at a mirror image. We initially confuse a mirror image for 'reality', and the realisation that we have done so is disorientating. (It's theoretically possible that we could have noticed their reversed faces before the image's status is revealed, but most people, I think, would not; more likely is a slight sense of something not quite right that doesn't reach the threshold of full consciousness.)

It is only in retrospect that what appeared indistinguishable from an image of the character – so indistinguishable that that is what we took it for – was in fact, like the opening of *Caché*, an image of an image. The fact that it was such an image was hidden in plain sight. The dwindling confidence of both 'Fred' and 'Pete' in their own identity is figured by the way these figures erode the confidence of the viewer. These figures are similar to other 'jarring

Distinguishing the Indistinguishable 113

Figure 6.3 Mirror images hiding in plain sight in Lost Highway.

moments' in *Lost Highway* discussed by Lucy Fife Donaldson, moments that 'undercut orientation in the space (and the narrative)' and thereby 'undermine the manner in which . . . images and bodies on-screen are comprehended via reference to real-world experience' (Fife Donaldson 2014: 103). Helpful as this description is, here I would prefer to say 'threaten to undermine'. Like the examples from *Vampyr* discussed in the Introduction, these mirror image figures are disorientating precisely *because* we (retrospectively) comprehend them, and do so 'via reference to real-world experience'; because, that is, we realise that we were originally *not* disorientated when we in a sense 'should have been'.

Hidden is, of course, the English version of the title of *Caché*. I referred earlier to the 'Owl Creek Bridge' interpretation of *Lost Highway* as potentially irresponsible; some have also seen Haneke's activity in *Caché* as in some sense irresponsible, as not playing fair. The film elicits the desire to solve the mystery of how, and by whom, the videotapes were produced, but there appears to be no possible realistic solution within the diegesis (I discussed what seems to me the inadequacy of George Wilson's treatment of this fact in Chapter 1). I want to suggest that because both films are *about* responsibility, and specifically about a refusal to accept it – in the case of *Lost Highway* we have a fairly familiar narrative about male violence, and in *Caché* something more of a postcolonial allegory about the conduct of France and the French towards Algeria and the Algerians – it is appropriate that the representational strategies the films use pose problematic questions about responsibility. This point can, I think, be connected to the reflexivity that is present in both

Figure 6.4 Hiding in plain sight at the end of Caché.

films. In *Caché*, for example, narrative cinema's convention that the camera is invisible is deconstructed by making certain images diegetic, but still not having the characters notice the camera. For example, at one point Anne and Georges pause the first videotape at a point where it seems that Georges must have been able to see the camera. It is only the diegesis that makes the image 'impossible': an identical image of Georges walking past the camera could have been used, as long as the image was not also supposed to exist, as an image, in the diegetic world. And in a further gesture of reflexivity, which is also an instance of hiding in plain sight, Georges asks 'How come I didn't see him?' and answers himself 'It'll remain a mystery' – an answer the audience is almost certain to assume will be falsified when the film's enigma is eventually explained, but which in fact turns out to be entirely accurate. There is, then, a reflexivity in the introduction of 'impossible' images into the diegetic world that plays on our readiness to accept that the images that make up a film are in some way 'not' images. Of course, diegetically, they are – usually – not, but were they not images, there could be no film. While the reflexivity 'breaks the rules' of ordinary narrative filmmaking, it also – like the example from *Daffy Duck & Egghead* discussed in the Prospectus – resembles the kind of joke that points out the obvious; there is also – again like the cartoon – something metaleptical about it, because the conditions of the film's production in our world seem somehow to have slipped into or infected the film's world.

On a first viewing, I suspect we probably try and see something *in* the opening image of *Caché* because it is held for such a long time, whereas we 'should' be seeing something *about* it. This is another instance of the unseen, which links directly to the film's closing shot (see Figure 6.4). In this much-discussed shot, the couple's son, Pierrot (Lester Makedonsky), speaks to the character played by Walid Afkir, unnamed in the film, who is the son of Majid (Maurice Bénichou), a man that Pierrot's father Georges mistreated when they were both boys, leading Georges to accuse him of being the source of the tapes; Majid eventually kills himself in Georges's presence. This final shot represents a kind of deliberate, staged unseen; it courts being mistaken for

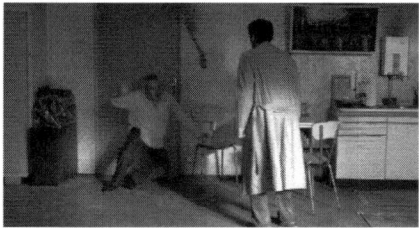 

Figure 6.5 *Instances of violence in* Caché *and* Lost Highway.

– indistinguishable with – a shot that contains no further narrative information. With a DVD and a remote control, however, we can pause and rewind or fast-forward – can do exactly what Anne and Georges do with the tapes they are sent – and appreciate just how carefully that which is hidden in it (the meeting of the two sons) is hidden in plain sight. Majid's son is in fact (just) visible from the very beginning of the shot, in the bottom right-hand corner of the screen (circled in the first image in Figure 6.4). He begins to move *exactly* as Pierrot comes into view (both young men are circled in the second image in Figure 6.4). But precisely because it takes rewatching, pausing, fast-forwarding and rewinding to discover all this, and because even when we have discovered it we are given no keys to how to interpret the meeting between the two young men – we hear nothing of what they are saying – the film's rather sardonic reflexivity comes into play again. Even if we spot the two young men and congratulate ourselves for our powers of observance, we are still left disorientatingly unsure of what to do with the knowledge we have gained. How do we know we are any different from Georges, constantly pausing and rewinding and constantly missing the point?

Whereas in the final scene what is in plain view is also hidden, in what is probably the most memorable scene in *Caché* Majid commits suicide by cutting his throat in full, excruciating view both of Georges and the viewer (Figure 6.5). Majid's death seems to me to represent a form of 'fast' imperceptibility rather than the 'slow' imperceptibility we normally associate with that word (think of the movement of glaciers, for example). By this I mean that Majid's death happens so rapidly that the boundary between before and after is itself almost imperceptible: Majid is alive, and then suddenly he is dead. That is one reason why the scene is so powerful. The imperceptibility of the moment of death itself could be said to figure its inconceivability. The fact that we are watching a moving image is, of course, crucial to this effect; we cannot 'capture' the feeling of the instantaneousness of death by pausing the film. Looking at the single image from *Caché* isolated in Figure 6.5, ironically, emphasises *continuity*, the process of Majid's body falling to the floor, whereas while watching the film the experience is of instantaneousness and the incommensurability of before (life) and after (death). If we freeze-frame the very brief sequence from *Lost Highway* of Fred surrounded by Renee's dismembered body something very different happens: we can easily see, in a way we cannot while watching the film, how laughable it all is, how it's all plastic and fake blood. (Freezing this image orientates – rather than disorientates – us, takes us 'outside' the diegesis.) To say this is not to catch out Lynch's filmmaking, to argue that *Lost Highway* would be a better film if the effects were better and that it only gets away with it by showing us the scene for such a short amount of time; it is rather to highlight the importance of what cinema *does not* show us, rather than *cannot* – just as it *could have* shown us the 'real' story of the man in the electric chair that, perhaps, generates *Lost Highway*.

It is precisely this relationship between what films show us, what they cannot show us and what they do not show us that I hope to have illuminated in this chapter. The relationship between what we see and what we do not see is a rich resource for all narrative films, and offers productive opportunities for disorientating viewers in ways that dramatise and illuminate the emotional states of characters, various narrative functions and also wider thematic or allegorical dimensions. In skilfully confusing the threshold between the discernible and the indiscernible – in making use of apparently indiscernible differences between images – filmmakers such as Tourneur, Haneke and Lynch have, in their different ways, exploited what I suggested at the beginning of the chapter we might refer to as 'figurality by indiscernibility', and have thereby shown themselves to have a powerful resource for figuring the possibilities and impossibilities of representation and its limits, whether these are personal, political, aesthetic or ethical.

CHAPTER 7

Homes for Displaced Figures:
Pedro Costa's Colossal Youth

White credits appear, in silence, on a black background. A busy but gentle murmur of voices, vehicles and nocturnal shufflings fades up. Then an image appears. It contains none of the sources of the sounds we can hear; instead, the camera looks up from an empty courtyard at the back walls of a collection of decrepit buildings, lit by a dim grey light. The sky and the borders of the image are jet black. Densely packed in on each other, most of the buildings are punctured by dark, blank windows. A chest of drawers appears at one of the first-floor windows. Someone pushes it all the way out; it falls with a violent crash on the ground one storey below. Other items of furniture follow: a single drawer; what might be a bedside cabinet; a chair; something that looks like a door. At the window we can just barely make out the figure responsible for these expulsions.

So begins Pedro Costa's 2006 film *Juventude em Marcha* (*Colossal Youth*).[1] We later realise that the figure in the shadows is Clotilde, wife of the film's protagonist, Ventura. Clotilde has kicked her husband out and proceeded, for good measure, to destroy his furniture. It is not uncommon for a film to begin with a domestic situation, an image of home that is then somehow disrupted – whether this image is of a comfortable (if a little indifferent) home, as in *Eyes Wide Shut* (Stanley Kubrick, 1999) or one that is from the outset uncomfortable and unsettling, as in *Lost Highway*. *Colossal Youth* does indeed begin with a domestic situation, but Costa represents it only via multiple displacements. We never see inside Ventura and Clotilde's home, nor do we see anything of Ventura's expulsion itself. Instead, the expulsion of the furniture serves as a metonym for the displacement of Ventura. Ventura's displacement could easily be seen as a metaphor for the wider story of the displacement of the inhabitants of the neighbourhood of Lisbon called Fontainhas. Between 2001 and 2005, the overwhelmingly Cape Verdean population (96.5 per cent) were expelled from their homes, which were certainly ramshackle but also (if only ambivalently) beloved. The inhabitants were moved into clean and bright but antiseptic and soulless new apartments in Casal da Boba and the old neighbourhood was knocked down (see Treno 2013). But this is not all that Ventura's expulsion signifies, because if it were we would simply have a story, common to many, told in microcosm through the experience of one participant (something Perez refers to as extended synecdoche (see Perez 2019: 95–9)), whereas *Colossal Youth* is something richer and more ambiguous that that. The film's opening shot actually exemplifies one of its characteristic procedures: it provides opportunities for the viewer to orientate themselves and at the same time obstructs their attempts at so doing.

How does this happen? When we encounter this scene during a first viewing of the film, what we are seeing is clear enough (furniture is being thrown from a window), but why it is happening is mysterious. The clarification which follows is itself displaced. We only see Ventura inform his daughter Bete that 'your mother's gone' after Clotilde, wielding a knife, delivers a monologue about swimming with sharks and leaving her son weeping on the shore. We do not even, at this point, have enough information to securely identify the woman with the knife with the figure that expelled the furniture: it is only two scenes later that Ventura reveals that Clotilde has stabbed him. To complicate matters still further, Bete doesn't let her father in but claims that he's 'got the wrong door and the wrong daughter'. We are not in a position to decide whether this is a daughter wanting rid of her father, a father who has indeed come to the house of the wrong daughter – or even if she isn't his daughter at all.

Beyond ambiguities about the contents of the diegesis, there are also ambiguities about the status of that diegesis. What mode of reality is being represented? The man who in the film is called Ventura is played by a non-professional actor, also called Ventura, who lives in the same parts of Lisbon where *Colossal Youth* was filmed, which brings us into proximity with documentary; *Colossal Youth* does, however obliquely, tell a true story. On the other hand, when Ventura tells Bete that 'I've been having this nightmare for thirty years', can we be sure that this is merely a metaphor, and that we are not 'literally' (literally within the fiction, that is) watching Ventura's dream? There are certainly invitations to see certain parts of the film, at least, as dreams. At one point, after one of several scenes set in a shack during the Carnation Revolution of 1974, Ventura wakes up on the floor in his new apartment, making it possible to construe the preceding scene as a dream. Could the film be Ventura's 'mindscreen' in Bruce F. Kawin's sense?[2] A fantastic or dreamlike logic often seems to be in operation, perhaps reflecting both Ventura's memories and the disorientation that his traumatic experiences have produced in him. Ventura tells Gustavo that he was stabbed by Clotilde, but also that the woman that stabbed him 'had Clotilde's face, but it wasn't her'. Towards the end of the film Ventura's friend Lento appears to be a ghost. Even if we were to decide that the film represents Ventura's mindscreen, however, it is not clear to what extent this would this actually aid us in our attempts at orientation. It seems likely that it would simply provide a quasi-diegetic *explanation* for our disorientation instead of a route out of it, an illusion of immediate clarity rather than a genuinely clarifying engagement with the experience of the film.

We should also note that the film's displacements do not *only* disorientate us. They are also thematic or, we could say, mimetic of Ventura's experience, which is one of profound disorientation. We identify with Ventura *because of* his disorientation: his confusion mirrors our own. Alex Pavey has noted that '[a] crucial shift in meaning' of the word 'occurred in parallel with the pathologization of disorientation that took place at the turn of the twentieth century: disorientation expands in the psychiatric literature to encompass not only spatial confusion, but also disruptions in *temporality* and *identity*' (Pavey 2017: 79).[3] At various moments Ventura – just like Laura Dern's characters in *INLAND EMPIRE* – exhibits confusion as to *where*, *when* and *who* he is. But although the expansion of disorientation beyond purely spatial senses has been immensely productive for thought, this particular triad still conceives too rigidly of the subject as an isolated individual, underplaying the extent to which disorientation is a fundamentally relational phenomenon. As I noted in my introduction, Amy Harbin offers an alternative triad which corrects this overemphasis: 'To become disoriented is, roughly, to lose one's bearings in relation to others, environments, and life projects' (Harbin 2016: xi). The members of Harbin's triad are more outward-facing, relational and transformative, more open to unexpected responses or alterations – and are all of profound importance in *Colossal Youth*.

Some degree of identification with characters is, of course, one of the most common – and the most productive – orientational strategies that narrative films invite, and *Colossal Youth* is no exception. The film does not, however, simply align our experience with Ventura's. Other characters might often be easier to identify with: Vanda, perhaps, through her narratives of hospitalisation, childbirth and motherhood, or even Lento, through his occasional irritation with Ventura's insistence that he memorise a letter to his wife. Some of the devices that are most commonly employed to facilitate identification (such as point-of-view shots and editing organised around eyeline matches) are absent from *Colossal Youth*; we are also *excluded* from Ventura's world because of his very mysteriousness, aided by cinematography that constantly makes him strange by framing him, in expressionist or film noir style, at stark angles against empty backgrounds. Almost all the spaces we see are framed so they are bounded on all sides. (Costa has spoken of his 'taste for the room, for confinement' (Costa 2008: 15, my translation).)[4] Even though the use of wide-angle lenses and frequent low angles tends to magnify the foreground and elongate the distance from the front of the space to the back, the boundedness of the spaces filmed means that this elongation is not expansive. The spaces are expanded and yet constricted at one and the same time, disconcertingly both displaced and condensed.[5]

Yet we should not let our disorientation distract us from what is simple about *Colossal Youth*: the film might be seen, ultimately, as tracing an arc from Ventura's initial expulsion from home to the final scene in which he is alone with his granddaughter in his daughter's bedroom, at home in some sense, however provisional and transitory.[6] In what follows I want to trace some of the displacements and disorientations that *Colossal Youth* generates, outlining the way it frequently destabilises or confuses distinctions – such as between fiction and documentary, fantasy and reality, memory and experience, metaphor and literalness – without rendering them inoperative. I will use the notion of figuration presented in Chapter 5 to assist in so doing, working towards the sense of figuration I outlined in that chapter. After setting things up with a discussion of the texture of the film's organisation – its use of particular motifs organised in networks – I will focus in turn on figure as person, as metaphor, and finally in a more general sense as a significant 'shaping' in and of space and time.

It is the one of *Colossal Youth*'s singular achievements that it does not merely break down distinctions but, precisely, displaces or disorients them. At moments in the film we might feel everything to be highly mysterious, only to come to puzzle over our very puzzlement: what is so mysterious about a man standing in an empty apartment? Jacques Rancière thinks that Costa's 'cinema is simultaneously a cinema of the possible and of the impossible' (Rancière 2011: 39). *Colossal Youth* does not merely disorientate us – which is not too difficult an achievement – but disorientates us by the very manner in which it orientates us. It can both orientate and disorientate at the same time.

NETWORKS OF SIGNIFICANCE

Colossal Youth contains a very focused repertoire of motifs; I identify the following as particularly important: furniture, falling, knives, departure, confusion of identity, work, waiting, appetite, the letter, locks, health. All these motifs have made an appearance by scene eleven, which is to say a quarter of the way through the film. (I count forty-four scenes in total – see the appendix for a scene breakdown of the film that also traces the appearance and recurrence of these motifs.) For three-quarters of the film, that is to say, we are dealing with the recurrence of motifs with which we are already familiar. The way that the different 'series' in the film function contributes to the sense of some kind of network. By this I mean that although all the components by which narrative films usually orientate their viewers are present (characters, spaces, events, objects, themes), and although there is certainly (sometimes) change within and among these components, any traditional sense of themes developing linearly, blossoming and becoming gradually enriched is largely absent. Instead, the film jumps between its components, so that viewers have to reconstruct a sense of development by connecting the motifs in memory, bridging the film's many ellipses for themselves.

This is not to argue that the themes and motifs are disconnected from one another, but neither do I mean to suggest, in structuralist fashion, that these motifs constitute a fully coherent framework of oppositions that underlies the film. The motifs do not lie beneath the surface of the film but rather on its surface, or one might say that they *are* its surface – they are part of what the film is made of. Thus to engage with these motifs is better described as having some kind of encounter with the film than as decoding it – as a process of tracing and exploring relationships rather than of deciphering a puzzle. The question of home unites a great many of the motifs (furniture, departure, work, appetite, locks), as does a focus on boundaries and transitions. Furniture is what is inside the home, work is what takes place outside it. Similarly, appetite tends to grow outside the home and be satisfied inside it. Locks – when they work – allow one to keep this boundary in operation, ensuring that that which should be inside the home stays there, and that that which should remain outside cannot get inside. But these boundaries that are likely to seem characteristic of home for many – perhaps most – viewers of the film will not necessarily seem so to everybody. The loss of home that *Colossal Youth* traces is also an interrogation of the meaning of the concept itself, in that it also involves the inscription of boundaries that, far from marking out a home, prove instead to be destructive of a particular understanding of it. As Costa said about the films that preceded *Colossal Youth*:

> In *Vanda*, and already in *Ossos* . . . you don't really know if you're in somebody's house, in everybody's house, or if this particular house, this living room, this room, isn't actually more of a plaza or a forum, an *agora*, a place where people go in order to say a bunch of things or to hide themselves. (Costa 2008: 15, my translation)

In this context a lock doesn't mark out a home, it prevents a home from being possible: 'They have locks, and we have a shot of a guy opening a door. They never opened doors, at least before. And I do not remember a key. Never. An idea of a key was nonexistent. In Fontainhas, the public space and private space was undetermined' (Eguchi 2008). Nevertheless, however public and private are divided up, home must always be a space that can be defined in contrast with spaces that are *not* home. Expulsion and exile (whether of

Ventura, the inhabitants of Fontainhas more generally, or of the Holy Family in the painting by Reubens that we see in the Gulbenkian) emphasise the home through narratives of its loss, pointing towards what Sara Ahmed calls 'a migrant orientation', which 'might be described as the lived experience of facing at least two directions: toward a home that has been lost, and to a place that is not yet home' (Ahmed 2006: 10).[7]

A clue as to how to approach the film's idiosyncratic thematic structure is provided by what a remark by Jean-Louis Comolli in which he is, I think, mistaken: 'Nothing happens from one shot to the next apart from this emptiness. There is no off-screen: everything is the *same* from one frame to the next, persistent and monotonous' (Comolli 2010: 70). While much might be the same from shot to shot, to say that everything is the same is a gross exaggeration. Many crucial things happen *between* the shots: Ventura's wounding by Clotilde, the return of Beatriz to Vanda and the death of Zita, to name just three. The recurrence of motifs not only underlines the many samenesses of the lives we are witnessing; it also reveals the way that change recontextualises repetition. It is clear that the *prospect* of change is very important, specifically the constantly looming change represented by the time when Fontainhas will no longer exist, but this time is difficult to locate precisely. The relationship of the diegesis to it is disorientating; we seem to be situated right on the edge, at the horizon, of Fontainhas's ceasing-to-be. In one scene Ventura tells Nhurro that nothing remains of Fontainhas 'but dirt, weeds, and rats', and yet Bete is still there – even if she's 'the only one left'. It is hard to decide if we should say that Fontainhas *has been* abandoned or *will soon* be abandoned. We hear the sounds of its demolition but do not witness it visually.

Particular spaces recur in the film as much as the motifs do, and not much appears to change within these spaces each time we see them. Revisited spaces are very much in the majority,[8] and they are clearly related to each other, but their relationships, too, are closer to those between points in a network than to a continuous topology. The fact that they are filmed in static shots also contributes to the sense of nodes in a network, of static points.[9] We cannot even see from one space to another: there are plenty of windows in *Colossal Youth* but they are almost all either jet black, as in the scene of the expulsion of the furniture, or a sheer, impenetrable white, as in Vanda's bedroom. We are very aware of the distinction between Fontainhas and the new apartment blocks but we have absolutely no idea how one would get from one to the other. We can only measure the distance between locations in terms other than the spatial. These spatial ellipses might, perhaps, mimic the gaps in Ventura's memory. We move between spaces by discontinuous leaps rather than by continuously changing passage.

A consequence of this is that rarely in cinema are the dual spatial and temporal senses of the word 'scene' as important as they are in *Colossal Youth*. Each scene is both a particular place (as in 'the scene of the crime') and a specific narrative event, such as a particular conversation (as in 'don't make a scene!'). The result is that the distinction that many films make use of between unique narrative events (such as the burning of Rosebud) and events representative of a recurrent action or type of action (a frosty evening between Kane and Susan) becomes very difficult to make. Scenes that on a first viewing can seem merely evidence of a repetitive and uneventful way of living – representative examples of the activities that take place in particular spaces – come to take on more and more particularity with each re-viewing. These scenes, spatial and temporal, lie between, and therefore connect, very different times and places even if they do not themselves change very much, at least not while we watch. It is in the way that it slowly makes its viewers aware of these connections that the film constructs its simultaneously orientating and disorientating networks of significance.

FIGURATION IN (AND OF) *COLOSSAL YOUTH*

The scene in *Colossal Youth* that takes place in the garden of the Gulbenkian both develops the figure of Ventura as a character, and enacts a more abstract figuration where day becomes night within a single shot. Ventura gives us in this scene some of the most concrete information we learn about him in the whole film: how he came to Lisbon from Cape Verde (even the exact date: 19 August 1972); how he worked on the construction of the Gulbenkian; how he was injured in a fall. Yet the speech in which he imparts this information is accompanied by a camera movement down from the canopy of trees with blue sky clearly visible (contrasting with the dungeon-like space of the museum's interior, which we have just exited) which then follows Ventura as he sits on a bench. He is now strongly illuminated, but not by the sky, which is scarcely visible any more, and is instead surrounded by deep shadows in a dramatic chiaroscuro.[10] Day transforms into night, or at least into a kind of less localised, more mythic time. The time of the narration is made ambiguous at the same time as the content of the narrative becomes ever more specific. Seemingly opposed tendencies shape a single sequence.

I shall now proceed to use the notions of the figure and of figuration to help unpack more fully some of these tendencies and the devices that exploit them, starting by exploring figures as persons, then as metaphors and finally in a more general sense as a way of referring to the shapes in and of space and time that *Colossal Youth* both *is* and *brings about*.

Figure as Person

In *Colossal Youth* we encounter actors playing characters very close to, or even at points indistinguishable from, the actors themselves. But a movement which brings the character close to the actor, performance close to non-performance, is not the only procedure at work here. The performances in *Colossal Youth* are in general focused upon the simple performance of gestures and the speaking of words rather than on the projection of such performances in order to convey discernible intent. There is a subtle range of possibilities on display which probe the distinction between 'acting' in the sense of representing a character and 'acting' in the simple sense of doing. The different modes of performance present in the film also relate to narration: many characters in *Colossal Youth* tell their own stories as much as they enact them. The film frequently shows us bodies, otherwise unmoving, in the act of speaking. Sitting in her room, always on the same corner of the bed, and watching television is both what Vanda enacts and what she *does*. She tells her own story of her experiences in hospital, and she tells it in much the way she would tell it to her friends were the camera not there.[11] Others, while still telling their own stories, perform for the camera more directly. Many of the people who appear in the film were asked to write their own texts, and to consider them as letters, which is to say specifically as words directed towards another (see Eguchi 2008).

Costa has frequently spoken of the way that his introduction to Fontainhas came when Cape Verdeans he met during the filming of *Casa de Lava* (1995) asked him to take letters back to their relatives in Lisbon. But even if we did not have Costa's account of his process, the content of the monologues and the conviction with which the non-professional performers deliver them would have suggested that they had a hand, at least, in their composition. The finished film contains traces of the 'documentary' of a particular kind of performance. Nhurro's monologue is one of these texts and is delivered almost directly to camera, with the actor's face in the centre of the frame; so is Clotilde's monologue at the film's opening. At the other extreme, Ventura is for most viewers the most distinctive figure in the film, and yet he is the one who has the largest quantity of dialogue likely to have been written for him by Costa.[12]

When we attend to the question of what kind of figures we are watching in *Colossal Youth*, then, it becomes clear that there is in the film a subtle and sometimes disorientating play of variations marking out the territory between the kind of acting we might expect in documentary (where the fiction is often that the camera's presence makes no difference), a kind of collaborative performance (such as in Nhurro's monologue, where text and delivery are largely the responsibility of the performer, with lighting, framing, etc., that of the filmmaker) and finally the relationship we expect in a fictional film (in which a performer speaks the lines and enacts the gestures required of them by the director). The procedures of representation and performance are not drawn attention to by drastic gestures of rupture but in a quieter fashion which rewards the viewer who becomes aware of the relevance of certain questions. The subtlety of these distinctions renders them likely to be initially disorientating, or at least lacking in orientational information: the distinctions between different modes of performance are not starkly underlined. Ultimately, however, they serve as territory by means of which the film's representational strategies can become discernible.

Figure as Metaphor

Pedro Costa has, in the past, expressed his aversion towards both metaphor and documentary, two categories that might seem inescapable in the discussion of his work. He has proclaimed both 'I don't like documentaries' ('I Died a Thousand Times', conversation with Nuno Crespo accompanying Costa 2013) and 'I don't like metaphors' (Costa and Chafes 2007: 128). To some extent these statements might derive from the filmmaker's wish to wrongfoot his interpreters. However, the forms of performance and representation that we have just examined show how Costa dramatises different responses to what I called the fiction of the camera's absence which marks many documentaries, and which I suspect might be one of the things Costa has an aversion to (as well as, presumably, the tendency of some documentaries to deliver a message with excessive clarity). The latter proclamation about metaphor, I would suggest, stems from a reluctance to include sequences that can be 'translated' into a message. Towards the end of Costa's earlier film *Ossos* (1997) there is a scene in which Tina attempts to help Clotilde (played by *Colossal Youth*'s Vanda Duarte) with the cooking and ends up spilling boiling water on her. After a pause, both girls laugh. The scene seems clearly to be saying that even when you attempt to help people, you often end up hurting them, but that this is something to be accepted and laughed at rather than struggled against.[13] Such direct metaphorical messages are rare in Costa's work, and particularly rare in the work after *Ossos*.

Other forms of metaphor, however, suffuse *Colossal Youth*. Clotilde's opening monologue is structured according to metaphors of fear, isolation and bravery. When she was a young girl she swam constantly, whereas 'none of the boys had the nerve to follow me'. But 'no shark ever got near' to her. She swam 'like a fish', which seems to have rendered her safe from the sharks. We might think a fish to be particularly vulnerable to a shark, but the simile also indicates the fact that she is at home in the water, neutralising the sharks' territorial advantage. Clotilde's sharks might be linked to the anaconda that Ventura and Vanda watch killing a crocodile on television; perhaps the sharks did not eat her because, unlike the anaconda's crocodile, she was not their natural prey. Costa, it seems, is happy deploying metaphors as long as the meanings they generate are sufficiently ambiguous.

The crucial figures, in the sense of metaphors or metonyms, in *Colossal Youth* are frequently binary in nature. Primary among these are the figures of the letter and the knife, both of which can connect people in ways that either damage or heal.[14] A letter is both an instrument of communication and a means of keeping communication private. It is 'what traverses absence' (Badiou 2009: 367) but it can conceal as much as it transmits. It communicates between its sender and receiver but, if it is sealed in an envelope and remains unopened until it reaches its destination, it also hides its contents from the messenger who delivers it. Actual letters were central to the lives of the residents of Fontainhas. As Daniel Eschkötter puts it, 'letters are the medium at the centre of the Fontainhas complex: letters that are recited, displayed, refused, carried around, reluctantly received' (Eschkötter 2016: 68, my translation). Ventura himself is also refused, reluctantly received and sometimes welcomed as he travels through the film; Emma Fajgenbaum describes him as resembling 'a lost soul on an odyssey' (Fajgenbaum 2019: 153). His character and its representation are intimately tied up with notions of communication, transmission and, nevertheless, separation.

Ventura seems to be the father of almost everybody we encounter in the film, a relationship at once material and significant. The narrative of the first part of *Colossal Youth* (after the destruction of the furniture and Clotilde's brandishing of the knife) involves Ventura's attempt to find out which of his children Clotilde was mother to. He tries Bete (who tells him that he's 'got the wrong door and the wrong daughter'), Gustavo (who asks 'what woman?') and Vanda (who tells him that her mother is in the cemetery). This narrative thread returns later when Ventura tells Paolo that his (Paolo's) mother has left him (Ventura). He is not contradicted, so we might think that Ventura's quest has been successful until we learn that Paolo's mother is called Lurdes. Ventura's eventual reconciliation with Bete and his telling her of how they met might indicate that he did not in fact have either the wrong door or the wrong daughter at the outset, but this is never confirmed. Beyond this narrative device, a straightforward metaphor is also in operation. When, after Zita's death, Vanda tells Ventura, 'Papa, Zita was your daughter, but she was my sister first', it is made clear that family relationships are something more than a matter of simple biology.

Ventura is also some kind of guardian figure. This image seems to have arisen from his actual role during the filming of Costa's earlier work *In Vanda's Room* (2000), concerning which the director has said that 'I think that I took him for a sentinel' (Costa 2008: 134, my translation). In *Colossal Youth*, is Ventura a guardian because he is a parent, or is it the other way round? Does he take on parental qualities because of his guardianship? His guardianship is also in contradistinction to that of the museum attendant at the Gulbenkian, who tells Ventura:

> Guarding this isn't like guarding the open-air market back home. Here you wield an iron hand in a velvet glove. There, it's just an iron hand . . . Here it's another world. An ancient, untroubled world. No one shouts or runs or spits on the floor. It's nice and easy . . . It's trouble when someone like you turns up. (*Colossal Youth*, 46′ 00″ – 46′ 45″)

Ventura's guardianship, on the other hand, is all about remaining with the Cape Verdeans. We never see Ventura actually defending anybody against violence or preventing the destruction of Fontainhas, but his presence and his witness, the way he is not simply one of the inhabitants but is also distinguished from them, so that it seems that he somehow accompanies them, is in itself a form of defence against the disorientating psychic violence that the displacement is enacting. (He is also a messenger, in that he is the only figure who appears able to move between Fontainhas and Casal da Boba; the movement that is the film's subject is elided, perhaps as a traumatic event that can only be represented indirectly.) The psychic violence that Ventura seems to have undergone (as well as actual violence: his fall from the scaffolding and his wounding by Clotilde) has not only precipitated his confusion but is also, perhaps, what suits him for such a role.

There is, though, another figure who briefly appears as a defender, namely Clotilde. In an excellent close reading of her only scene (the knife-wielding scene at the film's beginning) Annika Weinthal observes:

> Here, shortly before the opening of the main narrative, the camera looks metaphorically one more time deep into the memory of Fontainhas, out of which emerges Clotilde, the woman with the knife. The story that she tells is simultaneously her story and that of many others; is both concrete memory and a symbol of feminine power. (Weinthal 2016: 58, my translation)[15]

The memory that Clotilde speaks of derives from when she was young; it must of course have taken place in Cape Verde. Thus, immediately after the furniture crashes to the ground, signifying Ventura's expulsion and the wider expulsion from Fontainhas, we get the most direct representation there is in the film – a representation that is admittedly still oblique – of Cape Verde itself. Weinthal notes that the figures of Clotilde and her son could be seen as coming from Costa's earlier film *Casa de Lava*, which was set and filmed in Cape Verde, and in which we see many women 'who linger on the Cape Verdean islands in isolation and poverty, left behind by their husbands and fathers who have gone to Portugal to look for work' (*ibid.*). Clotilde's 'threatening gesture' ('Drohgebärde') can thus be interpreted in a multitude of ways. It 'can be understood simultaneously as a warning to the sharks, to the young men on the beach, and to the listener not to get too near to Clotilde' (*ibid.*). Whoever is listening to Clotilde's speech, at whom she brandishes her knife and stares so ferociously, is, as Weinthal reminds us, invisible. We could also consider ourselves, the viewers, as one more object of her threat. Is she warning us off, or perhaps warning us not to get close too lightly? Is Clotilde the figure of a more effective resistance that Ventura cannot offer? At the end of her single brief scene Clotilde withdraws into the darkness, but her knife blade still glints.

Figure as a Shaping in Space and/or Time

How else might we orientate ourselves with respect to this film, and why is it sometimes hard to do so? What role does the film's figuration, in the widest sense, have to play here? We might begin by noting the absence of establishing shots. Not only, as we have seen, are the spaces in which the film takes place dissociated from one another, but they are not even clearly situated in their immediate surroundings. What exactly do establishing shots, customarily, establish? We might say that they proceed from the assumption that we can separate space and event. A wide shot of a particular location announces it as a space in which events can take place. A tighter shot of the action serves to emphasise the uniqueness of temporal activity in contradistinction to the openness of space. Many different stories could take place within one space, but they could not take place within one space at the same time. The way that *Colossal Youth* simultaneously emphasises the temporal and spatial senses of 'scene' goes some way to undermining this. Without establishing shots, every space seen in the film is marked out as individual just as every moment in time is. We are not so much disorientated because the arrangement of the space is hard to discern; on the contrary, shots where this is the case (such as that of Clotilde brandishing her knife) are few and far between. But, as I have already noted, we do not know how the spaces we see are connected or articulated. We get four different views of Vanda's apartment, with minor variations: one of her bedroom, one of the hallway, one of the dining room, and one of the front door. But even by the end of the film we are none the wiser about how these spaces link up. As soon as we return to one of these four views we know exactly where we are, but we would still not know how to move to any of the others.

Even staircases and corridors seem, in *Colossal Youth*, more like spaces in their own right than transitions between other spaces. When they are connected these connections can be misleading. After he has been shown the first possible apartment in Casal da Boba, Ventura descends a flight of stairs. We are likely, I think, to assume that he is leaving the apartment. But then we hear a knock at a door, after which we see him in Vanda's bedroom. Going downstairs to an apartment seems peculiar; this only makes sense if we remember that we learned earlier that Vanda has a basement flat. Later on, Ventura sits at the foot of a flight of stairs as Vanda, Beatriz and Gustavo climb past him. Ventura follows and we hear a door close. But rather than any room in Casal da Boba, the next shot shows Ventura standing in the doorway of the shack he shared with Lento in the 1970s. When the passage between shots does seem to articulate different spaces – rather than underlining their isolation – it tends to do so across time and space rather than according to the logic of a realistic diegesis.

So how does *Colossal Youth* figure time? Rancière has written of Costa's 'still lives' (Rancière 2011), which might suggest that his compositions can be linked to the destabilisation of the dichotomy between the living and the dead that runs through Costa's cinema.[16] Vatchel Lindsay's excellent observation that '[i]t is a quality, not a defect, of all photoplays that human beings tend to become dolls and mechanisms, and dolls and mechanisms tend to become human' (Lindsay 1922: 25) seems somehow not to apply to *Colossal Youth*. We see very few mechanisms at all, and the figures, in all their stillness, never seem mechanical. Instead – just as in *Holy Motors*, but in a very different way – the distinction that is called into question is the notion that everything must be either alive or dead and cannot be both. We have seen how the temporality of the film seems poised at the exact moment when the neighbourhood could be said to be either dead (everyone has gone) or with minimal life remaining (Bete is still there). Are we close to the realm of the undead? As I have noted, at the end of the film Lento has become a ghost. Ventura's resemblance to the zombie Carre-Four, from *I Walked with a Zombie* (1943) by Costa's beloved Jacques Tourneur, has also been remarked upon (Costa 2008: 134).

Yet if we can speak of the life of Fontainhas, then clearly it is not only organisms that can be alive or dead; the environment, it seems, can become a figure.[17] Maybe, however, 'life' and 'death' are slightly too constrictive as categories, and it would be more helpful to think about methods of articulation: construction and animation. Ordinarily, non-living things (particularly, in this film, buildings) are constructed, whereas living things are animated. This might provide a way for a reformulation of Lindsay's observation to regain some of its pertinence: we see at times, for example, how the figure of

Ventura is constructed as a sharply outlined, curved dark shape against the bright straight lines of his new apartment. But if figures are in a sense constructed (in that we can see how, as images, they are put together), then rooms can also be animated. Despite the similar whiteness of the two rooms, the presence of Ventura together with Vanda and, eventually, Beatriz progressively animates Vanda's bedroom in a way that never happens in Ventura's apartment.

What of the figures that Ventura and Bete see as they lie on her bed and stare at her wall? (Ventura tells her: 'In the houses of the departed there are lots of figures to see'.) The figures on the wall also seem both constructed (each of them sees something different, apart — perhaps significantly — from a policeman that they both see) and animated. As Bete says, 'When they give us those white rooms we'll stop seeing these things.' The contrast between the richly textured, subtly illuminated greenish walls of Fontainhas and the starkly unforgiving white walls of Casal da Boba is one of the most striking visual aspects of *Colossal Youth*; imaginative life will be in grave danger of impoverishment in those deathly white spaces that cannot so easily be animated. We should, however, note the parallels in this scene with those of Vanda and Ventura watching TV. Here they look to screen right, there to screen left, but the compositions are similar and in both cases we see only the watching, not what is being watched. I see nothing to indicate that the television is condemned as imaginatively deadening: on the contrary, Vanda is wholly engaged both with the anaconda and her favourite soap opera, *Franklin*. Costa has no reason to be even-handed about the demolition — clearly the film condemns it — but neither does he simplistically romanticise a life without modern technology and media.[18]

As we have had reason to note a number of times thus far, the same phenomena which can help to orientate the viewer can also disorientate them. Take, for example, the length of time we spend in Vanda's room. This helps us come to know the space, but also makes us wonder exactly why we're spending such a long time there. The distinction between *waiting* and *doing nothing* is both suggested and destabilised. For example, it might initially seem as if there is a distinction in operation between waiting for something or someone (as Ventura clearly does in scene 3), and simply doing nothing (as with Ventura and Vanda in scene 6). But as the film continues it becomes increasingly difficult to be sure that sitting or standing quietly can ever be adequately described as *doing nothing*. When Ventura and Bete sit quietly together, for example, the sounds of Fontainhas being dismantled and people preparing to leave are quietly but clearly audible. Are Ventura and Bete, then, simply waiting to be relocated? Or are they, rather, actively *being*, existing in the space which they know they will only be permitted to occupy for a short while to come? Similarly, is Ventura doing nothing in the film's final scene, or is he looking after his granddaughter?

A related phenomenon takes place with regard to what activity might be required from us as viewers. The film's narration maintains the viewer at a certain 'distance' from the film's events, which enables some narrative ironies (irony being, traditionally, considered as a rhetorical figure). Volker Pantenburg argues that 'the realities on screen and of the audience are not linked by any direct form of empathy or identification. What unites them is a feeling of uneasiness' (Pantenburg 2010: 61). Uneasiness is, perhaps, a mild form of disorientation. One method by which *Colossal Youth* generates this uneasiness involves not flagging up the introduction of information which will have narrative significance. Thus it is possible to have a sense of inactivity, even perhaps something close to boredom, of time passing listening to idle conversation which seems to have little narrative import, only later to develop the feeling that we have not been paying enough attention, that we have missed crucial information.[19] This impression is itself part of the film's narrative and figurative strategies. I disagree, therefore, with Kiss and Willemsen's claim that 'understimulation does not disorient or mislead viewers', a view they derive from their sense that '[i]n art films, the main function of understimulating or underdetermined narration is usually to divert the viewers' attention away from the minimal action that these films present and towards the psychological or philosophical registers that underlie the narrative' (Kiss and Willemsen 2017: 45). The relationship between psychology and narrative is otherwise in *Colossal Youth*. To give one small example, Bete mentions Nhurro before we first meet him in the following scene. But we do not get any other signals that we should expect to meet this character, and hence are likely not to distinguish specifically narrative foreshadowing from other information whose significance is motivic or thematic. When we meet Nhurro we are reminded of some of the things that were said about him, but also of what we have forgotten, because we were not listening with our 'plot antennae' up; we become, as it were, retrospectively disoriented – we thought there could be no narrative information to miss, only to realise that we must have missed some. The film exploits any complacency about the ease of comprehending the 'minimal action' presented. The relative simplicity of the film's structure at this point (a character is mentioned for the first time and then introduced in the very next scene) is easy to miss and only becomes apparent on repeated viewings.

If the difficulty of describing any of what we see as genuine inactivity increases as the film goes on, there clearly is linear development in the film. One such linear sequence is the pattern of two characters being joined by a third, after which one of the first two leaves. This pattern occurs a number of times during the film within individual scenes, but is traced out over a larger time span in the pattern Ventura/Vanda, Ventura/Vanda/Beatriz and finally Ventura/Beatriz. The final pair only occurs in the last scene of the film, giving a degree of formal closure at the same time as the image of a grandfather together with his granddaughter raises questions about the relationship of the past to the future and whether they are necessarily coherently connected or whether there is an irreducible gap between them. Weinthal argues that 'Clotilde defends the memories of the inhabitants of Fontainhas against oblivion with her knife, because when the last house is demolished, it is not only a place of communal living that will go missing, but also a place of potential remembrance of shared origins' (Weinthal 2016: 58, my translation). Memory is not a secure repository of 'homeliness': if certain physical structures are destroyed, memory itself will eventually deteriorate.

In conclusion, we might say that *Colossal Youth* prompts us to consider whether the very concept of 'home' disturbs or confuses the distinction between the literal and the figurative. To say that a place is one's home is clearly not a metaphor but because emotions unveil the bluntness of the fact/value distinction and our tendency to align the literal with the factual, it doesn't seem quite right, either, to say that it is literally true. Can one, for example, be literally in love? In Costa's film home is not merely something that has been lost, but also something that (just like, I have argued, coherence in a film) has to be *achieved*. Love (of one's home, for example) might seem to be related to animation in my previous distinction between animation and construction: for instance, we more readily say that love 'grows' than that it is 'built'. And yet what makes a home a home in *Colossal Youth* is very much related to construction: the fact that the inhabitants of Fontainhas built their shacks themselves but did not build their new houses is crucial. As Costa puts it, talking about Casal da Boba: 'Yes, it's very simple: they're houses that they didn't build' (Costa 2008: 165, my translation).[20]

For all its bleakness, *Colossal Youth* is not without hope of the possibility of animation within these new, carelessly constructed apartments. At the very end of the film, Ventura sleeps on Vanda's bed as Beatriz plays on the floor beside it. The child initially seems a little disconcerted, but eventually she begins to laugh, and as she does so Ventura wakes up and passes his hand across his face. Both for characters and viewers, the film ends with a gesture, however provisional, of orientation rather than disorientation. Despite the excessive displacement that the film traces, as well as the ellipses and passages of stasis whose very emptiness disorientates us, we are finally given a tiny glimpse of the possibility that this house could, in time, achieve the status of some kind of home – at least for Beatriz's generation if not for Ventura's.

CHAPTER 8

Sink or Swim: Immersing Ourselves in Jean-Luc Godard's Adieu au langage

This book has been dealing with questions of orientation and disorientation in film, with the ways that films can cause us to lose – or to have difficulty getting – our bearings, and with the consequences of the various critical strategies we might employ in response. As I have had occasion to observe more than once, the language of orientation relies on a metaphor of territory; it envisages a film as some kind of place through which we pass, which may at times be more or less familiar, and may either supply or deny the signs necessary for us to be able to assess our 'location' in relation to the landscape that is the film. In *Colossal Youth* we encountered some situations where such signs seem to be insufficient or even lacking entirely. In common with much of his work, Jean-Luc Godard's 2014 film *Adieu au langage* presents almost the opposite situation: it contains such a surfeit of images, sounds, fragments of music and citations (both acknowledged and unacknowledged) that it can seem almost impossible to distinguish figure from ground, to separate elements that might serve as signs from those which are merely features of the landscape. This means that the film is often extremely confusing (in the ordinary sense). This confusion is generated both by the lack of obvious connections – those parts of the film that most exhibit what Brenez, as I mentioned in Chapter 5, calls 'figurality by overload' – and, as in *Holy Motors*, by the presence of connections that it is difficult to know what to do with. (This is particularly the case in those moments in that film that both offer a narrative and frustrate its comprehension.) As I also argued in my chapter on *Holy Motors*, however, I want to claim that the difficulty of perceiving a consistent diegesis in *Adieu au langage* should not lead us too quickly to assume that pursuing questions of diegesis could only result in a misdirected and fruitless quest. But, of course, it will not be possible to simply take the orientational strategies that worked elsewhere and apply them here; we need to look for new ones, guided by this film in particular. That we can – and should – look to confusing films themselves for guidance as to how we might go about orientating ourselves is, as I hope is becoming clear, one of the central claims of this book.

Daniel Morgan expresses the particular sensation of confusion that

Godard's recent work produces at the start of his book *Late Godard and the Possibilities of Cinema*:

> As any viewer of Godard's work over the past several decades can readily attest, his films and videos tend to evoke a feeling of being at sea . . . It's not so much a question of being able to identify every reference thrown our way – a task that seems not only fruitless but also pointless – as it is a problem of not knowing where to start, of not understanding what Godard is doing. (Morgan 2013: 1)

Morgan does not offer a formula for gaining orientation; his one general methodological stipulation is that 'only by staying with the intricate weave of sound, image, and text can Godard's late films and videos be approached and understood' (*ibid.*: 2). Appropriately enough, perhaps, *Adieu au langage* presents the viewer with problems of knowing 'where to start' right at the outset. It begins by presenting the viewer with an 'intricate weave' that includes a collection of endings. The film starts with a complex montage sequence in which, at one point, we read on the screen a phrase derived – as a number of the film's French viewers, at least, might perhaps be expected to recognise – from the final lines of Flaubert's *L'Éducation sentimentale* ('oui, c'est ce que nous avons eu de meilleur, dit Deslauriers').[1] We are also shown an excerpt from the end of Howard Hawks's 1939 *Only Angels Have Wings* in which Bonnie (Jean Arthur) realises that Geoff (Cary Grant) has given her the double-headed coin that had belonged to his beloved friend Kid (Thomas Mitchell) and was therefore, in telling her to flip the coin ('tails you go, heads you stay'), asking her, in his own way, to stay with him. Placing these citations at the beginning of the film allows them only the merest amount of context, making it very difficult to judge the mode in which we are invited to read them. The conceit of placing endings at the beginning suggests irony, but how much and of what kind? Will the film turn out to be a kind of essay film, along the lines of Godard's own *Histoire(s) du cinéma*, or is this merely the prologue to a more conventional narrative? It only takes a minute and a half, after all, before we encounter a title reading '1: la nature', after which we see a ferry arriving at shore and, soon after, meet some named characters. If we're a little lost at the beginning of *Adieu au langage*, this is not anything unusual. The same can be said for a great many films; even in the most straightforward narratives, it takes at least some time for us to orientate ourselves. What is more distinctive, and more bewildering, here is that we don't even know in quite what way we're lost. Right at the outset, the film problematises those notions of 'territory' on which the metaphor of orientation is based.

In the passage from Morgan I quoted above, it is interesting that he expresses the disorientation that Godard's films can provoke with an aquatic metaphor: 'a feeling of being at sea'.[2] *Adieu au langage* is full of images of (and references to) water and associated phenomena. Immediately after the opening montage sequence, as I have mentioned, we see a ferry arrive on the shores of Lake Geneva and later a woman drinks from a water fountain. The film proceeds to offer us a compendium of images of forms of water, including but not limited to: puddles, washing hands, rivers, thirst ('J'ai soif'), rain on windshields, snow (on cars and in a forest), Freudian speculations on the mythic associations of submersion in water with birth, rain, clouds, the sea, a shower, rapids, fog (mentioned on the soundtrack), a glass of water for painting watercolours, and so forth. I want to argue in this chapter that it may be appropriate to think of this film in terms of its strategies of *immersion*; immersion does not preclude orientation but it shifts the terms of the metaphor somewhat. The viewer is no longer securely placed on the land (even if lost) but in the very midst of things.

The notion of immersion also seems appropriate to this film because it is Godard's first feature in 3D. The stereoscopic illusions of depth created by 3D cinema technology are frequently discussed in terms of their immersive effects on the viewer. Delia Enyedi has usefully referred to the 'immersion aesthetic' of the film (Enyedi 2017) and, indeed, the film's images of water often look particularly remarkable in 3D, such as the early scene of hand washing in a fountain, or the waves on Lake Geneva. This kind of immersion is often regarded as sensual, as purely experiential and as having nothing to do with elements of film such as character and narrative. But the other aspect of film most frequently discussed in terms of immersion is, precisely, narrative; immersion is a common way of talking about the other sense, besides becoming confused or disorientated, in which we can get 'lost' in a film. The idea of being immersively lost in a narrative is interestingly in tension with that of being lost as a result of disorientation. We say that we are lost in a story when we are so engrossed in it that we can almost forget that it is merely a story, which in no way entails being lost in the sense of being disorientated; sometimes the result of the latter is, precisely, to prevent us from getting lost in the story, in the sense of being immersed in it.

From some of Godard's previous work, and some of the criticism written on it, one might expect that Godard's reaction to ideas of immersion, both in relation to 3D's illusionary potential and to narrative, would be to disrupt it, to render palpable – in broadly Brechtian fashion – the fact that immersion, whether in a 3D image or in a story, is simply illusion. Certainly, in *Adieu au langage*, Godard does frequently disrupt both these and other forms of immersion. But this can have complex dialectical effects. When, for example, the soundtrack is abruptly silenced or interrupted – which happens regularly in *Adieu au langage* – the immersive properties of sound are not simply undermined. They are also emphasised, because the sudden change makes strikingly evident the disappearance of that in which we were previously immersed. Thus I want to argue that Godard does not *only* disrupt immersion in this film; there are rather more complex relationships at play between immersion and the disruption of immersion which have profound consequences for our sense of orientation or disorientation. In this, Godard is maintaining something that has long been a feature of his work; Perez observes about 1964's *Bande à part* that '[i]f Godard is to be called Brechtian, it must be understood that, like Brecht, he seeks not merely to alienate us but concurrently to involve us, so that we enter into a transaction between distance and closeness, belief and disbelief' (Perez 2019: 169).

Godard does not only reinforce and exploit the non-immersive qualities of stereoscopic images, their tendency to create what Raymond Durgnat calls a 'depth too "laminated" to feel real' (Durgnat 1967: 116), although he does certainly radicalise this tendency. (At times the film almost generates the impression that objects can extend, paradoxically, in front of the foreground (negative parallax) and behind the background (positive parallax). When Josette (Héloïse Godet) sits in a slatted chair outside the cultural centre it somehow seems that she is in the foreground but that nevertheless the chair juts out towards us, further forward than the foreground.) But more nuanced procedures are also at work. The 3D treatment of the aforementioned scene of a woman washing her hands in the pool of a fountain, for example, puns on the notion that 3D images represent depth: the depth of the pool does indeed come across strongly, but what is more striking about the image is the way the stereoscopic image renders the *surface* of the water as a shimmering plane, covered in floating leaves and broken by the hands being plunged into it. (It might stand as an instance of what Godard's voice, much later in the film, refers to as the difficulty of fitting flatness into depth.) Indeed, many of the most striking three-dimensional images in the film emphasise surfaces, or at least textures, such as the almost tactile crenellations of waves on Lake Geneva that are seen starting just before twenty-three minutes into the film. Textures such as these both invite and resist immersion. They suggest a tactility, creating a sense that the viewer could almost touch the film, could immerse him- or herself in the sensory qualities of its world that go beyond what can be seen and heard but, at the same time, they make one also acutely aware that this is impossible.[3] They operate as a kind of interface between surface and depth.

I will try to show how the figuration that is at work in *Adieu au langage* both exploits and disrupts immersive phenomena and, in particular, water as a symbol (metaphor or metonym) for immersion. Whenever we encounter a phenomenon that has the capacity to clarify the film, there is almost always a contrary movement that is likely either to obscure it or to distract us from the fact that it has been clarified. The film might almost be seen to thematise this tendency via the pervasiveness of the theme of water and its highly contradictory properties. Water, after all, can literally support floating bodies and is a necessary support of life itself but one can also drown in it; it can be transparent, not obscuring vision – in fact it can clean away the murk obstructing a clear view – and yet it also tends to refract and distort whatever is seen through it. The film plays with surfaces and depths, with volumes and media (what we see and what we see through). See, for example, the various images of car windscreens, often splattered with rain, that both are and are not coterminous with the cinema screen, that seem to occupy the same space as the screen and yet also make us aware that this is impossible. There is transparency but there is also distortion. All of this emphasises water as a medium, and therefore reflexively emphasises the filmic medium as well. So water does not merely serve to immerse us in the film; it makes immersion itself into a theme. We are, I think, intended to recognise the mediated quality of every image, every word, every sound in the film, but we are not *only* intended to do this. The film also has immersive strategies of its own. But what are they? If it does not offer an immersive experience directed towards forgetting that one is immersed, what kind of immersion *does* the film offer?

HISTORY AND ARGUMENT

The body of *Adieu au langage* consists of two narratives, or two variations on the same narrative focusing on a couple consisting of a man and a woman. The segments concerning the first couple are labelled '1: la nature' and the second '2: la métaphore'. Early in the first 'la nature' section, the film makes various propositions concerning the historical and social milieu in which we are currently immersed. The didactic aspect of this part of the film is ironically acknowledged (one sequence begins with Davidson, played by Christian Grégori, announcing 'allez, en examen', or 'come on, exam time'), but this does not undercut the seriousness with which the film puts forward certain proposals. As Rick Warner summarises in his excellent article on the film, one of the most crucial references is to Jacques Ellul and his argument – made originally in the article 'Victoire d'Hitler?', published in *Réforme* on 23 June 1945, only weeks after VE day – 'that Hitler, despite his army's defeat, must be seen as having achieved a definitive political victory insofar as his conquerors put in place more cunningly veiled forms of mass control', even though in fact Hitler invented nothing, because he was merely continuing the work of figures such as Machiavelli, Richelieu and Bismarck (Warner 2016: 66). The conspiracy theory-like texture thereby introduced into the film recalls Deleuze's remarks towards the end of *Cinema 1* to the effect that one of the signs of the crisis of the action-image in post-war American cinema is the prevalence of a sense of 'a powerful concerted organisation, a great and powerful plot' in which '[o]ccult power is confused with its effects, its supports, its media, its radios, its televisions, its microphones' (Deleuze 2005: 214).[4] But here, rather than rupture, it is diachronic historical continuity that is emphasised, of a particularly dark kind.

There is, however, also an emphasis on synchronic discontinuity. When Davidson declares that Ellul foresaw almost everything, his voice is doubled on the soundtrack with a very slight delay, creating a kind of division within unity. Very shortly afterwards another male voice (apparently called Alain – this may perhaps be the young male student, unnamed in the credits, played by Jeremy Zampatti) declares that in 1793, at the height of the Terror, the Convention produced the civil code, the new calendar, the decimal system, the manufacture of steel, government accounting, and the Conservatoire de Musique. Given the extensive reference to what Ellul called 'Hitler's Victory', it seems clear that this cannot be read simply as an account of the need for destruction in order for there to be progress; the fact that the list of the Convention's achievements is read over images of a Nazi motorcade followed by a shot of the Tour de France might even satirise the notion of progress, as well as point to continuities in different forms of spectacle. But neither is there a sense that the achievements of the French Revolution are irreparably compromised by the Terror; they *are* compromised, perhaps, but in complex and ambivalent ways. Eschewing any contact with that which is compromised seems, for Godard, to be no solution at all. But where should we put the emphasis – on the Terror or on the decimal system, as it were?

The question of emphasis is crucial to the film's strategies of immersion and disorientation and the way that they facilitate multiple interpretations that nevertheless retain a relationship with one another. Digital media are a crucial site both for the exploration and exhibition of such fluidity, as both a prime contemporary example of the techniques that perpetuate 'Hitler's victory' (in that they can be argued to facilitate 'cunningly veiled forms of mass control') and also the very medium in which *Adieu au langage* exists. But Godard's sleight of hand is extensive. Ellul was in fact a Christian anarchist, and his article concludes by referring to 'the man Jesus Christ, who alone smashes the fate [les fatalités] of the world, who alone closes the jaws of Moloch, who alone will liberate men tomorrow from the servitude that the world is preparing for us today' (Ellul 1945, my translation). Does Godard mean to *détourne* Ellul by repurposing his argument about the spread of state power, or does he mean to introduce the possibility of ironically undercutting what appears to be his film's argument? The question of whether this film, and similar films by Godard, actually present arguments is a thorny one. Morgan is of the opinion that they do, arguing that '[i]f the contents of Godard's arguments are idiosyncratic, it is in part because we are called on to judge and make sense of them in new ways' (Morgan 2013: 7–8). But I wonder whether we should pause a moment. Why should we assume that they are the film's arguments, let alone Godard's arguments? Are we really dealing with arguments or merely with things that look or feel like arguments, or that invite one to treat them as such, an invitation one can also reject or at least treat with suspicion? Morgan does recognise this problem, but he swiftly elides the notion of making an argument with a broader notion of philosophy: 'In a sense, these questions are a version of a more common debate over the extent to which film can be said to do the work of philosophy' (*ibid.*: 25). But the various versions of the claim that 'films think' are, to me, more obviously various and able to be understood variously than the specific claim that a film *argues*. Hence what Morgan calls his 'fairly modest proposal' does not quite address the issue: 'We can say that a film (or video) raises questions of philosophy if and when considerations of these questions are necessary to arrive at a good interpretation of the way that film's images, sounds, and texts are put together' (*ibid.*: 26).

It seems in keeping with the way that *Adieu au langage* handles the many binary distinctions it deploys that it is possible to read its 'arguments' in contradictory ways. Early on in the film, for example, analogue and digital information technologies are literally juxtaposed. As Warner writes, '[g]athered around the bookstall, Davidson and the male student trade and fidget with their iPhones as Marie [Marie Ruchat], in the more immediate foreground, picks up and flips through the book in question. The shot thus stages a contrast between two media and the kinds of gestures they cultivate' (Warner 2016: 66). This is very helpful, but it seems to me equally possible to perceive similarity here as it is to recognise difference. We would be more secure, interpretationally speaking, if the Internet was simply being castigated for, say, its negative effects on attention span. In fact we see both phones *and* books. People look things up on their phones but still buy books at book sales. As if in answer to Davidson's ironic question about what people did with their thumbs before they used them on their phones, we see people thumbing through books. The full history of the information revolution in which we are currently immersed goes back at least to William Caxton's printing press rather than only to Tim Berners-Lee's World Wide Web. When boundaries dissolve, this can help us to see continuity as easily as it can erase the possibility of recognising difference.

Another example that it seems possible to read both as endorsed by the film and as attacked by it occurs at the film's beginning. The very first thing we see in the film is the phrase 'tous ceux qui manquent d'imagination se réfugient dans la réalité',[5] in white text on a black background, alternating with a large ADIEU in red capitals. Is reality the ultimate object of representation or merely a bolthole for those lacking creative potential? Or is this the wrong way to think about it? Marie Darrieussecq, from whose short piece in *Libération* the phrase derives, concludes that what the phrase indicates is that 'to be a writer, a poet, a playwright' (we might add, a filmmaker) is 'to want to create linguistic tools for describing a world perpetually in motion' (Darrieussecq 2014, my translation). Such a world, surely, is a *fluid* world, one which we do not merely inhabit but are, unavoidably, immersed. Whichever way we read it, however, what are we to make of the fact that it opens the film? Does this necessarily mean that the film is an endorsement of the remark, or might it be considered as an extended attempt to demonstrate its falsity, or at least to attempt to interrogate and challenge it? A different emphasis will have serious consequences for our reading of the film. Emphasis is often, here, a matter of choice, which is literalised by the two much-commented upon shots in which the image 'splits', the right-hand camera panning right and then back, while the left remains immobile.[6] To distinguish between the images we need to choose one of them, to close one eye so that we can see clearly, which also means that we can only see half of what there is to see. Throughout this book, I have indicated ways in which different strategic choices in dealing with disorientating phenomena can have incompatible or inconsistent results; *Adieu au langage* dramatises this with particular starkness.

One could, of course, accuse Godard of wanting to have his cake and eat it, of putting forward particular arguments but always retaining the possibility of retreating behind the defence that the argument was only presented, rather than actually being argued by the film. But – to stretch the metaphor to breaking point – it all depends on what kind of cake one takes Godard to be baking. Are we correct to see Godard himself as making arguments via his film, or are arguments themselves part of the material with which he works?[7] To put it another way, is the goal to persuade via argument, or is it to offer a range of arguments for assessment? Or perhaps these are not the only options – the texture of an argument may be what Godard is most keen to produce, or the feeling of being subject to an attempt to persuade, to name only two possibilities. This issue has long been pertinent to the interpretation of Godard's films. One might consider the discussion between Nana (Anna Karina) and Brice Parain (playing himself) towards the end of Godard's *Vivre sa vie* (1962). Though it is certainly plausible to see the film as endorsing the positions put forward in their discussion about thought, love and maturity, it is just as important that – contrary to what might be expected from an encounter between a young woman and an aging male philosopher – their discussion neither represents experience educating inexperience nor youthful freshness revitalising jaded age. Instead, as is indicated by the fact that the scene is shot in as close as the film gets to traditional shot/reverse shot, their exchange represents an encounter between equals, both of whom – for all their differences – seem equally vital and equally thoughtful.[8] Argument can be a component of Godard's cinema in a multitude of ways; making a firm decision as to whether the films themselves agree with their own arguments is not always a necessary or even a helpful thing to do.

DISTINCTION AND DIVISION

Whatever role argument has in *Adieu au langage*, however, in order to engage with it properly it is necessary to take heed of the distinctions that a given argument puts into play. Distinction, as well as division, are crucial to my understanding of the operation of immersion (and its disruption) in *Adieu au langage*. What distinctions are relevant? What parts can we distinguish in relation to which whole? Distinction is necessary for orientation (if we cannot distinguish one thing from another we have no hope of finding our way), and division is necessary to understand how a film, or anything else, fits together (if we cannot separate parts from wholes we can have no sense of how something is articulated). But, while closely related, these two concepts are themselves distinct: it is possible for two things to be distinguishable without their being divided from one another, and it is also possible for two indistinguishable things to be divided (like the two faces of Geoff's coin in *Only Angels Have Wings*). Hence the film's emphasis on pairs, which are themselves frequently paired (the two couples; the twin stereo channels of images and sounds;[9] there is also reference at two points in the film to 'two questions'), but also its frequent investigations into continuity (as in the historical examples referred to above, or the images of water, or references to certain mathematical ideas, in particular to the Riemann function, which is centrally concerned with the relationship between continuity and singularity). But how is the film's world related to – distinguished from, or divided from – our own world? Or is there no such division?

According to Rancière, a certain transformation occurred in this regard with the advent of Romanticism:

> It is not the case, as is sometimes said, that it [Romanticism] consecrated the 'autotelism' of language, separated from reality. It is the exact opposite. The Romantic Age actually plunged language into the materiality of the traits by which the historical and social world becomes visible to itself, be it in the form of the silent language of things or the coded language of images. (Rancière 2013: 32)

One might want to call Godard, in this sense, a Romantic filmmaker, or at least an heir to this aspect of Romanticism. But it is also an aspect that he interrogates, and in *Adieu au langage* he does this prominently through the image of the forest. We see a number of woods and forests, with the dog Roxy – a central character, on whom more later – wandering through them, and there are various references to forests. Both Gédéon (Kamel Abdeli) and Marcus (Richard Chevallier) declare that the Apache (Gédéon is more specific and refers to the Chikawa tribe) call the world 'the forest'. One shot resembles Courbet's painting 'L'Origine du monde', linking notions of worlds to 'forest' as slang for pubic hair.[10] There is also reference to the notion that showing a forest is easy, but showing a room with a forest nearby is difficult; these words are spoken over an image showing just that, as if to question the literalness of the statement.[11] We are not dealing here merely with a question of artistic operation per se but of its relation to the widest questions of history and society. How does narration (or fiction) relate to history? Is history a fiction (as Jean Baudrillard at times came close to claiming) or are fictions empirical (as Rancière insists)? Godard's equivocal answer might be 'yes and no' to both options. The forest can be used in relation to both these possibilities, because it is ambiguous whether the idea operates more as an image of the world in microcosm (metonymy) or an image of the world as a whole (metaphor).

Narrative, Hidden in Plain Sight

It would, I think, be false to claim that *Adieu au langage* does not present us with narrative, in the sense of microcosm, but it can frequently seem as if the narrative is handled as *material*, in a similar way to the abundance of quotations and citations. Warner, who does argue that *Adieu au langage* is a kind of essay film, writes that:

> From the early 1960s ... [Godard's] uses of the terms 'essay' and 'essayist' have implied not a formulaic type so much as a reflective disposition that inspires his very approach to working with sights and sounds, an activity of thought that forgoes a rigid choice between two generic options: staging a drama and carrying out a concerted critical inquiry. (Warner 2016: 62)

Drama and 'concerted critical inquiry' are, then, not mutually exclusive; Godard's dramas can be critical and his criticism can be dramatic. Nevertheless, *Adieu au langage* seems to me clearly to occupy different generic territory from, say, *Histoire(s) du cinéma*. This is largely down to the different roles of narrative in the two works. The question is both how *Adieu au langage* is put together, how it is articulated, and what it enunciates, with what degree of clarity: how articulate it is. Godard avoids classical continuity editing yet the film could not make sense without it. The film often eschews the clarificatory resources of classical continuity editing, such as when Roxy 'adopts' Josette and Gédéon at a petrol station – a simple cutaway to the dog in the car would have clarified this scene enormously. Yet we do need to use the expectations that classical continuity has created in us to make narrative sense of otherwise disjunctive montage. Take, as a simple example, the shots of Roxy indoors: since we are not explicitly shown that the house is that of the couple(s), we have to remind ourselves to consider that it might be so (even though nothing we see exactly suggests that it isn't).

One particularly surprising aspect of *Adieu au langage* is how straightforward some aspects of the organisation of the film come to seem, once one has grasped its principle. The moment-to-moment movement remains complex and unpredictable, but the middle ground divisions are in fact very simple. This can be seen in the structural parallels present in the main body of the film, the second appearances of '1: la nature' (which begins at about 15' 40") and '2: la métaphor' (starting circa 34' 35"). These sequences are dominated by conversations between unseen couples overheard while we look out of the windscreen of a car, exchanges in a house between – usually naked – couples, and passages involving Roxy. As has been mentioned, there are two couples in the film: in '1: la nature', Josette and Gédéon, and in '2: la métaphor', Ivitch (Zoé Bruneau) and Marcus. They are deliberately cast to look similar; rather than facilitating orientation, similarity here generates confusion. Clear views of the actors' faces are avoided during the early parts of the sequences under discussion, generating still further confusion. But though they do look similar, they are in fact clearly distinguishable, and on repeat viewing we can see that only one of the couples appears during their respective sections: the diegetic threads never tangle (at least not in this sense). Not only this, but they parallel each other remarkably straightforwardly.

In the '1: la nature' sequence beginning around 15' 40", the broad sequence is, in its barest outline, as follows. There is a conversation in a car. The couple (Josette and Gédéon) are naked in the house, and there is a discussion about shit and equality while the man sits on the toilet and defecates. Roxy is on a forest path. The ferry arrives again; we hear, off-screen, an explosion, screeching car brakes, and gunshots; the red-headed Marie can't hear (because of the explosion, presumably), says 'he says he's dying: then let him die', and reaches down: her hand comes up red; the Mercedes leaves the square which is familiar from the initial bookselling scene.[12] There is an extended sequence featuring Roxy, who then adopts the couple at a petrol station by getting in their car and refusing to leave. There is more material of the couple at home in front of the television, including an HD 'well-composed' and balanced shot of the two of them. More dialogue in the car follows. Roxy gets out for a walk. The couple leave Roxy by the lake while they go to watch *Frankenstein*. A helicopter lands, there is an explosion and Roxy appears to be blown up. The sequence after this, the '2: la métaphor' sequence starting at 34′ 36″, begins with a reiteration of an image of Ivitch behind the metal fence and the off-screen declaration 'Je suis à vos ordre' ('I am at your command' – literally 'order') with which the preceding 'métaphor' section concluded. There is a conversation in a car, then a brief appearance by Roxy. The couple (Ivitch and Marcus) are then naked in the house, and there is a discussion about shit while the man sits on the toilet and defecates. The ferry arrives again, the passengers disembark. A cafe. The booksale: there is a shot; we see water made red by blood and a man lolling in it. Then a sequence featuring Roxy (the water speaks to her) and another conversation in the car. The couple then appear at home once again, in front of the television, and there is a second HD 'well-composed' shot. They discuss having children but decide on a dog instead. There is a crane shot of a car park near a dock during which we can see the shadow of the crane (perhaps a reference to the opening of *Le Mépris*). Roxy comes into the house wet and whining. We see the couple at home yet again; at one point we hear a dog bark off-screen. There is another shot from the inside of a car, then it's back to the site of the booksale. Next we see a motorway at night; the couple discuss being on time or being first and there is mention of Riemann ('another German!'). Roxy is seen in the snow, beside a lake at sunrise or sunset, and then her head is seen from above while we hear 'One can imagine that Frankenstein was born here'. There is, again, a helicopter and an explosion (though a dog is harder to see – perhaps a paw is visible). Mary Shelley, Percy Bysshe Shelley and Byron appear; Mary is working on *Frankenstein*. The three sail off in a boat. Though difficult to follow from a verbal description, just as it is when watching the film, Table 8.1 will help to show how close the parallel sequences are, perhaps making 'je suis à vos ordre' into another pun.

Events that occur in both sequences follow, almost exactly, the same order. (The second sequence is longer and contains a longish section that is not paralleled in the first sequence.) The parallel narratives are not merely similar stories but similarly *structured* stories: the *syuzhets*, not just the *fabulas*, are similar. It *is* possible to perceive a fairly consistent diegesis, or at least to be clear on what it is that would need to be supplied in order to clarify things. After discovering the surprising simplicity of the structural parallels, another of the film's surprises is quite how cogent the narrative (or narratives) in the film turn out to be, despite their extensive lacunae. Thus, as I claimed at the beginning of this chapter, we do need to at least *look* for solutions to certain narrative problems, even if, in the final analysis, it is the search itself rather than its outcome which is of greatest importance.

Table 8.1 Adieu au langage

1: la nature (15' 38" – 34' 35")	2: la métaphor (34' 36" – 1 hr 2' 07")
	Ivitch behind the fence
car conversation	car conversation
naked in the house – toilet conversation	brief view of Roxy
brief view of Roxy	naked in the house – toilet conversation
ferry arrives – there is violence	ferry arrives – there is violence
extended Roxy sequence	extended Roxy sequence
car again – Roxy adopts the couple	car again
at home with TV – 'well-balanced' shot	at home with TV – 'well-balanced' shot
	discussion of children – decide on dog instead
	medium-length Roxy sequence
	couple at home
	car again
	the booksale again
	motorway
car – Roxy gets out	
they announce going to see *Frankenstein*	Roxy – discussion of *Frankenstein*
helicopter blows up Roxy	helicopter blows up Roxy (?)
	Mary and Percy Shelley with Byron

Which narrative problems, then, raise themselves urgently? Particularly thorny is the issue of the knife. We see a bloody bath in both strands, and a knife in '2: la métaphor'. Josette tells Gédéon, 'four years ago, you stabbed me; you've forgotten'.[13] Are the two couples representations of the same couple? All we would need to do to allow for this possibility is to locate '2: la métaphor' earlier than '1: la nature'. In this reading, the woman ('Ivitch' at this point) is threatened by her German husband. A man ('Marcus') offers to help her ('Je suis à vos ordre'). They begin an affair, but they have an argument (we see a fight in a shower) and he stabs her. Four years later (the opening of '1: la nature') the husband appears again, somebody is shot (neither 'Marcus' nor 'Gédéon'), and the man (now 'Gédéon') offers to help her, and they recommence their affair. I have no wish strongly to defend this reading; my point is merely that the film is coherent enough to allow it to be a possibility; an underdetermined possibility, perhaps, but one that rests on more than mere speculation. What is perhaps most surprising about taking the diegesis of *Adieu au langage* seriously is the fact that we can distinguish between *fabula* and *syuzhet* at all, even if we are left with some seemingly unanswerable enigmas. We might say that we can distinguish between *fabula* and *syuzhet* but not divide them.

TALKING DOG: THE QUESTION OF ROXY

It might be useful here to recall James Elkins's claim, quoted in Chapter 5, that '[a]n interpretation of a picture that stresses its "visual language," its linguistic structure, or its semiotic system, is not a reading made from somewhere "within" language and "outside" pictures, but simply an interpretation that lists only some of the qualities of the image' (Elkins 1998: 161). We can still see outside the water when we are immersed in it; distorted vision is still vision. Despite the long-standing conviction that 'for Godard language is pre-eminently the place of lies and the visual pre-eminently the place of truth' (Jameson 1992: 170), this pre-eminence has been the source of problems rather than a source of clarity, hence Godard's fascination with and reliance on language, and the difficulty of his oft-mentioned search for a 'just image' that is not 'just an image' ('une image juste / juste une image' in *Le Vent d'Est* (1970), recalled in *Notre Musique* (2004)). By immersing us in its complex and frequently disorientating images and sounds, all presented – like its narrative – in doubled forms that diverge almost as often as they cohere, *Adieu au langage* indicates that all acts of judgement have to take place from within some medium, somehow in the midst of things, rather than from without, from a securely distanced vantage point. Our orientation cannot rely on a secure perspective, because our view is always distorted by the medium itself. The indeterminacy that results does not simply undermine coherence or orientation, however; it is also – like language, and indeed like consciousness itself – a condition of possibility for orientation itself. *Adieu au langage* both exploits and allegorises this fact. Throughout the film we may suddenly pass at any moment into utterly different territory; the film's editing shows that a second, or even a microsecond, is, to quote one of the sources Godard draws on in the film, 'a thick thing – thick enough to separate two worlds, large enough to hold two worlds' (Simak 1988). But, however obscurely, these worlds are also shown to be articulated, or to hold out the possibility of articulation. This is the case even if this articulation confuses us, or (to put it in the language of Chapter 5) if we cannot easily parse the ways that the film's articulation is aligned with its signification, which is to say that we cannot easily give an account of its figuration. Recognising what it is that we would have to interrogate in order to do so is, however, simple enough: namely, those subjects, themes and images I have concentrated on in this chapter (argument, history, narrative, humanity and non-humanity, depth and fluidity).

Adieu au langage might, perhaps, be seen to demonstrate that in getting our bearings we may discover that we were not lost in the way we thought we were. The parallels in the two *syuzhets* – the stories of the two couples – are not only almost impossible to perceive without deliberate analysis (whereas one might have assumed that structural repetition always assists perceptual clarity), but the very parallels themselves, in asserting similarity, can serve to conceal difference. Local orientation can just as easily obstruct as clarify the passage to a more global orientation. But as well as seeing another instance of the dialectic whereby clarity can also serve to confuse, we might conclude from this that the source of our perplexity did not lie where we thought it did. Perhaps we were wrong about *where* we were lost. It is less the lack of diegesis in *Adieu au langage* that makes it hard to get our bearings than the very strength and abundance of diegetic cues that nevertheless – as in *INLAND EMPIRE* – resist being composed into a coherent whole, whether during viewing (largely due to the abundance of material we are asked to absorb), or during subsequent analysis and interpretation. We are forced to accept that we are often unable to gain enough distance to see the film *as a whole*; I have argued that this is a consequence of the particular sense of immersion that the film generates in the viewer.

But what of Roxy? How does she contribute to this film's 'particular sense of immersion'? The images of her death by helicopter recall the final images of Chris Marker's account of the New Left in the 1960s and 70s, *Le Fond de l'air est rouge* (*A Grin Without a Cat*; 1977, re-edited in 1993), which show wolves being culled from a helicopter, images that are juxtaposed with an international arms fair. The final words of the film's voice-over are 'some wolves still survive' ('il y'avait toujours des loups'). These same images are also deployed in chapter 4A of Godard's *Histoire(s) du cinéma*. Does Roxy, then, represent a kind of political defiance? It is difficult to tell, but *Adieu au langage* could at the very least be seen as an attempt to explore the internal life of the dog/wolf, rather than using her merely as an allegorical/political cipher, almost as a riposte to what Osip Brik wrote about the deer in Vertov's *A Sixth Part of the World*:

> Instead of a real deer, we get a deer as a symbolic sign with a vague conventional meaning. But since these deer were filmed without any thought about their possible use as conventional signs, their real nature as deer has resisted this turning them into symbols, and as a result we get neither a deer nor a sign, but a blank space. (*Lines of Resistance: Dziga Vertov and the Twenties* (Pordenone: Le Giornate del Cinema Muto (2004)), p. 227, quoted in Rancière 2014: 238)

At one point in *Adieu au langage* a voice-over tells us that the water spoke to Roxy, in a passage derived from Clifford D. Simak's 1951 time-travel novel *Time and Again*. The manner in which this is integrated into the film is, I want to argue, an example of a diegetic (rather than merely juxtapositional or collage) procedure. It has a climactic effect not only rhythmically (based on its location within the film) but also both thematically (Roxy and the water have earlier been juxtaposed but here they communicate) and diegetically. It is also allegorical: the non-human world ('goodbye to language'!) speaks. The situation could be post-apocalyptic (as in Simak's novel) but it also seems to refer to that which exists in parallel to humanity, but to which we can never have access because we have language. To represent this extra-linguistic world by means of and in terms of language is neither an absurdity nor an evasion: it is, rather, to refuse the all-too-easy gesture of claiming that cinema, simply by using means other than language (image and sound), can get *beyond* language.

The final section of the film, in which the couples are not seen, might seem to challenge my argument about the importance of the film's narrative. But does it not in fact emphasise the importance of Roxy as a diegetic centre, and not merely a symbolic centre? In a kind of *détournement* of Noël Burch's ideas about the primacy of diegesis (see Burch 1982)[14] rather than diegesis coming before narrative, a certain diegesis (i.e. Roxy's) is arrived at on the 'other side' of narrative. This might, in retrospect, be seen to be signalled right at the film's outset. The first appearance of the number 1 and the words 'la nature' seem to announce the commencement of the first section of the film proper. They are preceded by the image of the animal that, we learn later, is not merely 'a dog', but rather Roxy. If we were less certain that we knew how a Godard film was likely to operate, might we take the image of Roxy as the commencement of the diegesis? At 1hr 2′ 08″, another title appears, which moves from 'mémoire historique' to 'malheur historique'. It might be labelled as section 3, were it not that it in fact says '3D'. Its texture recalls the opening montage, featuring a sequence focused on the act of painting, what seem to be knights templar, arrivals at a train station and a bus stop, and so forth. Roxy is seen relaxing on a sofa and being ordered out of the house ('Roxy, tu sors!'). Roxy is then seen again on a sofa. Marcus and Ivitch, having clearly decided on a dog for now rather than children, discuss him off-screen: 'he seems depressed' – 'no, not at all, he's dreaming of the Marquesas Islands' – 'like in the Jack London novel' – 'exactly'.[15] (I disagree with Warner here, who seems to think that these voices belong to, or are at least somehow associated with, those of Godard and Anne-Marie Miéville (see Warner 2016: 75).) Nico Baumbach has argued, with respect to this sequence, that:

> Roxy suggests the possibility not of 'non-thought' but of another form of thinking uncontaminated by the symbolic or technological order – whether words or the distinction between being nude or clothed. Solitary like her caretakers, she is also a figure for freedom, not in the sense of the romantic masculine rejection of the law that might have attracted the younger Godard, but one that comes from fidelity. (Baumbach 2014: 41)

One of the characters in Simak's 1952 novel *City* (also cited in *Adieu au langage*) speaks of dogs having '[a] *different* mind than the human mind, but one that works with the human mind' (Simak 1988: 69). Fidelity is, of course, that which dogs most commonly stand for.[16] The passage from *City*, however, might give the symbolic function of canine fidelity in the film a melancholic turn, for there 'humanity' is only achieved by the race of dogs after human beings have suffered a final apocalyptic end. The end of Godard's film, like its beginning, juxtaposes beginnings and endings, but now the endings are either fantasies that were never fulfilled, or memories. In the '2: la métaphor' mirror scene Marcus proposes having children to Ivitch. Not yet, she says, and suggests a dog instead. We then see a young boy and girl running across a field. They seem at one and the same time to represent the couple as children ('imagine that you're still a little boy', Ivitch tells Marcus) and the children that they will never have, if it is Ivitch that shoots and Marcus that is shot (she is, after all, told to leave because the police are coming). We should not forget when we see the film's final images of Roxy that we have twice seen her blown up by a helicopter (shades, perhaps, of the way that Tarkovsky's *Ivan's Childhood* (1962) ends with images of Ivan, even though we have just learned of his execution by the Nazis).

I find that I disagree with Warner somewhat about Roxy's significance. Or, rather, I feel myself inclined to put the emphasis on one side of the equation whereas he emphasises the other. A voice-over at one point claims, explicitly citing Rilke, that we can only know what is outside through an animal's gaze. Warner argues that 'the film figures Roxy's gaze as an opaque medium that lets us indirectly and partially take 'what is outside' into account' (Warner 2016: 73). I think this is more or less right, but elsewhere Warner goes a little too far, such as when he writes that Roxy's powers of love and vision are designated by the film 'as falling beyond our reach – as belonging to a realm of sensation to which humans, as verbocentric and egocentric beings, have no direct access' (*ibid.*). The film certainly emphasises that there is a non-linguistic realm and a non-human realm, but it is not quite right to say that they fall 'beyond our reach'; we cannot occupy them, but we *can* have some kind of access (just not *direct* access). Roxy's gaze may be 'opaque', but it is an 'opaque *medium*'. This lets us take heed of the irony that it is with human vision that we see through Roxy's eyes, and through language that Rilke speaks of what is 'outside'.

The way this is conveyed has to do with performance. The humans in the film perform rather stiffly, at times in an almost Bressonian fashion. Roxy, who really does belong to Godard and Miéville, is in a sense not performing at all, and yet, because everything we see of her is mediated and selected, everything about her appearance becomes a performance.[17] But it is not easy to see how we could have reached this sensation without passing via narrative enacted by means of human performances. Thus the narrative in *Adieu au langage* could itself be considered a kind of signpost, a means of orientation towards something not in itself fundamentally about narrative. The discovery of a (relatively) coherent narrative, initially buried, changes our sense of the appropriate attention with which to watch the film, and thus opens the way to consider Roxy diegetically, initially in the standard sense (the dog is a character) and subsequently in an expanded sense that gets to the heart of the film's thematic concerns. If diegesis has to do with a character's world, what is the world of a dog and to what extent do we have access to it?

Warner has very helpfully tracked down the source of the sounds of dog and baby that conclude the film, a YouTube video entitled 'Husky Sings with Baby'. Watching the whole video, there really does appear to be echoing of rhythmic and pitched material between the two, but on the part of the *dog* rather than the baby. Ronald Bogue connects this moment to one of the songs we hear after the excerpt from 'Husky Sings with Baby', the popular French folk song 'Marlbrough s'en va-t-en guerre' ('Marlbrough Has Left for the War'):

> We are reminded of the two divergent destinies that await baby humans and canines: that of the infant, who will soon sing nursery songs of war with no foreseeable end, and that of the dog, who will live among humans, but will be able to run back and forth through the forest, which is what the Apaches called 'the world'. (Bogue 2017: 287)

Therefore I am not wholly convinced that *Adieu au langage*, at its conclusion, 'gestures towards a threshold beyond its current reach, toward the dawn of a new perceptiveness, the birth into the world of a language keyed to the potentialities that Roxy incarnates' (Warner 2016: 76–7). This seems to me at once too pessimistic ('Husky Sings with Baby' is, after all, a recording of something that really did happen in our world, not a construction of a utopian future) and too optimistic (the baby will, in the future, enter into language fully, while the dog never will). Given that the film begins with endings it makes sense to consider it as ending with new beginnings, but the final image is actually of a return: of Roxy rushing towards the camera, running towards the cameraman, who is in fact Godard himself. We are immersed in language and in consciousness; the film clearly presents this as a limited, and potentially tragic, situation, but not only this. Given that the film juxtaposes or conflates beginnings and endings, it is certainly also important that 'adieu', 'as Godard has stressed, means not only goodbye but is, in certain Swiss cantons, also a welcoming greeting' (Baumbach 2014: 41). Some critics, forgetting or in ignorance of this fact, have been too ready to see the film as primarily some kind of elegy, putatively for language but maybe also for cinema. Perhaps, however, this film also signifies Godard's *welcoming* of language, of the 'confusion' between the linguistic and non-linguistic that is human life. Just as much as it gestures towards that which will forever lie beyond the grasp of language, the film indicates its grasp of the fact that language is not merely 'the place of lies'; we should be suspicious of the orientation that language affords us, but not so suspicious that we try simply to reject it. The mediated access that language gives to what lies beyond it may indeed be inescapably mediated – we cannot escape our immersion – but it *is* access, nonetheless, and the fact that this access is often corrupted does not mean that it should not also be treasured.

Conclusion: Method-Free Orientation

Over the course of the discipline's still relatively short history, film studies has proposed a range of orientational strategies, including attending to: a film's authorship and the intentions behind it (perhaps assisted by information about its production history); patterns of comprehension based in universal or at least quasi-universal features of human cognition; the details of the particular means – often conceptualised as quasi-linguistic – by which films signify or produce meaning; the ways historical conditions find expression in particular films; genres and the webs of shared, public expectations they form, and how these webs shape and guide viewers' orientational presuppositions; the gender or sexual politics represented in a film, or implied by its means of representation; ideological phenomena, often expressed in unconscious contradictions between material conditions of production and explicitly stated content or intentions; or unconscious processes more generally, whether at work in a film's producers or its spectators. All these methods, and others besides, have made great contributions to our understanding of films. But they all have also, at one time or another, been proposed as secure methods of achieving true understanding of films or, to put it in the language of this book, of reliably keeping disorientation to a minimum.

It is my contention that, with regard to the aesthetic judgement of films – which is by no means detached from questions of authorship, cognition, signification, history, ideology and so forth, but is nevertheless not synonymous with them – the best orientational method is the absence of method. By this I do not mean that aesthetic criticism should not be methodical but that it should aim to avoid *general* methods, that the critic should be prepared to attend to the individual film and tailor their method to the demands of that film rather than arriving armed with a predetermined way of forcing the film to give up its secrets.[1] The most interesting forms of confusion and disorientation might then be seen not as calling for methodological rectification but as methodological resources in themselves. My method, for example, of working through a series of different strategies for reading *INLAND EMPIRE* by looking for what each strategy omits was prompted by the specific ways the film disorientated me. This strategy, I hope, both told us something about this film and clarified our understanding of the relationship between coherence and completeness in critical accounts of films more generally. A similar pattern pertains to all the critical writing in this book. In the introduction to his collection *A House Made of Light*, George Toles states: 'When I go to the movies I eagerly accept the first condition of my presence there: I am the one in the dark' (Toles 2001: 13). His pun emphasises the fact that a certain amount of disorientation, of not knowing what will happen, or why, is common to our experience of all narrative films, at least at the outset. But not only this; Toles's remark also implicitly suggests that we should not attempt to remedy this situation too eagerly. He goes on to remark that '[a]s a reader of film . . . it is never the task I set myself to *master* the narrative I am interpreting. It is more a matter of trusting the film to show me things – in its own terms, terms that I do not initially have at my disposal, living as they do within the form of the work itself' (*ibid.*: 18). A good critic, Toles implies, is open to being shown things by the film they are engaged with, and an excessive zeal for orientation risks closing down the possibility that the film might 'show [them] things' that they did not know before.

In this book I have tried to demonstrate that if there is not a 'right answer' as to how to respond to disorientation, neither are the choices we make in so doing indifferently arbitrary. The various ways that a film guides or applies pressure to our responses – or, indeed, refuses to do so – will shape these choices. My proposed definition of figuration ('signification significantly aligned with articulation') is intended to help us explore the process of attending and responding to these pressures in full acknowledgement of this process's individual, evaluative dimensions while also remaining closely attentive to detail. The itinerary, enquiry or quest offers itself as a model, as long as one keeps in mind that that this does not entail linear and clearly defined progress towards an unchanging goal. As Toles says, being lost is a 'renewable condition' (*ibid.*: 330), which implies that one can always get lost again, but also that any given experience of confusion or disorientation may turn out to be only temporary (otherwise the condition would not have to be renewed). Just as the acceptance of disorientation does not entail the celebration of disorientation for its own sake, the absence of a general method for the reduction of disorientation does not entail critical anarchy. I am suggesting that one's critical methodology must be formed anew with each film, not that there must be no methodology. But it would misrepresent the phenomenon of disorientation to attempt to construct a fool-proof method for fending it off in all circumstances; such a method would always itself be vulnerable to disorientation. The geographer Marcella Schmidt di Friedberg echoes my feelings when she writes at the end of her *Geographies of Disorientation*, a very wide-ranging survey of sources and implications of disorientation, that:

> A multi-layered phenomenon such as disorientation requires a kaleidoscopic perspective in that it cannot be easily captured using an axiomatic approach that would reduce it to a certain number of basic concepts and by following a sequence of logical steps, lead to a convincing conclusion. Indeed, it may be that the very nature of my research object has prevented me from developing a theory of disorientation. (Schmidt di Friedberg 2018: 219–20)

Nevertheless, the ways of thinking about metalepsis and figuration that I have defended do have methodological implications for the appropriate application of these concepts. I argued, for example, that examining metalepsis can serve as a tool for critically addressing some intriguing confusions, in Baumgarten's sense, of ontological and rhetorical matters, phenomena that are not always sufficiently understood simply by designating particular metalepses as either rhetorical or ontological. I also argued that fully accounting for the way many films disorientate us cannot be achieved without paying attention to both their narrative and figurative dimensions and to the relationships between them. Different films disorientate us in different ways, and rather than creating a taxonomy of different kinds of disorientation I have tried to show the productiveness of staying as attentive as possible to the specificity of our experience. For example, *Adieu au langage* can be described as a film that produces disorientation largely via what Brenez calls Godard's characteristic strategies of figurality by overload. We might respond to this by saying that the most appropriate critical response is a kind of surrender of the struggle to master, to comprehend, the film, that we should submerge ourselves in the film's whirl of detail and reject its gestures towards narrative as obvious traps for the credulous, as red herrings. If we did so, however, we would miss the original use the film makes of diegesis as part of its investigation of the relationship between the human and non-human worlds, between language and what is outside of language, and the fact that it is only by passing *through* the distinctive disorientation that the film's blend of essay and narrative provokes that we can come to this realisation. The more accurately we perceive our disorientation, the more we pay attention to it and follow where it leads, the greater our eventual understanding of the film in question is likely to be. Overall, *The Cinema of Disorientation* hopes to have demonstrated that responding appropriately to disorientation means not prejudging which methods will be appropriate for a given film, but instead allowing the film to guide the critic.

This approach to method echoes others. In the context of an exploration of the 'fragile and equivocal middle' on display in Kant's aesthetics between the facts that (a) one cannot persuade another person of something's beauty by argument alone and that (b) claims of beauty are not merely reports of subjective experience (which is to say that a claim about beauty is 'not really a claim about an object, but not really a claim about a subject either'), Simon Jarvis has argued that 'it is precisely *method* – wherever that means a procedure invariantly applied to differing objects – which would delete just the equivocality that has here been argued to be constitutive of the field of criticism. Method, that fear of error hardened into an imaginary guarantee against making mistakes, is in this case the error itself' (Jarvis 2002: 5 and 16). Similarly, with specific reference to film, Stanley Cavell remarks in his book on Hollywood comedies of remarriage that 'the way to overcome theory correctly, philosophically, is to let the object or the work of your interest teach you how to consider it' (Cavell 1981: 10). This sound advice is ignored sufficiently often for it to be worth restating and defending. It applies, of course, to film criticism in general but very disorienting films raise the stakes with a particular urgency; ignoring it means running a serious risk of critical irrelevance.

I want, finally, to offer a few remarks about beginnings and endings by returning to the film with which I also concluded this book's Prospectus. Toles has noted that to be on a quest does not, rather surprisingly, require that one be clear about one's goal (see Toles 2001: 330). *The Searchers* is very clearly a quest narrative, but its motivating factors are in many ways profoundly opaque. David Bordwell is not wrong to claim that 'goal-oriented characters' are crucial to many narratives, nor that comprehension of their goals is in itself a primary goal of the spectator: 'narrative comprehension and recall are centrally guided by the goal of creating a meaningful story out of the material presented' (Bordwell 1985: 157 and 34). We would be wrong, however, to conclude that the more explicitly the characters' goals are presented, the less confused either their situation, or ours as spectators, must necessarily be. In saying this we have returned full circle to where we began in the Introduction, with the notion that being lost can admit of degrees but that it does not exhibit a simple structure whereby the closer one gets to one's goal, the less lost one is. The critic may think themselves about to unlock the secrets of a film only for a new observation to throw their interpretation into crisis. At the end of John Ford's film, Ethan Edwards brings Debbie home after her long captivity with the Comanche. Of course, this was not his goal. Ethan's goal was to find her, yes, but then to kill her; for Ethan, to have been a Comanche's wife is worse than being dead.[2] But, of course, Ethan does not kill her. A number of critics have written about the way that *The Searchers* shows how our goals are not transparent to ourselves; George M. Wilson, for example, discusses the way that certain events of the film eventually reveal to Ethan 'what his search and his hatred have been about' (Wilson 1986: 48),

Figure C.1 *Confusion rectified?*

while Robert Pippin goes further and argues that '[w]hat we and he discover is that he did not know his own mind, that he avowed principles that were partly confabulations and fantasy' (Pippin 2010: 131).

But where does that leave us, the viewers, at the end of the film? At the very beginning – as the camera follows Martha out of the house to see Ethan arriving in the distance – we don't know what she knows but we do, for a moment, fully share her point of view. Confusion appears straightaway, however, linked both to the passage of time (Ethan lifts up little Debbie, mistaking her for her elder sister Lucy) and to the policing of racial boundaries (Ethan says to Martin that a 'fellow could mistake you for a half-breed', to which Martin replies that no, he's one eighth Cherokee, the irony being that this means that, for Ethan, it would be no mistake at all to take him for a 'half-breed'). These two confusions are recalled when Ethan finally catches up with Debbie and, famously, once again lifts her up in the air; this time he *does* recognise her, and he does not mistake her for a half-breed either, despite her appearance. Clarity seems to have been achieved. Ethan has either abandoned his original goal or perhaps, as mentioned above, has discovered that he was mistaken as to what his goal actually was. This resolution of confusion turns out to require a spatial division. Ethan's position with regard to the family has been ambiguous throughout the film (because of his love for Martha and the intensity of his racial hatred), but it has now become clear: he has become an excess preventing the whole from being whole and there is nothing for him to do but ride off into the distance.

Both Ethan and the others know their place (as Lieutenant Greenhill tells the Reverend Captain upon being told to tell his father 'where he's at': 'But he knows that, sir!'), even though what they know most importantly about these places is that they can no longer coincide. We the viewers, however, do *not* know where we're at, but remain awkwardly suspended, at least partially sympathetic to two parties who can never be properly brought together. Douglas Pye connects the difficult question of viewer sympathy to the film's more general treatment of race, and suggests that we are 'suspended' throughout: '*The Searchers* allows no comfortable identification with or disengagement

Figure C.2 *Ethan is shut out but the viewer is not shut in.*

from its hero (who is both monstrous *and* John Wayne) or easy detachment from other expressions by White characters of racial fear or hatred' (Pye 1996: 229). At the film's conclusion we are neither comfortably aligned with the family (of whom we see nothing once they cross the threshold) nor with Ethan, and the film's figuration, in trapping us on the threshold, expresses this; we feel Ethan's expulsion without also feeling ourselves part of the community that he has been expelled from. As the door closes on Ethan's retreating figure it does not enclose the viewer in the warmth of the family home but leaves only darkness. We do not know where we are, and so we leave the film as we entered it: disorientated. This is entirely appropriate given the complexity of what we have witnessed and must prepare to digest. In this and in many other instances, disorientation and confusion are not defects to be remedied; they are crucial to both *how* and *what* films mean.

Appendix

Colossal Youth: *Scene Breakdown*

1. *An unpeopled courtyard in Fontainhas, Lisbon, by night. Furniture is being thrown from a first floor window.* (**furniture** *[1]*; **falling** *[1]*) *A 'portrait' of Clothilde, wielding a knife.* (**knives** *[1]*) *Clothilde describes swimming, untroubled by sharks and how she watches, from the sea, her son crying on the beach, while other people watch her from the shore. She withdraws.* (**departure** *[1]*)
2. *Ventura arrives at his daughter Bete's door. She tells him he has the wrong door and the wrong daughter but he denies this. 'Your mother has left me,' Ventura says, 'I've been having this nightmare for more than thirty years.'* (**departure** *[2]*; **dream** *[1]*)
3. *Scene:* **waiting for Gustavo** *[1]*. *Ventura picks up his son (Gustavo) from a construction site we only hear but do not see.* (**work** *[1]*; **waiting** *[1]*)
4. *Ventura and Gustavo eat together. 'Not hungry?' Gustavo asks. 'No,' says Ventura.* (**appetite** *[1]*) *Ventura tells Gustavo that Clotilde has gone. 'She stabbed me with a knife . . . She had Clothilde's face, but it wasn't her . . . I don't know if it was her or another woman I slept with.'* (**departure** *[3]*; **knives** *[2]*; **dream** *[2]*; **confusion of identity** *[1]*)
5. **Outside the new apartments** *[1]*. *Ventura calls to Vanda, who appears, but only as a voice.*
6. **In Vanda's room** *[1]*. *Ventura and Vanda watch TV. Medium close framing, more darkness than light. Vanda wants, among other things — including the unemployment benefit she isn't getting — her daughter to be with her, but she isn't.* (**work** *[2]*) *Vanda's mother is dead (hence she is not Clothilde, we assume).* (**doing nothing** *[1]* [*importantly distinct from 'waiting'*])
7. **The shack** *[1]*. *Lento and Ventura play cards. Lento asks for a letter to send his wife and Ventura instantly begins reciting one.* (**the letter** *[1]*) *Ventura asks Lento to write it down, but 'there are no pens in the shack'.*
8. **Outside Bete's house** *[1]*. *Ventura waits outside what we will only later discover is Bete's house. He says 'I brought chicken,' but is not let in. Eventually he leaves.* (**waiting** *[2]*)
9. **Outside the new apartments** *[2]*. *Ventura meets André Semedo, housing officer and former locksmith.* (**locks** *[1]*) *They exchange details of their origins in Cape*

Verde. (***departure*** *[3]*) *Semedo points to the flat he will show Ventura: 'It's full of light.'*

10. **Apartment number one**. *Semedo: 'Temple, shack, household god.' Semedo wipes the wall where Ventura has touched it.* (***wiping*** *[1]*) *The apartment is unfurnished.* (***furniture*** *[2]*) *Ventura descends the stairs.*

11. **In Vanda's room** *[2]. Wider framing than before and the room now lit by a bright window covered with material. Vanda tells the story of how she gave birth.* (***hospitals*** *[1]*) *'I'm not fucking sick!' she told the medical staff.* (***health*** *[1]*) *She demanded food, was told she shouldn't eat, but also felt nauseous.* (***appetite*** *[2]*) *She threatened suicide. Ventura, about children: 'Raising them is hard work, but it's worth it.' Ventura calls Vanda Zita by mistake, quickly correcting himself.* (***work*** *[3]*; **confusion of identity** *[2]*) *Ventura stands in the hallway of Vanda's apartment.* (***waiting*** *[3]*)

12. **Waiting for Gustavo** *[2]. Ventura seems to look directly at the camera, but his eyes are deeply shadowed so it is hard to be sure. Construction noises off-screen and this time an argument as well.* (***waiting*** *[4]*; ***work*** *[4]*) *A cat crosses the frame.*

13. *Ventura and Gustavo eat together again. Gustavo is working even though it is a holiday.* (***work*** *[5]*) *Ventura asks after Gustavo's wife and daughter.*

14. **The shack** *[2]. Ventura recites the letter again.* (***the letter*** *[2]*) *Still life of a bright blank window, darkness inside the room, and richly hued glass bottles.*

15. **The Gulbenkian** *(inside). First we see only a painting. Then a different shot also shows Ventura. A guard whispers to him, Ventura moves off, and the guard wipes the floor where he was.* (***wiping*** *[2]*) *Portraits of both Ventura (who moves his head to look to his left, screen right) and, less tightly framed, the guard (who moves his head to look to his right, screen left). The guard escorts Ventura out, unlocking a door like a jailer.* (***locks*** *[2]*) *They ascend a staircase and birdsong can be heard.*

16. **The Gulbenkian** *(garden). Travelling shot moves from the tree canopy to Ventura who sits down on a bench. Ventura tells the story of how he came to Portugal from Cape Verde (19 August 1972), sitting next to a man on the plane who didn't eat.* (***departure*** *[4]*; ***appetite*** *[3]*) *He worked building the Gulbenkian. The museum attendant speaks about how his life working here is easier than it was in Cape Verde, although it causes trouble when someone like Ventura turns up.* (***work*** *[6]*) *Ventura was injured in a fall here.* (***falling*** *[2]*)

17. *Scene:* **the shack** *[3]. Ventura is bandaged. He isn't hungry.* (***appetite*** *[4]*) *He plays cards with Lento and keeps reciting the letter.* (***the letter*** *[3]*) *Ventura is now hungry.* (***appetite*** *[5]*) *Lento now has two pens, but no paper: he scribbles on a desk. Ventura brings in a bottle and then a record player. They listen to the Os Tubarões song 'Labranta braço'. Lento's scribbling makes the record player stick, so Ventura eventually stops him by gently putting his hand on top of Lento's.*

18. **In Vanda's room** *[3]. Very similar framing to 11. Vanda's very young daughter, Beatriz, is now present. Vanda's cough (familiar from* No Quarto da Vanda*)*

has returned. (**health** [2]) Vanda: 'Mama just wants to raise you. Then I can die.' (**departure** [5]) Ventura talks to Vanda about going to visit Bete. The two daughters appear not to know each other, but share things such as a love of shrimp. 'Dance, baby, dance!'

19. **Outside Bete's house** [2]. Jagged shadows. Ventura sings and is let in. Bete: 'You know you have a dead son?' She has heard people talk about Nhurro, 'but I doubt my brother is alive.' Ventura and Bete sit in silence; outside are the sounds of the evacuation and demolition of Fontainhas: moving furniture, tools. (**waiting** [6]; **furniture** [3]) Sneezing. Ventura stands outside the house.
20. **Nhurro's furniture shop**. (**furniture** [4]) Ventura asks, 'Are you clean, Nhurro?' 'I'm not the same Nhurro you left in that hole, in that shanty town.' (**confusion of identity** [3]) Nhurro recites a 'letter' to his mother, who says 'I'm expecting you.' (**waiting** [7]) She is awaiting relocation from Fontainhas; his father has returned to Cape Verde to die. (**depature** [6]) Nhurro's father can't read. How can Nhurro's father have returned to Cape Verde if he is Ventura's son? (**confusion of identity** [4])
21. **The shack** [4]. Ventura murmurs the letter to himself. (**the letter** [4]) Sound of gas. Another still life with bottles. Ventura's footsteps. Liquid in one of the bottles vibrates. (**waiting** [8])
22. Scene: **apartment number two**. We begin in the ground floor entranceway. André Semedo (a former locksmith) tells Ventura: 'We seem to be having trouble with the keys. How did you get in?' Ventura says the door was open. (**locks** [3]) This apartment looks identical to the last one, again unfurnished. (**furniture** [4]) Ventura points to the ceiling just as Semedo had pointed to the apartment in 9 and says 'It's full of spiders.' Semedo: 'How many children do you have?' Ventura: 'I don't know yet.' (**confusion of identity** [5]) Ventura has some trouble with the intercom, thinking it to be a doorbell. Ventura repeatedly opens a door that closes by itself. Framed so the vertical of the corner of the room is not true, so the door appears to be falling due to gravity. (**falling** [3])
23. Ventura sits surrounded by debris, stuffing papers into his pockets. He blows his nose.
24. **At Vanda and Gustavo's dining table** [1]. Vanda and Ventura. Vanda wants to take Beatriz to Fátima on pilgrimage. Ventura says he will come too and pay for the trip. (**departure** [7]) Vanda: 'The cripple wants to come too.' Gustavo arrives. Vanda: 'I've had enough of these couches.' She found a table but didn't bring it home, and when she returned it had gone. (**furniture** [5]; **departure** [8]) Vanda talks of white shapes that 'look like ghosts. My daughter sees them too.' Ventura tells again the story of how Clothilde ('or a woman just like her') destroyed his furniture and stabbed him. (**furniture** [6]; **knives** [3]) Vanda offers Ventura some fruit but he says he's full. She leaves and he accepts an apple. (**appetite** [6]) Ventura asks Gustavo 'You're married to Vanda?' (**confusion of identity** [6]) Pattern of 2–3 – different 2: Ventura/Vanda; Ventura/Vanda/Gustavo; Ventura/Gustavo.

25. **The shack** *[5]*. *Strong wind outside. Lento enters and Ventura continues reciting the letter.* (**the letter** *[5]*)
26. **Apartment number two** *[2]*. *Very dark image: all we can make out is a hand and a rectangle of light from a window. There is silence. Sound of a doorbell tells us we are in the new apartment. Ventura is lying on the floor and gets up to answer the door.* (**furniture** *[7]*) *(Can the preceding scene now be reinterpreted as a dream?) Paulo ('the cripple') has come calling, by coincidence. Paulo knocks on doors to beg, succeeding by being concerned about the health of the occupants.* (**health** *[3]*) *But his friend has tried to scam money by pretending that Paulo has died and needs funeral expenses, etc. So is Paolo, not Nhurro, the brother presumed to be dead that Bete spoke of?* (**confusion of identity** *[6]*) *Ventura: 'Your mother left me, Paolo.'* (**departure** *[9]*) *Paolo now sells toys outside schools.*
27. **The shack** *[6]*. *One brief shot.*
28. **In the park**. *Ventura buys food from a street vendor. Sits on a bench with Lento.*
29. **The shack** *[7]*. *A window is being boarded up.* (**work** *[7]*) *Lento and Ventura seen from outside the shack, framed in a window. Lento tells the story of the carnation revolution, which is happening, diegetically, at the same time as this narration, although from the perspective of the majority of the film this scene takes place in the past. Ventura: 'I went to confession. The priest asked me if I ever ate human flesh.'* (**appetite** *[7]*) *Ventura tries to get Lento to work on learning the letter, but Lento insists that it's futile because no letters will now reach Cape Verde.* (**the letter** *[6]*) *Lento is holding a machete.* (**knives** *[4]*) *He boards up the window we are looking through.*
30. **Outside Bete's house** *[3]*. *Sawing and barking of dogs can be heard. Ventura and another man (Xana). Xana: 'Another one departing . . . Zita, Lina's daughter. The usual poison.'* (**departure:** *[10]*) *Ventura: 'It wasn't poison she took. It was all the poison taken for her before she came into the world.' Bete emerges and Xana leaves. 2–3–2: Ventura/Xana; Ventura/Xana/Bete; Ventura/Bete. Ventura and Bete go inside and look at patterns on the wall. They both see different things. Bete asks Ventura, 'did you see him?' Ventura only replies 'I was in real pain. I just heard someone crying in the street.' In Portuguese, 'the street' ('na rua') is a near-homophone for Nhurro. Bete: 'When they give us those white rooms, we'll stop seeing these things.'*
31. *Ventura in a passageway between steep buildings like a canyon.*
32. *Outside a door we haven't seen before* (**outside Vanda's apartment** *[1]*). *Distant muffled music from a stereo. Then* **at Vanda and Gustavo's dining table** *[2]*. *The muffled music can still be heard. Waiting – Vanda is crying.* (**doing nothing** *[4]*) *They are mourning Zita. Vanda: 'Papa, Zita was your daughter, but she was my sister first.'*
33. **The shack** *[8]*. *Close-up of a gas lamp and a machete.* (**knives** *[5]*) *A 'portrait' of Ventura, still with bandaged head, in a blue and black striped top. He recites the letter.* (**the letter** *[7]*) *Lento: 'That's an awful letter, Ventura.'*

34. **The hospital**. (***hospitals*** *[2]*) *Ventura comes to visit Paulo in his hospital bed. Paulo's wife is also present but does not speak. Paulo: 'I had too much anaesthesia.' He wants to work: 'Goldsmith would be perfect. That's the trade I learnt as a kid... I even did wedding rings.' Paolo wants Ventura to come with him to see his mother. The last time he went, with Nhurro (Ventura: 'My Nhurro?'; Paolo: 'Yes') was a disaster. Paolo's mother is called Lurdes, but in 26 Ventura told Paolo that 'your mother left me', so we had assumed she was Clothilde.* (**confusion of identity** *[7]*)
35. *Ventura at the bottom of a flight of stairs rising to screen left. We hear Vanda, Beatriz and Gustavo. They pass him, but only Gustavo pays him any attention, putting his hand on his shoulder.*
36. **The shack** *[9]*. *Ventura: 'The shack floor is shaking.' (Remember the liquid in 21.) Lento brings in a radiator. Lento: 'I can't write and you won't write.' Lento tries to connect the electricity but falls from the pylon.* (***falling*** *[4]*) *Ventura's bare feet. The bandage falls on them.*
37. **In Vanda's room** *[4]*. *Vanda talks about the graves of her mother and Zita. 'Papa, your socks don't match.'*
38. **Outside Bete's house** *[4]*. *Bete and Ventura at the dining room table. Ventura: 'I brought your mother grilled chicken at the hospital the day you were born.' (Remember the chicken in 8.) Ventura met Bete's mother on Independence Day. He sings 'Labranta braço' from 17. (Political history is now folded into personal history.)*
39. *An alleyway.*
40. *Ventura goes up the stairs he descended in 10.*
41. *Lento opens a fire-blackened door and lets Ventura in. The whole apartment has been incinerated. They hold hands. Ventura: 'They say you jumped from a window with your wife and children.'* (***falling*** *[5]*) *(Time converges: Lento's burnt flat is in one of the new apartment blocks – he says he and Ventura will be neighbours – but it can't be as they weren't built back then.) Lento: 'I threw a match on the mattress because of our problems.' Lento asks if Ventura can see Clothilde. Ventura: 'Stop it, there's no-one there.' Lento finally recites the letter.* (**the letter** *[8]*)
42. *An outdoor shot panning right. Reflections of light from a river on trees. A road and low-rise buildings beyond. Birdsong. A bridge to the right. Ventura and Lento row past in a boat.*
43. **Outside Vanda's apartment** *[2]*. *Ventura knocks on the door. Vanda comes out and Ventura goes in to look after Beatriz. Vanda listens at the other door, to screen left, then lets herself in.* (**locks** *[4]*) *Ventura stands in Vanda's hallway as he did in 11.* (**waiting** *[9]*)
44. **In Vanda's room** *[5]*. *The TV is on quietly. Children can be heard playing outside. Ventura lies on his back on the bed.* (**waiting** *[10]*) *Beatriz plays on the floor by the bed, perfectly framed in the bottom right corner of the screen. The series 2–3–2 (Ventura/Vanda; Ventura/Vanda/Beatriz; Ventura/Beatriz) has finally been completed. Cut to black. Sound continues: Beatriz chatters contentedly. Fade to music.*

Notes

INTRODUCTION

1. I do not want to give the impression that disorientation relates primarily to details of plot or motivation. Certainly, confusion about *what* is going on or *why* it is going on often leads to disorientation, but we can also feel disoriented in other ways – emotionally or morally disoriented, for example, or even what we might call stylistically disoriented if, say, we can get no grasp on how the stylistic dimensions of a film relate to its other aspects; some viewers feel disoriented in this way in relation to the range of colour schemes and film stocks used in Andrei Tarkovsky's *Mirror* (1975), for example.
2. In evaluating a disorientating film a crucial question is, precisely, whether or not such a justification can be discovered. Many viewers, for example, have found the spatial confusion of the later parts of David Fincher's *Alien*³ to be a failing, whereas Stephen Mulhall argues that it is productive and related to a deliberate attempt to dismantle the significance of conventional plot:

   > [T]he audience acquires no overall sense of the geography of the refinery, and is barely capable of distinguishing one shaven-headed male from another ... But Fincher is not here trying, and failing, to generate the usual structure of suspense and fear: the terrain of this final hunting of the beast is unsurveyable, and the unfolding of its events is disorientating and uncompelling, because Fincher has already lost ... any faith in the significance of such narrative artefacts. (Mulhall 2016: 54)

3. Daniel Morgan describes this as resulting, ultimately, from the way Dreyer 'trades on an underlying *desire* we have to identify with the camera, to be with it as it moves through the world' (Morgan 2016: 241). He notes perceptively that the notion that viewers identify with the camera is taken by many theories of camera movement as 'conceptual bedrock' when it is in fact 'the expression of a deep *epistemological fantasy*' (ibid.).
4. Stanisław Lem's polemic against structuralism does a good job of pointing out methodological, empirical and logical problems with Todorov's argument; see Lem (1974).
5. Although films can be many things besides aesthetic objects (historical phenomena, commercial productions, occasions for experiences, fulcrums of community) I see no reason for film studies to reject the study of films as texts as the

field expands into neglected or novel areas; to do so would not be to correct but to diminish our understanding of films.
6. Some scholars, of course, are engaged in doing exactly that. The work of Barry Salt (see Salt 1992) is a pioneering example; more recently members of the Stanford Literary Lab have extended their study of the intersection of big data and literary criticism to film (see Kanatova et al. 2017).
7. I find the following suggestion by Joseph North to be attractive: '[T]he practices of a materialist aesthetics would help us consistently to feel the inextricability of formal and social modes of value; they would be a way of teaching ourselves to be struck by the *value* of experiences, in the full sense of value, which includes the moral, the social, the political, the historical' (North 2019: 182). *The Cinema of Disorientation* was not conceived as a work of 'materialist aesthetics' but I hope that much of what it has to say is at least consistent with such a practice.
8. Coëgnarts and Kravanja draw on Conceptual Metaphor Theory, in which 'what we call "abstract" concepts are defined by systematic mappings from bodily-based sensorimotor source domains onto abstract domains' (Coëgnarts and Kravanja 2012: 2).
9. I also have a more technical reservation about an aspect of Sobchack's work which she shares with some of her followers, namely her approach to metaphor and figuration. She writes that 'except insofar as all language is metaphorical or as it is specifically identified in this present work, I do not use metaphor. (For example, the term film's body in this work is meant to be empirical, not metaphorical.) My prose is also engaged in serious punning' (Sobchack 1992: xviii). It is not at all clear to me why metaphor is to be avoided but 'serious punning' to be recommended, nor am I convinced that Sobchack is successful in avoiding metaphor. Insofar as I do understand it, I think this approach is regrettable. I shall return to these issues in Chapter 5.

Prospectus

1. It might have been possible to reserve disorientation for the more extreme states of confusion, but since one can be profoundly confused or slightly disorientated such a usage would seem to me artificial.
2. I subscribe to Gilberto Perez's view that '[a] term having various senses . . . isn't necessarily a disadvantage to critical thinking' (Perez 2019: 150).
3. Except insofar as it is a subcategory of the general affective phenomenon of confusion, I am not in this book specifically focusing on confusion in the sense of muddling things up, of confusing one thing 'for' another. For a detailed study of this from the perspective of analytic philosophy, see Joseph L. Camp, Jr (2002).
4. One might compare this to some remarks by Wittgenstein in the *Philosophical Investigations* on 'knowing' and 'saying'. Consider what it means to *know* 'how many metres high Mont Blanc is' or 'how a clarinet sounds' and the possibility of *saying* either of these things. For Leibniz, presumably, the height of Mont

Blanc would be a 'distinct' idea and the sound of a clarinet a 'confused' one. See Wittgenstein (2009: 41), §78.

5. Some recent thinking continues to see a fundamental link between aesthetics and forms of confusion: for Jacques Rancière, '[w]hat aesthetic "confusion" initially tells us is that there is no such thing as art in general' (Rancière 2009: 6).
6. I should clarify that Kant himself – who, as Paul Guyer notes in the passage cited below, may not have had first-hand acquaintance with Baumgarten's *Aesthetica*, although there is no doubt that he was familiar with the earlier *Metaphysica* (first published in 1739) – was unconvinced by Leibniz's distinctions and uses confusion largely in its pejorative sense. He remarks in the *Prolegomena to Any Future Metaphysics* that before him (i.e. before Kant) 'philosophical insight into the nature of sensory cognition had previously been perverted by making sensibility into merely a confused kind of representation' (Kant 2004: 41). See also the 'remark' at the end of section XI of the First Introduction to the Third Critique and Paul Guyer's discussion in Kant (2000: 360–1), n. 19.
7. I should also note the possibility of a subliminal debt to Adam Lowenstein's article on Ben Wheatley, 'A Cinema of Disorientation' (Lowenstein 2016), which I had read but did not recall when deciding on the term. I discuss Lowenstein's article further in Chapter 2.
8. That being said, these approaches are not mutually exclusive. While both Aydemir's and Landry's articles contain much sensitive and illuminating analysis, I find them occasionally unconvincing in their detailed readings, which has implications for their political conclusions. Aydemir, for example, in discussing *Elephant*'s theme of whether or not one can discern somebody's homosexuality simply from their appearance makes no mention of the film's use of this as a figure for the possibility of spotting a potential perpetrator of a high-school massacre, and whether or not this enriches the film's sexual themes or troublingly instrumentalises them. Similarly, Landry argues that *Phoenix* is fundamentally concerned with its protagonist Nelly's traumatised body, whereas I would question whether this is really so. The film is very hard on characters who do not ask about Nelly's experiences in a concentration camp, but Landry does not for me convincingly demonstrate that the film is much more interested in them; Nelly appears to suffer no long-term physical trauma and when she finally becomes 'herself' again this is represented – for me problematically – as largely a matter of clothing, hair dye and makeup.
9. The detail and subtlety of Lehman's subsequent argument and the way he incorporates a great many of the film's thematic and narrative patterns suggests that he may not, in fact, think that 'visual rhyme' is really the *sole* motivation for the motif.
10. Pippin does note the connection; see Pippin (2010: 114).
11. The contrasting way that the death of Martin's (Jeffrey Hunter) 'accidental' wife Look (or Luke, or Wild Goose Flying in the Night Sky, played by Beulah Archuletta) is represented has implications for the racial politics of the film. We look out from within the teepee at Ethan looking in, but we are then shown

Look's dead body. It takes two shots to represent an event – death – that earlier, with the death of Martha, took only one shot. Look's death, precisely because we *can* look directly on her dead body, is figured by the film as the less traumatic of the two deaths.

12. If it didn't risk outrageous pretentiousness I might at this point quote the Preface to Hegel's *Phenomenology*: 'Nor is the *result* which is reached the *actual* whole itself; rather, the whole is the result together with the way the result comes to be' (Hegel 2018: 5).

CHAPTER 1

1. Among these films are *Der Andere* (1913), *Der Student von Prag* (1913), *Der Golem* (1915) and *Das Cabinet des Dr. Caligari* (1920) (see Andriopoulos 2006). The interest of cinema in doubles, twins, changelings and the like has never abated, being recently represented by Richard Ayoade's adaptation of Dostoyevsky in *The Double* (2013). Gilbert Cohen-Séat, originator of the filmology movement, argued that cinema 'ends by creating a universe which is added to our universe' (*Essai sur les principes d'une philosophie du cinéma* (Paris: Presses Universitaires de France, 1946: 24)), quoted in Lowry (1985: 35).
2. Although this is not an argument I will develop in detail, I think a case could be made that orientation (and disorientation) are particularly appropriate concepts for engaging with films because comprehending a film always involves coordinating multiple channels, a process that could almost be said to be a synonym for orientation. See Schmidt di Friedberg (2018: 1, 44 and 117, but also – more or less – *passim*).
3. Souriau was, significantly, '[t]he first scholar to use the term diegetic in the modern sense' (Winters 2010: 226).
4. The French notion of a cinematic 'field' (champ) – the segment of the represented world that we can see which exists in depth but is nevertheless bounded by the screen – is also not precisely covered by any of Souriau's levels.
5. I shall have more to say about *Caché* in Chapter 6.
6. '*Réique*' is a neologism coined by Souriau that might be translated as 'thingly'.
7. A few further remarks on Walton's notion of fiction. Walton argues that 'Paris is an object of *A Tale of Two Cities* because *A Tale of Two Cities* makes it fictional of Paris that it exists, that it was the site of knittings by a certain Madame Defarge, and so on' (*ibid.*: 106). But it is very odd to say that a book by Dickens 'makes it fictional of Paris that it exists'. That Paris exists is not fictional, no matter how many books about it Dickens had written, and neither is Paris's existence fictional within the fiction (for Madame Defarge, for example, it is clearly a fact). This seems to me a very odd use of the term 'fictional'. Why not say that some of the things that are true within fictional worlds are also true within our worlds? Perhaps the answer is because this would indicate how close to metalepsis fictions always are, something Walton is reluctant to acknowledge. See Newsom (1994) for a stimulating discussion related to this point.

8. Despite the helpfulness of his distinction between the *world-of* and the *world-in* films, between 'films as artistic worlds distinct from fictional story-worlds', I find that Daniel Yacavone neglects this point when he writes, for example, that '[c]inematography, camera placement and movement, editing, staging, design, music, and lighting, may all be seen to take up what amount to a particular *perspective upon* the represented *world-in* of some films' (Yacavone 2015: xxi and 124). This is certainly true, but it is also true that these elements, and others like them, are our only means of access to the *world-in* the film: our sense of the *world-in* a film (the fictional ontology of its diegesis), therefore, derives from the *world-of* the film (its rhetoric). I also discuss this point in Lash (2017: 173–4).
9. To the viewer who remained sceptical about the 'Wise Up' sequence, one could demonstrate its non-arbitrariness, its location in networks of patterning in *Magnolia*. A song (Mann's version of Harry Nilsson's 'One') unites all the characters early on in the film but causes no alarm because it conforms to the conventions of non-diegetic music. (It is the sense that the characters are singing to a non-diegetic song that makes the 'Wise Up' sequence feel metaleptical.) We have also seen what Toles calls the 'overtly choreographed' earlier, in some very elaborate Steadycam shots, but again this artifice is covered by convention. The way the sequence relies on coincidence ties into what is one of the film's major themes, announced as such at its very outset (a narrator relates some – fictional – historical coincidences and asserts that 'this is not just a matter of chance'). The way that the sequence borders on breaking the fourth wall connects both to Jim's (John C. Reilly) act of pretending to be in a police documentary and to the film's final shot in which Claudia (Melora Waters) looks directly at the camera. And, finally, the sequence has a structural role: the surprise it generates by shifting the viewer's sense of the film's range of possibility prefigures the effect of the climactic – and notorious – rain of frogs.

CHAPTER 2

1. It is important to note that densely embedded narratives, while obviously providing ample opportunity for presenting generic multiplicity, by no means necessarily do so. Dense embedding can easily exist without a kaleidoscope of genres, as happens in *The Saragossa Manuscript* (Wojciech Has, 1965).
2. Ashbery was a very appropriate choice given his passion for one of the film's main influences, Raymond Roussel's *New Impressions of Africa* (see Peranson 2015).
3. It is tempting to make a connection here with the Wachowski's own gender transitioning, although this aspect of the film seems to me rather soft-pedalled. There was, in fact, a certain amount of controversy about casting and race in *Cloud Atlas*, including criticism by the Media Action Network for Asian Americans, who saw the treatment of different races as asymmetrical (see Zakarin 2012).

4. This neatness operates at various scales. One tiny example is the way a sequence in the Zachry narrative involving a bridge cuts directly to Timothy Cavendish's train, which crosses the frame along almost exactly the same line as that along which Zachry's pursuers had crossed the bridge.

CHAPTER 3

1. Some have suggested that we should. Michael Atkinson, reviewing *INLAND EMPIRE*, claims that the frustration experienced by many critics and viewers comes about because they have 'expected a narrative clarity where there is none, and searched for irrelevant codes and readings even as they ignored the sensual experience they had, dozily lost in the underlit corridors of Lynch's imagination' (Atkinson 2007). Though I would challenge such readings, they are far from inexplicable; Jennifer Pranolo's statement that *INLAND EMPIRE* is 'arguably Lynch's most inscrutable work to date' is perfectly reasonable (Pranolo 2011: 477).
2. The sense that the visitor has somehow brought about this strange sequence reminds me of a remark made by Tom Gunning about the fondness of another director, also interested in the fantastic and in the uncanny powers of the gaze, for metaleptical effects: '[Fritz] Lang at points seems to confuse the clear separation between diegetic story and action and extradiegetic style, as characters seem to exert control over the visual devices of the film itself, especially its editing' (Gunning 2000: 16).
3. Similar notions make frequent appearances in Lynch's *oeuvre*, most recently in Mike's repeated question in *Twin Peaks: The Return* (2017): 'Is it future or is it past?'
4. G. Smalley takes things to extremes: 'She [Dern] possibly plays as many as six or seven characters, depending on whether you chose to see the woman who fights with her husband when she announces she's pregnant, the woman at the outdoor barbecue, or the woman who hangs out with the prostitutes as having a separate identity or not' (Smalley 2010).
5. Some viewers have deemed the answer to be yes; the website *Halfborn*, for example, insists that Nikki is a fantasy whereas 'Sue Blue and Billy Side are real people' (Blackman 2009).
6. Harring's voice does appear in the film, belonging to one of the rabbits.
7. This last point of course connects Niko to Nikki in more than name because the screwdriver wound she receives is in more or less the right place to have created just such a wound.
8. Pranolo sees it as a 'fleshy metonym for the various "holes" in *Inland Empire*' (Pranolo 2011: 492), but it seems to me that it would be more properly described as a metaphor.
9. Tanner's remark comes from his enthusiastic response to the possibilities opened up by this metaphor of smuggling, as occasioned by Joseph McElroy's 1966 novel *A Smuggler's Bible*.

Chapter 4

1. This drama – of which George M. Wilson's 'rhetorical figures of narrational instruction' (Wilson 1986: 49), referred to in my introduction, are perhaps a subset – was known in the Middle Ages by the name *ductus*:

    > *Ductus* is the way by which a work leads someone through itself: that quality in a work's formal patterns which engages an audience and then sets a viewer or auditor or performer in motion within its structures, an experience more like travelling through stages along a route than like perceiving a whole object. (Carruthers 2013: 190)

2. This thought is related to the discussion in the last chapter concerning what we can learn from *Lost Highway* about the extent to which films trade on the *promise* of a coherent (non-paradoxical) *fabula*, rather than there being anything in the nature of linear storytelling which requires such a *fabula* to exist in order for us to be able to engage with them.
3. This account of coherence need not contradict the notion referred to above that our sense of coherence can fluctuate during a viewing. Particularly during a first viewing, we do not know precisely what kind of whole the parts will come to make up; our sense of coherence can therefore fluctuate as our expectations about the nature of this whole shift. (One could describe my account of *INLAND EMPIRE* as an attempt to trace an unusually difficult instance of this process.)
4. Manohla Dargis wrote in the *New York Times*, for example, that '[a]lthough the movie doesn't have an obvious narrative through line, its episodes are nonetheless deeply connected by mood, visual style and Mr. Lavant' (Dargis 2012).
5. This conclusion is offered explicitly in contrast to V. F. Perkins's views and while, as I say, I am in sympathy with it, Berliner's treatment of Perkins does not entirely do justice to the subtlety and sophistication of his arguments; I try to show in Lash (2017) how one could reach a similar conclusion by following Perkins's own principles, even if so doing entails disagreeing with some of his explicit judgements. In fact Perkins himself told John Gibbs in 1997: 'I think that *Film as Film* slightly overdoes coherence really' (Gibbs 2019: 48).
6. Compare, for example, the opening montage (combined with Scott Walker's music) of the otherwise much more diegetically straightforward – albeit still confusing – *Pola X*.
7. Thanks to Gareth Evans for this observation.
8. Carax has said: 'I use cinema as language to create the science fiction world but hopefully the film is not about cinema' (Asdourian 2012).
9. In the next sequence, Oscar plays a man called M. Vogan. In the Merde sequence there is a sardonic joke: a group of tombstones all invite one to 'visit my site' and contain a web address; one of these is www.vogan.fr.
10. This phenomenon recalls Murray Smith's observation about Raoul Ruiz's *La vocation suspendue* (1978) that '[t]he disorienting effect of [the film's] inconsistencies

is exacerbated by the fact that the inconsistencies are themselves inconsistent' (Smith 1995: 126).
11. For some viewers the question as to whether this is the case becomes active early in the film. A number of students of mine became concerned about the question of how many of the people we see are performing within the diegetic world after the finger-biting episode. Does Jamie the photographer's assistant *really* lose her fingers?
12. Morgan raises this same question with regard to the moment Lavant, or Oscar, or the movement capture artist, falls on the treadmill (see Morgan 2015: 7).
13. During his conversation with the Man with the Birthmark, Oscar bemoans the fact that the cameras have become invisible. Oscar, it seems, can't believe in his performances any more precisely because of the absence of signs that cinema is *not* real.
14. Auerbach's understanding of the figural is rather different from the notions of figures and the figurative most useful to me; see the next chapter for clarification.
15. The cause of death is unconfirmed but, adding pathos to the death of Kylie Minogue's character, it is rumoured to have been suicide (Thomson 2014).
16. I would argue that *Holy Motors* challenges the generalisability of Murray Smith's account of *La vocation suspendue*. Smith claims that, in Ruiz's film, 'profound disorientation at the level of character recognition threatens the very legibility of narrative . . . It is only when the most basic level of character engagement is secure that we are at all likely to respond emotionally to the mimetic functions of characters' (Smith 1995: 138). In *Holy Motors*, however, 'profound disorientation at the level of character recognition' turns out not to prevent emotional intensity.
17. Naremore elsewhere (Naremore 2007: 29) mentions Diane Arbus in this connection, and Arbus is in fact explicitly – if rather sarcastically – cited in *Holy Motors*.
18. I am reminded of the original conclusion to Stanley Cavell's *The World Viewed*:

> A world complete without me which is present to me is the world of my immortality. This is an importance of film – and a danger. It takes my life as my haunting of the world . . . So there is reason for me to want the camera to deny the coherence of the world, its coherence as past: to deny that the world is complete without me. But there is equal reason to want it affirmed that the world is coherent without me. That is essential to what I want of immortality: nature's survival of me. It will mean that the present judgement upon me is not yet the last. (Cavell 1979a: 160)

We might see the way *Holy Motors* wrestles with coherence as a kind of allegory for, or literalisation of, this wish simultaneously both to deny and to affirm the coherence of the world, a wish that Cavell sees as fundamental to the condition of film viewing.

CHAPTER 5

1. I like Arnold Isenberg's remark that '[i]t seems silly to ask how music can be *light-hearted*, as if you already knew how a *heart* can be *light*' (Isenberg 1973: 9).

2. A figure in this sense is something less rounded, more schematic, than a 'character'. Incidentally, in French, a 'figurant' is the kind of actor we would call in English an 'extra'.
3. Genette traces this tendency back to César Dumarsais's *Des Tropes* (1730), which did much 'to place at the center of historical thought the opposition between the literal and the figurative . . . and therefore to turn rhetoric into a consideration of figuration, a turnstile of the figurative defined as the other of the literal, and of the literal defined as the other of the figurative – and to enclose it for a long time to come in this meticulous vertigo' (Genette 1982: 105).
4. Jacques Aumont refers to this phenomenon with a metaphor based in hygiene: 'traditionally, the figure is a sort of contamination of the verbal by the iconic' (Aumont 1991: 191). Aumont also offers a useful corrective to any tendency too rigidly to oppose uncoded (iconic) visual resemblance to language's code-based methods of signification. In fact, visual recognition also involves highly abstract procedures: 'the work of recognition uses not just the elementary properties of the system of vision, but also the capacities for coding which are already quite abstract' (*ibid.*: 57).
5. Such a view seems to me to resonate with the remarks by Sobchack about *To the Wonder* and *Upstream Color* that I discussed in the introduction, and to be similarly problematic.
6. Barker, I suspect, inherits this way of thinking from Sobchack. I also find it problematic in Sobchack's writing; see the final footnote to the introduction.
7. Note the other words to which the notion is cognate, owing to the history of its translation from Greek rhetoric into Latin: 'The Greek term σχῆμα, for instance, which is reasonably consistently used in Greek rhetoric to denote what the later rhetorical tradition will call a 'figure', is variously translated and/or referred to by Roman rhetoricians as *forma* or *conformatio*, *exornatio*, or *figura*' (Matzner 2016: 31). Thus words such as 'scheme', 'form' and 'ornament' might also be in our minds.
8. Recall the remarks by Klevan about context and meaning that I quoted in the introduction.
9. Perez suggests that 'at least with regard to the film image, we may leave that distinction aside and subsume simile under metaphor' (Perez 2019: 57), but he does so because he is assuming that the comparison in question is enacted by means of montage; I think the example from *Tess* indicates that both terms have their uses. Perez is correct, however, in indicating some ways in which the distinction between tenor and vehicle is not always pertinent or helpful with regard to film (see Perez 2019: 57–8).
10. As Perez explains, in classical rhetoric tropes – which alter the meaning of words – may be distinguished from figures which do not, and hence '[w]e may . . . distinguish film tropes . . . which alter the meaning of images, from figures of arrangement such as crosscutting or the reverse angle', which do not, at least not to the same extent (Perez 2019: 53). I think such a distinction is potentially quite helpful but I have not maintained it in this book because of potential confusion

with the now common use of 'trope', with regard to film, to refer to familiar patterns and conventions. I have tended, instead, to use the term 'figure' for both figures and tropes, both so as to avoid confusion with this use of 'trope', and to underline the connection with the *processes* of figuration in which I am most interested.

11. This definition might usefully be compared with Stephen Heath's definition of 'figure' in *Questions of Cinema*:

> The circulation between agent, character, person and image, none of which is able simply and uniquely to contain, to *settle* that circulation, the figure it makes in a film. What obtain are specific regimes of the articulation of the different instances, particular versions of coherence, of the balancing out of the circulation; whether, as is most often the case by a hierarchization in the interests of character or by some pattern of movement between character and image. The articulation can fail to balance, slip into an overlaying that does not simply cohere. (Heath 1981: 182)

12. We should note that Brenez, perfectly willing to problematise her own distinctions, ends her article with an example of a filmmaker who 'conceives of representation *as* figuration', namely Robert Bresson (Brenez 1990: 19).
13. This claim might recall Barthes's denigration of representation when compared to figuration, according to which representation is 'when nothing emerges, when nothing leaps out of the frame' (Barthes 1975: 57), but I would prefer to retain a more mutable relationship between the two, such as I think we see in Rancière's discussion of *They Live by Night* or in Brenez's claim, cited in the preceding footnote, that it is even possible to conceive of 'representation *as* figuration'.
14. That is to say, if it is a recommendation to be wary of Kiss and Willemsen's insistence, to which I have already referred more than once, that we at all times strictly separate 'the cognitive effort of narrative comprehension' from 'the variety and richness of simple or complex perceptual and interpretive responses', then I think it is sound (Kiss and Willemsen 2017: 45). Recall Heath's definition of 'figure', cited above. Martin would, I think, agree with this: sometimes coherence is achieved by 'hierarchization in the interests of character', but many times other procedures may be more relevant.
15. Merleau-Ponty writes in 'The Film and the New Psychology' that '[i]t is impossible to understand perception as the imputation of a certain significance to certain sensible signs, since the most immediate sensible texture of these signs cannot be described without referring to the object they signify' (Merleau-Ponty 1964: 51).

Chapter 6

1. We could say that the figures I will discuss complicate and exacerbate a basic condition of narrative cinema, as described by Robert Pippin: 'We don't understand what we see unless we can bring to bear what we can't see but must be able to take into account (sometimes in error, as we are eventually shown)' (Pippin 2016: 221).

2. More specifically, we might say they concern *morally* disorientated characters, referring to Murray Smith's concept of moral orientation (see, for example, Smith 1995: 189). Via a discussion of Jean-Pierre Melville's *Le Doulos* (1963) Smith makes the important points that 'moral structures themselves have important effects on the putatively more basic, informational structures of narrative and narration' and that 'the mistaken inferences that a playful – or duplicitous – narration like that of *Le Doulos* encourages us to make, often involve emotional as well as cognitive factors (bearing in mind, of course, that emotions themselves have a cognitive component, and are not irrational factors opposed to cognition)' (*ibid.*: 223). I am in complete agreement with these points, though I am not wholly persuaded by Smith's reading of the film itself.
3. In all my examples indistinguishability is directed more at the viewer than at the characters; any discussion of situations where diegetic characters also encounter indistinguishable images would of course have to reckon with examples such as the hall-of-mirrors conclusion of Welles's *The Lady from Shanghai* (1947).
4. Tourneur's work is one of the primary influences on Pedro Costa, so this example is intended to serve as something of an oblique bridge to the next chapter's analysis of *Colossal Youth*.
5. V. F. Perkins has argued that our comprehension of films cannot rely only on what we see; for one thing it will rely on knowledge we bring from outside the film: 'intra-textual understanding depends on extra-textual information not only about facts but about values' (Perkins 1990: 6).
6. Saige Walton discusses this effect; see Walton (2016: 68ff.).
7. Elkins himself argues precisely this: see Elkins (1998: 261).
8. It seems possible that Haneke got this idea from Lynch in the first place, though I don't believe this has been confirmed; *INLAND EMPIRE* might be returning the favour by giving the Rabbits' room the same number as that of Majid's apartment in *Caché*: 47.
9. A possible further line of enquiry, which I shall not pursue here, would be to connect this (and Elkins's categories) with Alain Robbe-Grillet's notion of 'dysnarration' (or 'disnarration') – the narration of that which did not happen. See, for example, Prince (1988), who distinguishes the disnarrated from the unnarratable and the unnarrated; Deleuze also refers to disnarration in the famous 'Powers of the False' chapter in Deleuze (2013).

CHAPTER 7

1. Literally *Youth on the March* but known in English as *Colossal Youth*, after the only album (from 1980) by Young Marble Giants, thus indicating the filmmaker's interest in punk and post-punk music.
2. Kawin argues that if we see the images that comprise a narrative film to be organised by an off-screen presence – broadly, by some kind of narrational agent – 'it does not seem necessary to deny the possibility that the organizer, as a persona of the artist or even just as a character, can be fictitious, and that he can include

an image of himself (or an indicator of his offscreen presence) in the filmed field without compromising his status as narrator' (Kawin 1978: 4).
3. Pavey's 'Disorientation: The History and Pathology of a Concept' (Pavey 2017: 74–84) gives a helpful overview.
4. Cyril Neyrat has described *Colossal Youth* as 'a chamber film, in the sense of the term *chamber music*' (Neyrat 2010: 16).
5. Costa has remarked on the technical difficulty of achieving these effects, and how 'it took a very long time to find the position of the camera':

> In width, depth, and height, there is only one point where the three dimensions come together, only one possible place where the verticals are straight, and it's sometimes very hard to find because if you move a millimetre one of them becomes curved or starts to move left ... In *Colossal Youth* there are lots of angles, of verticals and horizontals, of doors, windows and perspectives, it was a terrible job and sometimes really maddening, almost mathematical. (Costa 2008: 98–9, my translation)

6. Other narratives also exhibit relatively conventional structures of resolution. Ventura's relationships with both Lento and Bete eventually achieve reconciliation: Lento finally learns the letter (even if he has had to die to do so), and Bete does at last relent and let Ventura in. There are also a number of smaller cohesive narratives, such as Vanda's about giving birth and the 'letters' of Nhurro and Paolo.
7. There is also the merest gesture towards voluntary and beneficial departures from home, when Vanda discusses wanting to go to Fátima on pilgrimage in thanksgiving for her daughter's health. The irony is that we feel this desired departure to be the least likely of fulfilment.
8. Locations that do not recur – the Gulbenkian, its garden, the first apartment Ventura is shown and Nhurro's furniture shop – are the exception rather than the rule.
9. There are only four exceptions: the rightward pan in the shot in which Ventura first appears (scene 2); the rightward pan in the apartment in 10; the pan down from the sky and left to the bench in 16; and the rightward pan in 42.
10. The effect is, of course, in fact achieved by using mirrors to direct the daylight, as one can see in Aurélian Gerbault's documentary *All Blossoms Again* (2006). This chiaroscuro is taken to greater lengths in Costa's most recent film, *Vitalina Varela* (2019). During most of the film – until we finally emerge fully into daylight at the very end – limited patches of vibrant illumination serve only to increase the depth of the darkness that surrounds them.
11. Vanda Duarte will certainly have become very used to Costa's presence, not only in the making of this film but the long process of filming *In Vanda's Room* (2000) in the years previous to the making of *Colossal Youth*.
12. The main exception is the scene in the garden analysed above.
13. Thanks to Gareth Evans for a helpful conversation about this scene.
14. In Costa's short films *Tarrafal* (2007), *The Rabbit Hunters* (2007) and *O nosso homem* (2010) these two figures are directly combined in a closing shot of a deportation notice pinned up with a knife.

15. The following citations from the same article are also my translations.
16. Consider, for example, the dead father in *O Sangue* who nevertheless writes a letter, or the long tracking shot in *Ossos* in which the boy carries what seems to be a dead baby in a plastic bag, only for the baby to turn up alive and well.
17. I don't think, incidentally, that the figures in *Colossal Youth* ever become environments: there are no shots anywhere in the film with more than three people in them; the human beings represented in the film are always figures, not backgrounds or environments as they can become in crowd scenes, for example. The distinction between figure and ground is always clear.
18. Likewise, though it may seem brutal when Semedo tells Ventura that 'unpaid electricity bill means no light', is it definitely worse than falling from a pylon trying illegally to get on-grid, as Lento does? Costa's sensitivity to questions of the aestheticisation of poverty might be indicated by a reflexive reading of Paolo's claim that the doctors are taking pictures of and filming his treatment and sending the photos and films to the USA.
19. Perez observes about Straub-Huillet (among Costa's most profound influences), that those who find the sequences in the car in their *History Lessons* (1972) boring 'are bored not for lack of action but for lack of a scheme of meaning that would subsume all that action going on in the streets' (Perez 1998: 284).
20. This theme is continued, and the necessity for building homes to be a *shared* endeavour underlined, in *Vitalina Varela*. Vitalina berates her dead husband for the shoddy job he did building his Portugese home (at one point a piece of ceiling falls on her head while she takes a shower), in contrast to the 'incomparable' home they built together (in forty-five days) in Cape Verde.

Chapter 8

1. 'yes, it was the best time we ever had, said Deslauriers'
2. Disorientation and confusion seem both to have a close connection with aquatic imagery. Ami Harbin writes that an 'oceanic metaphor' is 'used strikingly often to describe disorientations' (Harbin 2016: 2), and Martine Beugnet points out that '[o]ne of Leibniz's favoured examples of clear and confused perception is that of the sea, which we identify although we cannot distinctly perceive it: we hear the roar of the sea, made of all the crashing waves, writes Leibniz, and we identify it as the sound of the sea even though we cannot distinguish the sound of each individual wave' (Beugnet 2017: 2).
3. Nick Jones writes that 'just as a sculpture might emphasise its constituent material (be it iron, wood, glass, etc.), this film stresses and revels in the immaterial material of stereoscopic depth' (Jones 2018).
4. Deleuze seems here to mean 'confused' in a sense closer to Baumgarten than the familiar pejorative meaning. His specific subject is the change across Fritz Lang's *Mabuse* films, and his point, not that the effects of 'occult power' are simply mistaken for that power itself but that a genuine change has taken place:

Mabuse's power 'no longer passes through a production of secret actions, but rather through a monopoly of reproduction' (Deleuze 2005: 214).

5. 'those who lack imagination take refuge in reality'
6. I wonder if there is in these shots something of the opening of the famous sequence in *Vampyr* in which Allan Gray's dream self leaves his sleeping body.
7. We might recall here Frederic Jameson's discussion of Godard's *Passion* (1982), in which he refers to 'Godard's themes . . . only distantly resembling ideas, and serving as the various lights that strike his aesthetic object in rotation, tinting it, highlighting a relief, flooding another side or aspect, and then plunging the collective substance – the totality of the film's relationships – back into the chiaroscuro of a Rembrandt' (Jameson 1992: 176).
8. Stanley Cavell does not seem to agree:

   > Or take Godard's use of the sound of philosophy, in those longish dialogues his women elicit from actual philosophers. It is a good perception that recognized this sound for the cinema, that found that in an environment of nonsense and insinuation and cynicism the sound of sense still falls sweetly upon the human ear. But Godard hasn't seen it through, because he does not care whether what the philosopher says is valid or not – that is, he listens to it the way his girls do, or the way a bourgeois audience does, somewhere within embarrassment, envy, contempt and titillation. And while his talent and wit lead him to remark that philosophy is now stimulated by pretty girls, either he fails to recognize the humor and sadness of this, or else he sees nothing further . . . Godard's girls walk away intact from these confrontations. Is this supposed to show that they are unseducible? So are prostitutes. Anyway, they are seduced – by slogans, advertisements, and illicitness. (Cavell 1979a: 100)

   While, as always with Cavell, there is much in this that is thought-provoking, I find the sexual politics rather troubling. On what basis exactly does Cavell draw his conclusions about the ways 'Godard's girls' listen to philosophy? What if, in *La Chinoise*, the philosopher has *not* concluded 'that the girl before him is an unloving and dangerous nitwit' (*ibid.*: 101)? Could he be paying her the respect of not concluding that?

9. This is not strictly accurate – in cinemas the film was presented in surround sound, and 5.1 channel audio is available on DVD and Blu-ray.
10. At other moments there are some rather questionable jokes about this, which seem to refer to the fact that, as Zoé Bruneau explains in her book *En attendant Godard*, she shaves her pubic hair and thus had to wear a merkin to film the nude scenes (Bruneau 2014: 30–1). At one point we hear that there is 'no more forest', and at another she stands in a doorway and holds a rug in front of her naked body.
11. Warner points out that this phrase is a reference to Godard's own *Cahiers du cinéma* review of Alexandre Astruc's 1958 film *Une Vie* (Warner 2016: 64).
12. What we see and hear, as well as what we can't see and can't hear, are crucial in this sequence. Albertine Fox interestingly suggests that the language of the obvious and obscure might introduce an unconscious bias towards the visual, one which 'constrains the focus to narrative comprehension in terms of visual

coherence, and overlooks the power of the spectator's aural imagination' (Fox 2018: 183). Unfortunately for my purposes she does not explore the role of the 'aural imagination' in making narrative and diegetic inferences or speculations but moves immediately to suggest that we listen to *Adieu au langage* 'as though it were a piece of sonic art or poetry rather than attempting to comprehend it in terms of its adherence to a storyline of visible events' (*ibid.*: 183–4).
13. This is somewhat reminiscent of *INLAND EMPIRE*, but amnesia is not a theme insisted upon in *Adieu au langage* in the way it is in Lynch's film.
14. In Burch's account, narrative is not a *sine qua non* for cinematic diegesis; distinguishing diegetic production from diegetic reception, and referring to diegetic *process* in order 'to encompass the two', he declares that 'one of my contentions is that this process can be triggered off in a filmic context independently of the presence of any narrative structure, and that one may consequently see it, rather than narrative, as the true seat of cinema's "power of fascination"' (Burch 1982: 16).
15. This appears to be a conflation of *Call of the Wild* (1903) (and/or *White Fang* (1906)) with *The Cruise of the Snark* (1911).
16. The juxtaposition of themes of fidelity and of relationships with the non-human underlines the relevance of the film's references to *Frankenstein*.
17. Performance on film does not, of course, have a simple relation with intention since directors often choose takes because of things that the actors may not have been exactly conscious of.

Conclusion

1. Robert Pippin recently made some remarks to this effect after delivering a paper on Hitchcock's *Vertigo*: 'If we take the film as a case study then our conclusions that are derived from it are just confirmational of [our theories] . . . When I read this paper and there are Film Studies people in the audience, they say, "What the hell are you doing? . . . What's your theory?" . . . I'm just trying to understand the goddamn film!' (see Pippin 2017b). Lest I be misunderstood, let me emphasise that I in no way intend to argue that all of film studies' attempts at explaining disorientation have been regrettable attempts to explain it away. I was at pains in the first paragraph of the conclusion to emphasise that we have learned a great deal from the wide variety of explanatory methods it has employed. I wish merely to suggest that – where the *aesthetics* of disorientation and confusion are concerned – to aim at reliability of method is to run the risk of distorting the phenomena under investigation.
2. And not only Ethan: for Laurie, too, as we learn in her extraordinary outburst at Martin – whose goal *is* to bring Debbie back alive – in which Laurie even claims that Martha, Debbie's mother, would have thought it better for her to be killed than rescued.

Bibliography

Adorno, Theodor (2004) *Aesthetic Theory*. London: Continuum.
Affeldt, Steven G. (1998) 'The Ground of Mutuality: Criteria, Judgement, and Intelligibility in Stephen Mulhall and Stanley Cavell', *European Journal of Philosophy*, 6 (1), pp. 1–31.
Ahmed, Sara (2006) *Queer Phenomenology: Orientations, Objects, Others*. Durham, NC and London: Duke University Press.
Andrew, Dudley (1983) 'The Primacy of Figure in Cinematic Signification', in Stephen Heath and Patricia Mellencamp (eds), *Cinema and Language*. Frederick: University Publications of America, pp. 133–40.
Andrew, Dudley (1984) *Concepts in Film Theory*. Oxford: Oxford University Press.
Andriopoulos, Stefan (2006) 'The Terror of Reproduction: Early Cinema's Ghostly Doubles and the Right to One's Own Image', *New German Critique*, 99, pp. 151–70.
Asdourian, Raffi (2012) 'Leos Carax Discusses the Surreal Journey to Make 'Holy Motors'', *Film Stage*, 18 October 18 <https://thefilmstage.com/features/interview-leos-carax-discusses-the-surreal-journey-to-make-holy-motors/> (last accessed 16 July 2018).
Atkinson, Michael (2007) 'Absurdia: Lynch's Semiconscious Menagerie Unleashed', *The Stranger*, 18 January <http://www.thestranger.com/seattle/absurdia/Content?oid=137174> (last accessed 11 July 2018).
Aumont, Jacques (1991) *The Image*. London: BFI.
Aydemir, Murat (2016) 'Queer Orientation with Gus Van Sant's *Elephant*', *Culture, Theory and Critique*, 57 (1), pp. 32–47.
Badiou, Alain (2005) 'The False Movements of Cinema', in *Handbook of Inaesthetics*, trans. Alberto Toscano. Stanford, CA: Stanford University Press pp. 78–88.
Badiou, Alain (2009) *Logics of Worlds: Being and Event II*. London: Bloomsbury.
Barker, Jennifer M. (2009) *The Tactile Eye: Touch and the Cinematic Experience*. Berkeley, Los Angeles and London: University of California Press.
Barney, Richard A. (ed.) (2009) *David Lynch Interviews*. Jackson, MS: University Press of Mississippi.
Barthes, Roland (1975) *The Pleasure of the Text*, trans. Richard Miller. New York: Hill & Wang.
Barthes, Roland (1990) *S/Z*, trans. Richard Miller. Oxford and Cambridge, MA: Basil Blackwell.
Baumbach, Nico (2014) 'Starting Over', *Film Comment*, no. 38 (December), pp. 34–41.
Berliner, Todd (2010) *Hollywood Incoherent: Narration in Seventies Cinema*. Austin, TX: University of Texas Press.
Beugnet, Martine (2017) 'Introduction', in *Indefinite Visions: Cinema and the Attractions of Uncertainty*. Edinburgh: Edinburgh University Press, pp. 1–13.
Bierce, Ambrose (2000) *Tales of Soldiers and Civilians and Other Stories*. Harmondsworth: Penguin.
Biles, Jeremy (2013) '*Holy Motors*', *Journal of Religion and Film*, 17 (1), p. 41.

Blackman, Jeremy (2009) 'Halfborn' website <http://xixax.com/halfborn/> (last accessed 10 July 2018).
Blatter, Helene (2006) *'Inland Empire* – Just Don't Expect to See the 91', *The Press-Enterprise*, September <http://www.thecityofabsurdity.com/inlandempire/intInlandEmpire04.html> (last accessed 11 July 2018).
Bloom, Harold, Paul de Man, Jacques Derrida, Geoffrey Hartman, and J. Hillis Miller (1979) *Deconstruction and Criticism*. London and Henley: Routledge & Kegan Paul.
Bluestone, George (1957) *Novels into Film: The Metamorphosis of Fiction into Cinema*. Berkeley, Los Angeles and London: University of California Press.
Bogue, Ronald (2017) 'Deleuze and Roxy: The Time of the Intolerable and Godard's *Adieu Au Langage*', in Colin Gardner and Patricia MacCormack (eds), *Deleuze and the Animal*. Edinburgh; Edinburgh University Press, pp. 275–92.
Bordwell, David (1985) *Narration in the Fiction Film*. London: Methuen.
Brenez, Nicole (1990) 'Comme Vous Êtes: Representation et Figuration, Invention de l'image Cinematographique', *Admiranda*, 5, pp. 9–19.
Brenez, Nicole (2007) *Abel Ferrara*, trans. Adrian Martin, Contemporary Film Directors. Urbana, IL and Chicago: University of Illinois Press.
Brenez, Nicole (2011) 'An Archeology of the Figure and the Figural in Cinema after Kracauer', lecture delivered 22 November <http://www.kracauer-lectures.de/en/winter-2011-2012/nicole-brenez/> (last accessed 16 July 2018).
Brinkema, Eugenie (2014) *The Forms of the Affects*. Durham, NC and London: Duke University Press.
Brown, William (2014) 'Complexity and Simplicity in *Inception* and *Five Dedicated to Ozu*', in Warren Buckland (ed.), *Hollywood Puzzle Films*. London, Routledge, pp. 125–39.
Bruneau, Zoé (2014) *En Attendant Godard*. Paris: Maurice Nadeau.
Buckland, Warren (2013) 'The Acousmatic Voice and Metaleptic Narration in *Inland Empire*', in Carol Vernalis, Amy Herzog and John Richardson (eds), *The Oxford Handbook of Sound and Image in Digital Media*. Oxford: Oxford University Press, pp. 236–49.
Burch, Noel (1982) 'Narrative/Diegesis – Thresholds, Limits', *Screen*, 23 (2), pp. 16–33.
Carruthers, Mary (2013) 'The Concept of Ductus, or Journeying through a Work of Art', In *Rhetoric Beyond Words*. Cambridge: Cambridge University Press, pp. 190–213.
Camp Jr, Joseph L. (2002) *Confusion*. Cambridge, MA and London: Harvard University Press.
Cavell, Stanley (1979a) *The World Viewed: Reflections on the Ontology of Film*. Cambridge, MA: Harvard University Press.
Cavell, Stanley (1979b) *The Claim of Reason*. Oxford and New York: Oxford University Press.
Cavell, Stanley (1981) *Pursuits of Happiness: The Hollywood Comedy of Remarriage*. Cambridge, MA and London: Harvard University Press.
Cavell, Stanley (2015) *Must We Mean What We Say?* Cambridge: Cambridge University Press.
Cecchi, Alessandro (2010) 'Diegetic versus Nondiegetic: A Reconsideration of the Conceptual Opposition as a Contribution to the Theory of Audiovision', *Worlds of Audiovision* <http://www-5.unipv.it/wav/index.php?option=com_content&view=article&id=71%3Adiegetico-vs-extradiegetico&catid=25%3Aworlds-of-audiovision&lang=en> (last accessed 6 March 2020).
Chion, Michel (1995) *David Lynch*, trans. Robert Julian. London: BFI.
Clayton, Alex (2016) 'V. F. Perkins: Aesthetic Suspense', in *Thinking in the Dark: Cinema, Theory, Practice*. New Brunswick, NJ and London: Rutgers University Press, pp. 208–16.
Coëgnarts, Maarten and Peter Kravanja (2012) 'Towards an Embodied Poetics of Cinema: The Metaphoric Construction of Abstract Meaning in Film', *Alphaville: Journal*

of Film and Screen Media, no. 4 <http://www.alphavillejournal.com/Issue%204/HTML/ArticleCoegnarts&Kravanja.html> (last accessed 6 March 2020).

Comolli, Jean-Louis (1980) 'Machines of the Visible', in Teresa de Lauretis and Stephen Heath (eds), *The Cinematic Apparatus*. New York: St. Martin's Press, pp. 121–42.

Comolli, Jean-Louis (2010) 'Frames and Bodies – Notes on Three Films by Pedro Costa: *Ossos, No Quarto Da Vanda, Juventude Em Marcha*', *Afterall: A Journal of Art, Context and Enquiry*, 24 (Summer), pp. 62–70.

Costa, Pedro (2008) *Dans La Chambre de Vanda: Conversation, Collage, Documents* (book accompanying Capricci DVD of the film). Nantes: Capricci.

Costa, Pedro (2013) *Casa de Lava*. Lisbon: Pierre von Kleist editions.

Costa, Pedro and Rui Chafes (2007) *Fora! / Out!* Museu Serralves.

Currie, Gregory (1995) *Image and Mind: Film, Philosophy and Cognitive Science*. Cambridge: Cambridge University Press.

Daly, Fergus and Garin Dowd (2003) *Leos Carax*. Manchester and New York: Manchester University Press.

Dargis, Manohla (2012) 'It's Not About the Destination, but About the Dizzying Ride', *The New York Times*, 16 October <https://www.nytimes.com/2012/10/17/movies/holy-motors-from-the-french-filmmaker-leos-carax.html> (last accessed 13 July 2018).

Darrieussecq, Marie (2014) 'La Résonance d'une phrase', *Libération*, 24 January <http://next.liberation.fr/culture/2014/01/24/la-resonance-d-une-phrase_975334> (last accessed 18 July 2018).

Deleuze, Gilles (2005) *Cinema I: The Movement-Image*, trans. Hugh Tomlinson and Barbara Habberjam. London and New York: Continuum.

Deleuze, Gilles (2013) *Cinema II: The Time Image*. London: Bloomsbury.

Durgnat, Raymond (1967) *Films and Feelings*. London: Faber & Faber.

Dyer, Geoff (2012) *Zona*. Edinburgh and London: Canongate.

Eagleton, Terry (1990) *The Ideology of the Aesthetic*. Oxford: Blackwell.

Ebert, Roger (2012) *Cloud Atlas* (review) <https://www.rogerebert.com/reviews/cloud-atlas-2012> (last accessed 20 June 2019).

Eguchi, Kenichi (2008) 'Pedro Costa: The Trembling Moment', *Outside in Tokyo*, 2 April <http://www.outsideintokyo.jp/e/interview/pedrocosta/index.html> (last accessed 17 July 2018).

Elkins, James (1998) *On Pictures and the Words That Fail Them*. Cambridge: Cambridge University Press.

Elliott, Kamilla (2003) *Rethinking the Novel/Film Debate*. Cambridge: Cambridge University Press.

Ellul, Jacques (1945) 'Victoire d'Hitler?' *Réforme*, 23 June <http://1libertaire.free.fr/EllulContreHitler.html> (last accessed 18 July 2018).

Enyedi, Delia (2017) 'Auteur 3D Filmmaking: From Hitchcock's Protrusion Technique to Godard's Immersion Aesthetic', *World Academy of Science, Engineering and Technology, International Journal of Humanities and Social Sciences*, 11 (3), pp. 644–8.

Eschkötter, Daniel (2016) 'Costas Nachleben', *Film-Konzepte*, 41 (January), pp. 60–9.

Fajgenbaum, Emma (2019) 'Cinema as Disquiet: The Ghostly Realism of Pedro Costa', *New Left Review*, 116/117 (March/June), pp. 135–59.

Fife Donaldson, Lucy (2014) *Texture in Film*. Basingstoke: Palgrave Macmillan.

Fox, Albertine (2018) *Godard and Sound: Acoustic Innovation in the Late Films of Jean-Luc Godard*. London and New York: I. B. Tauris.

Fujiwara, Chris (1998) *Jacques Tourneur: The Cinema of Nightfall*. Baltimore, MD and London: Johns Hopkins University Press.

Genette, Gérard (1972) *Figures III*. Paris: Editions du Seuil.
Genette, Gérard (1982) *Figures of Literary Discourse*, trans. Alan Sheridan. New York: Columbia University Press.
Genette, Gérard (2004) *Métalepse*. Paris: Éditions du Seuil.
Gibbs, John (2019) Interview with V. F. Perkins, 22 May 1997, *Movie: A Journal of Film Criticism*, 8, pp. 45–52.
Gonsalves, Joshua D. (2010) ' 'I'm a Whore': 'On the Other Side' of *Inland Empire*', in François-Xavier Gleyzon (ed.), *David Lynch in Theory*. Prague: Litteraria Pragensia Books, pp. 117–31.
Goodwin, Jonathan (2014) 'The Separate Worlds of David Lynch's *Inland Empire*', *Quarterly Review of Film and Video*, 31 (4), pp. 309–21.
Greimas, Algirdas Julien (1988) *Maupassant: The Semiotics of Text: Practical Exercises*, Vol. 1. Amsterdam and Philadelphia: John Benjamins.
Grote, Simon William (2010) *Moral Philosophy and the Origins of Modern Aesthetic Theory in Scotland and Germany*. PhD thesis, UC Berkeley.
Gunning, Tom (2000) *The Films of Fritz Lang: Allegories of Vision and Modernity*. London: BFI.
Harbin, Ami (2016) *Disorientation in Moral Life*. Oxford: Oxford University Press.
Heath, Stephen (1981) *Questions of Cinema*. London and Basingstoke: Macmillan.
Hegel, Georg Wilhelm Friedrich (2018) *The Phenomenology of Spirit*, ed. and trans. Terry Pinkard. Cambridge: Cambridge University Press.
Hynes, Eric (2015) 'The World of Never-Were and Almost-Was: An Interview with Guy Maddin and Evan Johnson on *The Forbidden Room*', *Reverse Shot*, 13 October <http://reverseshot.org/archive/entry/2117/maddin_johnson_interview> (last accessed 25 September 2019).
Isenberg, Arnold (1973) *Aesthetics and the Theory of Criticism*. Chicago and London: University of Chicago Press.
James, Henry (1966) *The Portrait of a Lady*. London: Penguin.
Jameson, Fredric (1992) *The Geopolitical Aesthetic: Cinema and Space in the World System*. Bloomington, Indianapolis and London: Indiana University Press and BFI Publishing.
Jarvis, Simon (2002) 'An Undeleter for Criticism', *Diacritics*, 32 (1), pp. 3–18.
Jones, Nick (2018) Unpublished manuscript on 3D cinema.
Kaes, Anton, Nicholas Baer and Michael Cowan (eds) (2016) *The Promise of Cinema: German Film Theory 1907–1933*. Oakland, CA: University of California Press.
Kanatova, Maria et al. (2017) 'Broken Time, Continued Evolution: Anachronies in Contemporary Film', *Stanford Literary Lab Pamphlets*, April.
Kant, Immanuel (1991) *Political Writings*, ed. Hans Reiss, trans. H. B. Nisbet, 2nd edn. Cambridge: Cambridge University Press.
Kant, Immanuel (2000) *Critique of the Power of Judgement*, ed. Paul Guyer, trans. Paul Guyer and Eric Matthews. Cambridge: Cambridge University Press.
Kant, Immanuel (2004) *Prolegomena to Any Future Metaphysics*, ed. and trans. Gary Hatfield. Cambridge: Cambridge University Press.
Kawin, Bruce F. (1978) *Mindscreen: Bergman, Godard, and First-Person Film*. Princeton, NJ: Princeton University Press.
Klevan, Andrew (2018) *Aesthetic Evaluation and Film*. Manchester: Manchester University Press.
Kiss, Miklós (2012) 'Narrative Metalepsis as Diegetic Concept in Christopher Nolan's *Inception* (2010)', *Acta Universitatis Sapientiae: Film and Media Studies*, 5, pp. 35–54.
Kiss, Miklós and Steven Willemsen (2017) *Impossible Puzzle Films: A Cognitive Approach to Contemporary Complex Cinema*. Edinburgh: Edinburgh University Press.

Kovács, András Bálint (2007) *Screening Modernism: European Art Cinema, 1950–1980*. Chicago and London: University of Chicago Press.
Kracauer, Siegfried (1987) 'Cult of Distraction: On Berlin's Picture Palaces', trans. Thomas Y. Levin, *New German Critique*, 40 (Winter), pp. 91–6.
Lachenmann, Helmut (2004) 'Philosophy of Composition: Is There Such a Thing?' in *Identity and Difference*, eds F. Agsteribbe, S. Beelaert, P. Dejans and J. D'hoe. Leuven: Leuven University Press.
Landry, Olivia (2017) 'A Body Without a Face: The Disorientation of Trauma in *Phoenix* (2014) and New Holocaust Cinema', *Film-Philosophy*, 21 (2), pp. 188–205.
Lash, Dominic (2017) 'Film as Film in the Twenty-First Century: The Function and Evaluation of Diegesis and Disruption', *Screen* 58 (2): pp. 163–79.
Lehman, Peter (2004) ' "You Couldn't Hit It on the Nose": The Limits of Knowledge in and of *The Searchers*', in *The Searchers: Essays and Reflections of John Ford's Classic Western*, eds Arthur M. Eckstein and Peter Lehman. Detroi, MI: Wayne State University Press, pp. 239–63.
Lem, Stanislaw (1974) 'Todorov's Fantastic Theory of Literature', trans. Robert Abernathy, *Science Fiction Studies*, pp. 227–37.
Lewinsky, Mariann (1997) *Eine verrückte Seite: Stummfilm und filmische Avantgarde in Japan*. Zürich: Chronos.
Lim, Dennis (2015) *David Lynch: The Man from Another Place*. New York: Amazon.
Lindsay, Vachel (1922) *The Art of the Moving Picture*. New York: Macmillan.
Lowenstein, Adam (2016) 'A Cinema of Disorientation: Space, Genre, Wheatley', *Critical Quarterly*, 58 (1), pp. 5–15.
Lowry, Edward (1985) *The Filmology Movement and Film Study in France*. Ann Arbor, MI: UMI Research Press.
Luhmann, Niklas (2000) *Art as a Social System*. Stanford, CA: Stanford University Press.
Lynch, David, and Kristine McKenna (2018) *Room to Dream*. Edinburgh: Canongate.
Lyotard, Jean-François (2011) *Discourse, Figure*, trans. Antony Hudek and Mary Lydon. Minneapolis and London: University of Minnesota Press.
McElroy, Joseph (2003 [1966]) *A Smuggler's Bible*. Woodstock and New York: Overlook Press.
McGann, Jerome J. (1988) 'The Cantos of Ezra Pound, the Truth in Contradiction', *Critical Inquiry*, 15 (1), pp. 1–25.
McGowan, Todd (2010) 'The Materiality of Fantasy: The Encounter with Something in *Inland Empire*', in *David Lynch in Theory*, ed. Francois-Xavier Gleyzon. Prague: Litteraria Pragensia Books, pp. 8–23.
Martin, Adrian (1997) 'Ultimatum: An Introduction to the Work of Nicole Brenez', *Screening the Past* <http://www.screeningthepast.com/2014/12/the-ultimate-journey-remarks-on-contemporary-theory/> (last accessed 16 July 2018).
Martin, Adrian (2012a) *Last Day Every Day: Figural Thinking from Auerbach and Kracauer to Agamben and Brenez*. New York: punctum books.
Martin, Adrian (2012b) 'Adrian Martin Interview about His Book *Last Day Every Day: Figural Thinking from Auerbach and Kracauer to Agamben and Brenez* on Vimeo' <https://vimeo.com/55990130> (last accessed 16 July 2018).
Martin, Adrian (2014a) *Mise en Scène and Film Style*. Basingstoke: Palgrave Macmillan.
Martin, Adrian (2014b) 'Where Do Cinematic Ideas Come From?' *Journal of Screenwriting*, 5 (1), pp. 9–26.
Martin, Adrian (2018) *Mysteries of Cinema: Reflections on Film Theory, History and Culture 1982–2016*. Amsterdam: Amsterdam University Press.

Martin, Adrian and Girish Shambu (eds) (2012) 'Hail Holy Motors', *Lola*, 3 (December) <http://lolajournal.com/3/index.html> (last accessed 16 July 2018).

Martin, Niall, and Mireille Rosello (2016) 'Disorientation: An Introduction', *Culture, Theory and Critique*, 57 (1), pp. 1–16.

Matzner, Sebastian (2016) *Rethinking Metonymy*. Oxford: Oxford University Press.

Merleau-Ponty, Maurice (1964) *Sense and Non-Sense*, trans. Hubert L. Dreyfus and Patricia Allen Dreyfus. Evanston, IL: Northwestern University Press.

Metz, Christian (2016) *Impersonal Enunciation, Or the Place of Film*, trans. Cormac Deane. New York: Columbia University Press.

Morgan, Daniel (2013) *Late Godard and the Possibilities of Cinema*. Berkeley, Los Angeles and London: University of California Press.

Morgan, Daniel (2015) 'The Curves of a Straight Line: *Holy Motors* and the Powers and Puzzles of Cinematic Forms', *Krystalbilleder: Tidsskrift for Filmkritik*, 5, pp. 30–45.

Morgan, Daniel (2016) 'Where Are We? Camera Movements and the Problem of Point of View', *New Review of Film and Television Studies*, 14 (2), pp. 222–48.

Morsch, Thomas (2012) 'Permanent Metalepsis: Pushing the Boundaries of Narrative Space', in *Screen Dynamics: Mapping the Borders of Cinema*, trans. Felix Koch. Vienna: Austrian Film Museum and SYNEMA, pp. 108–25.

Mozaffar, Omer M. (2012) 'Six Keys to *Cloud Atlas*' <https://www.rogerebert.com/far-flung-correspondents/six-keys-to-cloud-atlas> 27 October (last accessed 24 June 2019).

Mulhall, Stephen (2016) *On Film*, 3rd edn. London: Routledge.

Naremore, James (1998) *More Than Night: Film Noir in Its Contexts*. Berkeley, CA: University of California Press.

Naremore, James (2007) *On Kubrick*. London: BFI.

Naremore, James (2014) *An Invention Without a Future*. Berkeley, Los Angeles and London: University of California Press.

Nash, Mark (1976) 'Vampyr and the Fantastic', *Screen*, 17 (3), pp. 29–67.

Neofetou, Daniel (2012) *Good Day Today: David Lynch Destabilises the Spectator*. Alresford: Zero Books.

Neyrat, Cyril (2010) 'Rooms for the Living and the Dead', in booklet accompanying *Letters from Fontainhas*, Criterion DVD Box Set, pp. 10–17.

Newsom, Robert (1994) 'Fear of Fictions', *Narrative*, 2 (2), pp. 140–51.

North, Joseph (2019) 'Two Paragraphs in Raymond Williams: A Reply to Francis Mulhern', *New Left Review*, 116/117 (March/June), pp. 161–87.

Pantenburg, Volker (2010) 'Realism, Not Reality: Pedro Costa's Digital Testimonies', *Afterall: A Journal of Art, Context and Enquiry*, 24 (Summer), pp. 54–61.

Pavey, Alex (2017) *Crime, Space and Disorientation in the Literature and Cinema of Los Angeles*. PhD thesis, University College London.

Peirce, Charles Sanders (1966) 'Some Consequences of Four Incapacities', in *Selected Writings (Values in a Universe of Chance)*. New York: Dover, pp. 39–72.

Peranson, Mark (2015) 'Lost in the Funhouse: A Conversation with Guy Maddin and Evan Johnson on *The Forbidden Room* and Other Stories', *Cinema Scope* <https://cinema-scope.com/cinema-scope-magazine/lost-funhouse-conversation-guy-maddin-evan-johnson-forbidden-room-stories/> (last accessed 25 September 2019).

Perez, Gilberto (1998) *The Material Ghost: Films and Their Medium*. Baltimore, MD: Johns Hopkins University Press.

Perez, Gilberto (2019) *The Eloquent Screen: A Rhetoric of Film*. Minneapolis, MN and London: University of Minnesota Press.

Perkins, Victor F. (1990) 'Must We Say What They Mean? Film Criticism and Interpretation', *Movie*, 34, pp. 1–6.
Perkins, Victor F. (1993) *Film as Film: Understanding and Judging Movies*. New York: Da Capo Press.
Pier, John (2016) 'Metalepsis (revised version; uploaded 13 July 2016)', in *The Living Handbook of Narratology*, ed. Peter Hühn et al. <https://www.lhn.uni-hamburg.de/node/51.html> (last accessed 3 January 2020).
Pippin, Robert B. (2010) *Hollywood Westerns and American Myth: The Importance of Howard Hawks and John Ford for Political Philosophy*. New Haven, CT and London: Yale University Press.
Pippin, Robert B. (2016) 'Responses', in Ludwig Nagl and Waldemar Zacharasiewicz (eds), *Ein Filmphilosophie-Symposium mit Robert B. Pippin*. Berlin and Boston: Walter de Gruyter, pp. 219–37.
Pippin, Robert B. (2017a) *The Philosophical Hitchcock:* Vertigo *and the Anxieties of Unknowingness*. Chicago and London: Chicago University Press.
Pippin, Robert B. (2017b) CCT MFS Film & Philosophy, University of Chicago, 'The Philosophical Hitchcock' <https://www.youtube.com/watch?v=LIpg7WHe7AY> (last accessed 18 July 2018).
Pomerance, Murray (2008) *The Horse Who Drank the Sky: Film Experience Beyond Narrative and Theory*. New Brunswick, NJ and London: Rutgers University Press.
Pranolo, Jennifer (2011) 'Laura Dern's Eternal Return', *Screen*, 52 (4), pp. 477–92.
Prince, Gerald (1988) 'The Disnarrated', *Style*, 22 (1), pp. 1–8.
Pye, Douglas (1996) 'Double Vision: Miscegenation and Point of View in *The Searchers*', in Ian Cameron and Douglas Pye (eds), *The Movie Book of the Western*. London: Studio Vista, pp. 229–35.
Rancière, Jacques (2001) *La Fable Cinématographique*. Paris: Éditions du Seuil.
Rancière, Jacques (2009) *Aesthetics and Its Discontents*. Cambridge and Malden: Polity Press.
Rancière, Jacques (2011) 'The Politics of Pedro Costa', trans. Emiliano Battista. Masters of Cinema *Colossal Youth* DVD booklet.
Rancière, Jacques (2013) *Aisthesis: Scenes from the Aesthetic Regime of Art*. London: Verso.
Rancière, Jacques (2014) *The Intervals of Cinema*, trans. John Howe. London: Verso Books.
Rancière, Jacques (2016) *Film Fables*, trans. Emiliano Battista. London: Bloomsbury.
Rapold, Nicolas (2015) 'Interview: Guy Maddin and Evan Johnson', *Film Comment*, 25 September, <https://www.filmcomment.com/blog/interview-guy-maddin-and-evan-johnson/> (last accessed 25 September 2019).
Rayns, Tony (2015) 'Film of the Week: *The Forbidden Room*', *Sight and Sound*, 11 December <https://www.bfi.org.uk/news-opinion/sight-sound-magazine/reviews-recommendations/film-week-forbidden-room> (last accessed 20 June 2019).
Romney, Jonathan (2015) 'The Infernal, Ecstatic Desire Machine of Guy Maddin', *Film Comment*, 51 (5), pp. 34–9.
Rourke, Brian (2016) ' "A Man I Once Knew": Old Tales and Bad Times in David Lynch's *Inland Empire*', *Senses of Cinema*, no. 79 (July).
Roussel, Raymond (2011) *New Impressions of Africa*, translated Mark Ford. Princeton, NJ and Oxford: Princeton University Press.
Routt, William D. (2000) 'For Criticism: Parts One and Two', *Screening the Past* <http://www.screeningthepast.com/2014/12/de-la-figure-en-general-et-du-corps-en-particulier-linvention-figurative-au-cinema/> (last accessed 16 July 2018).
Ryan, Marie-Laure (2006) *Avatars of Story*. Minneapolis and London: University of Minnesota Press.

Salt, Barry (1992) *Film Style and Technology: History and Analysis*, 2nd expanded edn. London: Starword.
Sanders, Ted J. M., Wilbert P. M. Spooren and Leo G. M. Noordman (1992) 'Toward a Taxonomy of Coherence Relations', *Discourse Processes*, 15(1), pp. 1–35.
Schmidt di Friedberg, Marcella (2018) *Geographies of Disorientation*. London and New York: Routledge.
Silvia, Paul J. (2009) 'Looking Past Pleasure: Anger, Confusion, Disgust, Pride, Surprise, and Other Unusual Aesthetic Emotions', *Psychology of Aesthetics, Creativity, and the Arts*, 3 (1), pp. 48–51.
Sylvia, Paul J. (2010) 'Confusion and Interest: The Role of Knowledge Emotions in Aesthetic Experience', *Psychology of Aesthetics, Creativity, and the Arts*, 4 (2), pp. 75–80.
Simak, Clifford D. (1977) *Time and Again*. London: Magnum Books, Methuen Paperbacks Ltd.
Simak, Clifford D. (1988) *City*. London: Mandarin.
Smalley, G. (2010) '48. *INLAND EMPIRE* (2006)', 16 February <http://366weirdmovies.com/inland-empire-2006/> (last accessed 11 July 2018).
Smith, Murray (1995) *Engaging Characters: Fiction, Emotion and the Cinema*. Oxford: Oxford University Press.
Sobchack, Vivian (1992) *The Address of the Eye: A Phenomenology of Film Experience*. Princeton, NJ: Princeton University Press.
Sobchak, Vivian (2014) 'Stop Making Sense: Thoughts on Two Difficult Films from 2013', *Film Comment*, 50 (1), pp. 50–3.
Souriau, Étienne (1951) 'La Structure de l'univers Filmique et Le Vocabulaire de La Filmologie', *Revue Internationale de Filmologie*, 2 (7–8), pp. 231–40.
Souriau, Étienne (2015) *The Different Modes of Existence*. Minneapolis, MN: Univocal.
Taggart, VanCleeve (n.d.) 'An Interpretation of David Lynch's *INLAND EMPIRE* (A Woman in Trouble)'.
Tanner, Tony (1987) *Scenes of Nature, Signs of Men: Essays on 19th and 20th Century American Literature*. Cambridge: Cambridge University Press.
Thomson, David (2014) 'Yekaterina Golubeva, 1966–2011', *Sight and Sound*, 26 March http://www.bfi.org.uk/news-opinion/sight-sound-magazine/comment/obituaries/yekaterina-golubeva-1966-2011> (last accessed 16 July 2018).
Toles, George E. (2001) *A House Made of Light: Essays on the Art of Film*, Vol. 28. Detroit, MI: Wayne State University Press.
Toles, George E. (2016) *Paul Thomas Anderson*. Urbana, IL, Chicago and Springfield, IL: University of Illinois Press.
Treno, Pedro (2013) 'Requiem for a Demolition: The Fontainhas Neighbourhood in Pedro Costa's Cinema' <https://www.academia.edu/19890540/Requiem_for_a_demolition_The_Fontainhas_neighbourhood_in_Pedro_Costas_cinema> (last accessed 17 July 2018).
Walters, James (2008) 'Making Light of the Dark: Understanding the World of *His Girl Friday*', *Journal of Film and Video*, 60 (3–4), pp. 90–102.
Walton, Kendall (1990) *Mimesis as Make-Believe: On the Foundations of the Representational Arts*. Cambridge, MA and London: Harvard University Press.
Walton, Saige (2016) *Cinema's Baroque Flesh: Film, Phenomenology, and the Art of Entanglement*. Amsterdam: Amsterdam University Press.
Warner, Rick (2016) 'Godard's Stereoscopic Essay: Thinking in and with *Adieu au langage*', in Seung-Hoon Jeong and Jeremi Szaniawski (eds), *The Global Auteur: The Politics of Authorship in 21st Century Cinema*. London and New York: Bloomsbury.

Weinthal, Annika (2016) 'Gezückte Messer: Gesten Der Widerständigkeit in *Juventude Em Marcha*', *Film-Konzepte*, 41 (January), pp. 55–9.
Wheatley, Catherine (2011) *Caché*. London: BFI.
Wilson, George M. (1986) *Narration in Light: Studies in Cinematic Point of View*. Baltimore, MD and London: Johns Hopkins University Press.
Wilson, George M. (2011) *Seeing Fictions in Films: The Epistemology of Movies*. Oxford: Oxford University Press.
Winters, Ben (2010) 'The Non-Diegetic Fallacy: Film, Music, and Narrative Space', *Music and Letters*, 91 (2), pp. 224–44.
Wittgenstein, Ludwig (2009) *Philosophical Investigations*. Chichester: Wiley-Blackwell.
Wood, Robin (2003) *Hollywood from Vietnam to Reagan . . . and Beyond*, expanded and revised edn. New York and Chichester: Columbia University Press.
Yacavone, Daniel (2015) *Film Worlds: A Philosophical Aesthetics of Cinema*. New York: Columbia University Press.
Yacavone, Daniel (2016) 'Film and the Phenomenology of Art: Reappraising Merleau-Ponty on Cinema as Form, Medium, and Expression', *New Literary History*, 47, pp. 159–86.
Yu, Chang-Min (2016) 'Figures for Figuring Out', *Film Criticism*, 40 (1) <http://dx.doi.org/10.3998/fc.13761232.0040.135> (last accessed 16 July 2018).
Zakarin, Jordan (2012) '*Cloud Atlas* Slammed for Lack of Asian Actors, "Yellow Face" Makeup By Advocacy Group', *Hollywood Reporter*, 25 October <https://www.hollywoodreporter.com/news/cloud-atlas-asian-actors-yellow-face-manaa-383070> (last accessed 21 September 2019).

Filmography

Adaptation (Spike Jonze, 2002)
A Sixth Part of the World (Dziga Vertov, 1926)
A Star Is Born (George Cukor, 1956)
Adieu au langage (Jean-Luc Godard, 2014)
Alien³ (David Fincher, 1992)
All Blossoms Again (Aurélian Gerbault, 2006)
A Page of Madness (Teinosuke Kinugasa, 1926)
Bad Timing (Nicholas Roeg, 1980)
Bande à part (Jean-Luc Godard, 1964)
Blue Velvet (David Lynch, 1986)
Boy Meets Girl (Leos Carax, 1984)
Caché (Michael Haneke, 2005)
Casa de Lava (Pedro Costa, 1995)
Ceddo (Ousmane Sembène, 1977)
Céline et Julie vont en bateau (Jacques Rivette, 1974)
Citizen Kane (Orson Welles, 1941)
Cloud Atlas (Tom Tykwer, Lana Wachowski and Lilly Wachowski, 2012)
Colossal Youth (Juventude em Marcha) (Pedro Costa, 2006)
Daffy Duck & Egghead (Tex Avery, 1937)
Das Cabinet des Dr. Caligari (Robert Wiene, 1920)
Days of Eclipse (Alexander Sokurov, 1988)
Deliverance (John Boorman, 1972)
Der Andere (Max Mack, 1913)
Der Golem (Paul Wegener and Henrik Galeen, 1915)
Der Student von Prag (Paul Wegener and Stellen Rye, 1913)
Dr. Strangelove (Stanley Kubrick, 1964)
Elephant (Gus Van Sant, 2003)
eXistenZ (David Cronenberg, 1999)
Eyes Wide Shut (Stanley Kubrick, 1999)
Eyes Without a Face (Les Yeux sans visage) (Georges Franju, 1960)
Forbidden Planet (Fred M. Wilcox, 1956)
Hable con ella (Pedro Almodóvar, 2002)
Hiroshima mon amour (Alain Resnais, 1959)
Histoire(s) du cinema (Jean-Luc Godard, 1988–98)
History Lessons (Straub-Huillet, 1972)
Holy Motors (Leos Carax, 2012)

'Husky Sings with Baby', <https://www.youtube.com/watch?v=Nyk1HXvCNks> (accessed 18 July 2018; uploaded to YouTube by danm923, 14 March 2011)
Inception (Christopher Nolan, 2010)
INLAND EMPIRE (David Lynch, 2006)
In Vanda's Room (Pedro Costa, 2000)
Invasion of the Body Snatchers (Don Siegel, 1956)
Ivan's Childhood (Andrei Tarkovsky, 1962)
I Walked with a Zombie (Jacques Tourneur, 1943)
J'accuse (Abel Gance, 1938)
Khrustalyov, My Car! (Aleksei German, 1998)
Kind Hearts and Coronets (Robert Hamer, 1949)
La Chinoise (Jean-Luc Godard, 1967)
La nuit américaine (François Truffaut, 1973)
Last Year at Marienbad (L'Année dernière à Marienbad) (Alain Resnais, 1961)
Laura (Otto Preminger, 1944)
Le Doulos (Jean-Pierre Melville, 1963)
Le Fond de l'air est rouge (A Grin Without a Cat) (Chris Marker, 1977/1993)
Le Mépris (Jean-Luc Godard, 1963)
Les Amants du Pont-Neuf (Leos Carax, 1991)
Le Vent d'est (Jean-Luc Godard, 1970)
Lost Highway (David Lynch, 1997)
Mabel's Dramatic Career (Mack Sennett, 1913)
Magnolia (Paul Thomas Anderson, 1999)
Mauvais sang (Leos Carax, 1986)
Meshes of the Afternoon (Maya Deren and Alexander Hammid, 1943)
Mirror (Andrei Tarkovsky, 1975)
mother! (Darren Aronofsky, 2017)
Mulholland Dr. (David Lynch, 2001)
My Darling Clementine (John Ford, 1946)
New Rose Hotel (Abel Ferrara, 1998)
Night of the Demon (Jacques Tourneur, 1957)
Notre Musique (Jean-Luc Godard, 2004)
Oldboy (Park Chan-wook, 2003)
Only Angels Have Wings (Howard Hawks, 1939)
O nosso homem (Pedro Costa, 2010)
O Sangue (Pedro Cosa, 1989)
Ossos (Pedro Costa, 1997)
Passion (Jean-Luc Godard, 1982)
Passion (Brian de Palma, 2012)
Persona (Ingmar Bergman, 1960)
Phoenix (Christian Petzold, 2014)
Pola X (Leos Carax, 1999)
Psycho (Alfred Hitchcock, 1960)
Seconds (John Frankenheimer, 1966)
Sherlock Jr. (Buster Keaton, 1924)
Syndromes and a Century (Apichatpong Weerasethakul, 2006)
Synecdoche, New York (Charlie Kaufman, 2008)
Tarrafal (Pedro Costa, 2007)

Tess (Roman Polanski, 1979)
That Obscure Object of Desire (Luis Buñuel, 1977)
The Big Sleep (Howard Hawks, 1946)
The Double (Richard Ayoade, 2013)
The Forbidden Room (Guy Maddin and Evan Johnson, 2015)
The French Lieutenant's Woman (Karel Reisz, 1980)
The Lady from Shanghai (Orson Welles, 1947)
The Locket (John Brahm, 1946)
The Master (Paul Thomas Anderson, 2012)
The Passenger (Michelangelo Antonioni, 1975)
The Purple Rose of Cairo (Woody Allen, 1985)
The Rabbit Hunters (Pedro Costa, 2007)
The Saragossa Manuscript (Wojciech Has, 1965)
The Searchers (John Ford, 1956)
The Seventh Victim (Mark Robson, 1945)
The Shining (Stanley Kubrick, 1980)
The Suspended Vocation (Raúl Ruiz, 1978)
The Testament of Dr. Mabuse (Fritz Lang, 1933)
They Live By Night (Nicholas Ray, 1948)
Three Women (Robert Altman, 1977)
Tokyo! (Michel Gondry, Leos Carax and Boon Jong-Ho, 2008)
To the Wonder (Terrence Malick, 2012)
Timecrimes (Nacho Vigalondo, 2007)
Twin Peaks: The Return (David Lynch and Mark Frost, 2017)
Une Vie (Alexandre Astruc, 1958)
Upstream Color (Shane Carruth, 2013)
Vampyr (Carl Th. Dreyer, 1932)
Vertigo (Alfred Hitchcock, 1958)
Vitalia Varela (Pedro Costa, 2019)
Viva Zapata! (Elia Kazan, 1952)
Videodrome (David Cronenberg, 1983)
Vivre sa vie (Jean-Luc Godard, 1962)
Way Down East (D. W. Griffith, 1920)
Wild at Heart (David Lynch, 1990)

Index

3D, 135–6, 148

Adieu au langage, 18, 24, 133–51, 155, 179n
Adorno, Theodor, 16
affect, 2, 6, 9–11, 13, 14, 16, 28, 35, 36, 56, 58, 63, 67, 83, 99, 105, 166n
Affeldt, Steven J., 17
Ahmed, Sara, 122
allegory, 14, 64, 67, 82, 84–7, 113, 172n
Anderson, Paul Thomas, 19, 34–6
Andrew, Dudley, 92, 95, 101
Ashbery, John, 45, 169n
Auerbach, Erich, 84–5, 92, 172n
Aydemir, Murat, 18, 167n

Badiou, Alain, 30, 126
Bae, Doona, 41, 50
Balzac, Honoré de, 29
Barker, Jennifer M., 94, 173n
Barthes, Roland, 59, 101, 174n
Baumbach, Nico, 148, 150
Baumgarten, Alexander, 13–14, 15, 28, 36, 82, 94, 96, 155, 167n, 177n
    his sense of confusion pertaining to aesthetic cognition, 13–14
Berliner, Todd, 73, 171n
Berry, Halle, 41, 50
Big Sleep, The, 31
Biles, Jeremy, 79
Blue Velvet, 61
Bluestone, George, 97
Bogue, Ronald, 150
Bordwell, David, 4, 5, 8, 156
Boy Meets Girl, 74
Brenez, Nicole, 21, 22, 92, 100–1, 102, 104, 105, 108, 133, 155, 174n
Brinkema, Eugenie, 10–11

Broadbent, Jim, 41, 50
Brown, William, 7
Buckland, Warren, 27, 53
Burch, Noël, 148, 179n

Caché [*Hidden*], 24, 32, 105, 108–9, 111, 112, 113–15, 175n
Carax, Leos, 18, 23, 69–87, 171n; see also *Boy Meets Girl*; *Holy Motors*; *Les Amants du Pont-Neuf*; *Mauvais Sang*; *Pola X*
Casa de Lava, 124, 127–8
Cavell, Stanley, 4, 16–17, 156, 172n, 178n
Céline et Julie vont en bateau, 19, 28
Chion, Michel, 52
Clayton, Alex, 36, 47
Cloud Atlas, 23, 27, 34, 39–50, 63, 169n
Coëgnarts, Maarten, 7–8, 166n
cognitivist film studies, 5–8, 10, 36, 40–1, 174n, 175n
coherence, 21, 23, 50, 51–2, 56, 57, 59, 61, 63, 69–87, 121, 132, 145–7, 150, 154, 171n, 172n, 174n, 178–9n
    distinguished from cohesion and consistency, 71–2
Colossal Youth, 18, 24, 117–32, 133, 175–7n
    scene-by-scene breakdown, 159–63
Comolli, Jean-Louis, 93, 122
Costa, Pedro, 18, 24, 117–32, 175–7n; see also *Casa de Lava*; *Colossal Youth*; *In Vanda's Room*; *Ossos*
Currie, Gregory, 5, 7

Daffy Duck & Egghead, 20, 114
Daly, Fergus, and Garin Dowd, 73–4, 85
de Man, Paul, 95
Deleuze, Gilles, 63, 92, 99, 138, 175n, 177–8n

Deliverance, 1–2, 9
Dern, Laura, 30, 51, 54, 56, 57, 59, 60–3, 64, 65–6, 119, 170n
diegesis, 7, 14, 23, 28, 31–7, 48–50, 53–4, 58, 64, 69–84, 97–9, 102, 105, 108–9, 112–14, 116, 118–19, 122, 129, 133, 143–5, 147–50, 155, 168n, 169n, 170n, 171n, 172n, 175n, 179n
   relationship to metaphor, 97–8
   as a rhetorical production, 37, 109
Dowd, Garin *see* Daly, Fergus
Dreyer, Carl Th., 2–3, 20, 165n
Durgnat, Raymond, 136

Eagleton, Terry, 14
Ebert, Roger, 39, 44, 48
Elephant, 18, 167n
Elkins, James, 104, 109–10, 112, 146, 175n
Elliott, Kamilla, 97–8
Ellul, Jacques, 137–8

fabula, 34, 58–9, 144, 145, 171n; see also *syuzhet*
Fife Donaldson, Lucy, 113
figuration, 5, 13, 20–2, 23, 24, 34, 80, 91–104, 105–16, 120, 123–32, 136, 146, 154–5, 158, 166n, 173n, 174n
   definition of, 95
Forbidden Room, The, 23, 27, 39–41, 45–50
Ford, John, 21, 84, 156
Frankenstein, 144–5, 179n

Genette, Gérard, 20, 27–8, 29, 35, 75, 94–5, 96, 173n
genre, 7, 17–18, 23, 28, 39–50, 80, 83, 110, 153, 169n
Godard, Jean-Luc, 18, 24, 104, 133–51, 155, 178n; see also *Adieu au langage*; *Histoire(s) du cinema*; *Vivre sa vie*
Golubeva, Yekaterina, 85, 87
Goodwin, Jonathan, 56–7, 58, 67
Greimas, A. J., 61
Grote, Simon William, 14
grotesque, 86

Haneke, Michael, 24, 32, 105, 113, 116, 175n; see also *Caché*
Hanks, Tom, 41, 44, 49–50
Harbin, Ami, 1, 62, 119, 177n

Harring, Laura Elena, 54, 62, 170n
Hawks, Howard, 31, 134
Hiroshima mon amour, 27
Histoire(s) du cinema, 134, 142, 147
Hitchcock, Alfred, 10–11, 179n
Holy Motors, 18, 23, 69–87, 101–2, 109, 129, 133, 172n
Hynes, Eric, 39–40, 46

I Walked with a Zombie, 129
If on a winter's night a traveller, 41–2
imperceptibility, 102, 105, 110–11, 115–16
In Vanda's Room, 127, 176n
indistinguishability, 105–16, 124, 141, 175n
INLAND EMPIRE, 6, 18, 23, 30, 37, 51–68, 69, 75, 84, 119, 147, 153–4, 170n, 171n, 175n, 179n
Ivan's Childhood, 149

James, Henry, 82
Jarvis, Simon, 16, 156
Johnson, Evan, 39–40, 46–7

Kant, Immanuel, 15, 16, 155–6, 167n
Kinski, Nastassja, 62, 98
Kiss, Miklós, 6–8, 27, 36, 41, 131, 174n
Klevan, Andrew, 8
Kracauer, Siegfried, 17
Kravanja, Peter, 7–8, 166n
Kubrick, Stanley, 53, 63, 79, 86, 117

Lachenmann, Helmut, 77
Landry, Olivia, 18, 167n
Lang, Fritz, 19, 170n, 177–8n
Last Year at Marienbad [*L'Année dernière à Marienbad*], 19, 72
Latour, Bruno, 33
Lavant, Denis, 69, 74, 77, 78, 79–81, 171n, 172n
Lehman, Peter, 21, 167n
Leibniz, Gottfried Wilhelm, 14, 166–7n, 177n
Les Amants du Pont-Neuf, 73–4
Lim, Dennis, 52, 59
Lindsay, Vatchel, 129
literalness, 15, 21, 53, 63, 65–7, 73, 80, 91–4, 97–8, 101, 118, 120, 132, 137, 139, 140, 142, 144, 172n, 173n

López, Cristina Álvarez, 75
Lost Highway, 24, 58–9, 105, 111–13, 115–16, 117, 171n
Lowenstein, Adam, 40, 167n
Lucas, Peter J., 55, 57, 62, 65
Luhmann, Niklas, 96
Lynch, David, 1, 18, 24, 51–68, 105, 111–13, 115, 116, 170n, 175n, 179n; see also *INLAND EMPIRE*; *Lost Highway*

McGowan, Todd, 56
Maddin, Guy, 39–40, 45–8
Magnolia, 34–6, 40, 169n
Mann, Aimee, 35, 169n
Marey, Étienne-Jules, 74, 85, 86
Marker, Chris, 147
Martin, Adrian, 73, 101–3, 174n
Matzner, Sebastien, 93, 96, 99, 173n
Mauvais Sang [*The Night is Young*], 74
Merleau-Ponty, Maurice, 8–9, 174n
Meshes of the Afternoon, 53
metalepsis, 20, 23, 24, 27–37, 40–1, 48–50, 51, 65, 66, 75, 78, 81, 93, 155, 168n
"metaleptical explanation", 31–2, 35
metaphor, 1, 7, 16, 21, 53, 65, 67, 70, 92–4, 97–8, 103, 117, 118, 120, 123, 125–8, 132, 133–5, 140, 142, 166n, 170n, 173n, 177n
metonymy, 21, 93, 117, 126, 136, 142, 170n
Metz, Christian, 30
Mirror [*Zerkalo*], 19, 165n
Mitchell, David, 41–2
Morgan, Daniel, 79–80, 133–4, 139, 165n, 172n
Morsch, Thomas, 28
Mozaffar, Omer M., 43, 50
Mulholland Dr., 54, 62

Naremore, James, 19, 79, 86, 87, 172n
narration, 6, 21–2, 23, 28, 30, 34, 42, 105, 109, 123, 124, 131, 142, 171n, 175n
Nash, Mark, 4
Neofetou, Daniel, 58
Night of the Demon, 106–8

"Occurrence at Owl Creek Bridge, An", 111–12, 113

Only Angels Have Wings, 134, 141
Ossos, 121, 125, 177n

Passenger, The, 7–8, 11
Passion, 103
Pavey, Alex, 66, 119, 176n
Peirce, C. S., 71
Peranson, Mark, 46, 47, 169n
Perez, Gilberto, 3, 84–5, 93, 118, 136, 166n, 173n, 177n
Perkins, V. F., 5, 7, 36, 97, 100, 171n, 175n
Persona, 30
phenomenological film studies, 8–10, 11, 94
phenomenology, 7, 8–10, 11, 16, 34, 94, 168n
Phoenix, 18, 167n
Pippin, Robert B., 21, 58, 157, 167n, 174n, 179n
Pola X, 74, 85, 171n
Pomerance, Murray, 75–6
Pound, Ezra, 52
Pranolo, Jennifer, 65–6, 67, 170n
Psycho, 10–11, 82
Pullman, Bill, 58, 111
Purple Rose of Cairo, The, 28
puzzle films, 6, 18, 41
Pye, Douglas, 157–8

Rancière, Jacques, 98–100, 101, 120, 129, 141–2, 167n, 174n
reflexivity, 62–3, 70–1, 75, 78, 81, 84, 86–7, 114–15, 137, 177n
rhetoric, 10, 20, 22, 23, 28, 34–7, 40, 45, 48–9, 53, 66, 81–2, 94, 100, 105, 131, 155, 169n, 171n, 173n
Richards, I. A., 98, 103
Rosello, Mireille, 6
Rourke, Brian, 52, 58, 59
Routt, William D., 94, 102, 103
Roxy, 142, 143–5, 146–50
Ruiz, Raúl, 19, 171–2n, 172n

Saragossa Manuscript, The, 27, 169n
Schmidt di Friedberg, Marcella, 154–5, 168n
Scob, Édith, 69, 83
Searchers, The, 21–2, 156–8
Silvia, Paul J., 6
Simak, Clifford D., 146, 147–9

Sobchack, Vivian, 8–10, 11, 166n, 173n
Souriau, Étienne, 30–4, 71, 168n
Sparks, 46, 85
Stenger, Isabelle, 33
Sturgess, Jim, 41, 49, 50
Suspended Vocation, The [*La Vocation suspendue*], 19, 171–2n, 172n
synecdoche, 93, 118
syuzhet, 34, 58–9, 144, 145, 148; see also *fabula*

Taggart, VanCleeve, 56, 57, 62
Tanner, Tony, 67, 170n
Tarkovksy, Andrei, 19, 149
Tess, 97–8
That Obscure Object of Desire, 61–2
They Live by Night, 98–100, 101, 174n
To the Wonder, 9, 173n
Todorov, Tzvetan, 4, 165n
Toles, George, 35–7, 154, 156, 169n
Tourneur, Jacques, 106–8, 116, 130, 175n

Upstream Color, 9, 173n

Vampyr, 2–5, 8, 10, 20, 21, 113, 178n
Ventura, 117–32, 176–7n
Viertel, Berthold, 29–30
Vivre sa vie, 140–1

Wachowski, Lana and Lily, 39, 169n
Walters, James, 87
Walton, Kendall, 35, 168n
Walton, Saige, 175n
Warner, Rick, 137, 139, 142, 148, 149–50, 178n
Wayne, John, 22, 158
Weinthal, Annika, 127–8, 132
Wheatley, Catherine, 109
Whishaw, Ben, 41, 50
Wild at Heart, 61
Willemsen, Steven, 6–8, 36, 41, 131, 174n
Wilson, George M., 22, 32, 113, 156, 171n
Wittgenstein, Ludwig, 17, 166–7n
Wood, Robin, 72–3

Yacavone, Daniel, 9, 169n
Yu, Chang-Min, 92